Chiaroscuro

Chiaroscuro
Essays of Identity

Revised Edition

Helen Barolini

The University of Wisconsin Press

The University of Wisconsin Press
2537 Daniels Street
Madison, Wisconsin 53718

3 Henrietta Street
London WC2E 8LU, England

1   3   5   4   2

Printed in the United States of America

Library of Congress Cataloging-in-Publication Data

Barolini, Helen, 1925–
   Chiaroscuro : essays of identity / Helen Barolini.–Rev. ed.
   236 pp.   cm.
   Includes bibliographical references and index.
   ISBN 0-299-16084-X (pbk.)
   1. Barolini, Helen, 1925– –Authorship. 2. American literature–
Italian American authors–History and criticism–Theory, etc.
3. Italian American women–Intellectual life.   4. American
literature–Italian influences.   5. Italian Americans in literature.
6. Italian Americans–Civilization.   7. Group identity in
literature.   I. Title.
PS3552.A725C47   1999
814'.54–dc21   98-48742

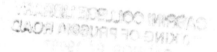

Contents

v

Foreword

Chronicling aspects of my personal and writing life, these fourteen essays span a period of twenty-five years and fall quite naturally into three areas of focus: family memoir, emergence as a writer, and the larger context of Italian American identity.

Responding first to an internal directive, I had to find not only geographic Italy, the land of my immigrant grandparents, but also what the idea of Italy meant to my sense of identity, to my feelings of myself. What did it mean to be American of Italian background? Why did I feel not quite American? And to make it more complicated, how did the circumstance of my being female of Italian American background affect me as a writer? Unraveling that conundrum awoke in me an awareness of how Italian Americans have seldom received recognition as literary authors and the toll this has taken on the writing.

Innocently, once, I thought of writing as pure act, untethered to anything but language and story, certainly not to gender or ancestry. But one writes from one's skin, and I, too, write from who I am, not from abstraction. That's no longer a matter of unkind fate, it's a fact and a choice. In writing I re-create my world and give myself my history.

And who I am, I found, is almost a hyperbole for all women who write, for that condition is intensified through the Italian American experience: the tension between family and self is greater; the pull of tradition more present; the fear of autonomy and distance more harrowing; the neglect and disparagement by the outside more real.

Certainly the momentous times I've lived through in the last half of this century had a deep effect on me, from the spectacular emer-

gence of Black writers into American literature followed by the flowering of other minority writers, to the clarion call of the women's
movement in the sixties and seventies. Both movements were liberation and stimulus to me as a late-blooming writer.

I have added to this revised collection an updated Introduction
to my 1985 collection *The Dream Book: An Anthology of Writings by
Italian American Women* since it amplifies themes present in the
shorter pieces. There seemed to be a mystery surrounding Italian
American women writers: Where were they? Why did they and
their work remain so unknown? What was the thread or pattern of
these lives that might explain them? Those questions I addressed in
my original Introduction.

The Dream Book called forth a response from writers and readers
of both genders and many ethnic backgrounds. Amy Lin, for instance, responding as an Asian American to the issue of marginal-
ization from the national literature, tells in *Feminisms: An Anthology of
Literary Theory and Criticism* of finding solace and solidarity through
reading the Introduction to *The Dream Book.* Male scholars and writers also found relevance in *The Dream Book,* and mirabile dictu, so
did Italian scholars who had so long ignored their American kin.
And most gratifying of all were the responses from an audience of
readers: "This volume signifies awakening" . . . "[it] gives voice to a
group usually unperceived as authors" . . . "the book touches something in almost everyone's experience" . . . "finally in print an expression of our experience and concerns" . . . "a wonderful and important contribution" . . . "a special gift" . . . "such an affirmation!"

The Dream Book had become a fortuitous agent of change. Other
collections followed (*From the Margin* in 1991 and *The Voices We Carry*
in 1994), and Italian American studies began to blossom within an
academy which had long ignored the field. This development affected not just women writers but all those who had worked in
seeming isolation and from the outsider position. And so, brought
up to date, the Introduction is offered once again as a document of
our times.

The essays in *Chiaroscuro* are quite interconnected—themes reap-
pear, urgencies are reiterated. In "Bianca, the Gulf War, Saroyan
and Me," for instance, I relate the story of a young woman who
could have been one of the contributors to *The Dream Book* if her life
had not come to a premature end. And in the final essay, "Turtle

out of Calabria," I find that if things move slowly, still there is reason to continue the slow march, still reason to write, to keep going on, to stay the course, to hold onto deeply held convictions.

Hastings-on-Hudson, New York   HELEN BAROLINI

Acknowledgments

The author thanks the following for permission to reprint essays: "Bianca, the Gulf War, Saroyan and Me," *Trivia* (Summer 1992); "The Finer Things in Life," *Arizona Quarterly* (Spring 1973); "Shutting the Door on Someone," *Southwest Review* (Autumn 1990); "Buried Alive by Language," *Word Out!* (Winter 1990); "How I Learned to Speak Italian," *Southwest Review* (Winter 1997); "The Case of the Missing Italian American Writers," *MultiAmerica,* ed. Ishmael Reed (Viking Penguin, 1997); "The Way of the World," *FRA NOI* (August 1985); "Reintroducing the Dream Book" appeared in a slightly different version as "Italian American Women Writers" in *New Ethnic American Literature and the Arts: The Italian American Heritage* (Garland, 1998). The first edition of *Chiaroscuro: Essays of Identity* was published in 1997 by Bordighera, Inc.

Chiaroscuro

The Way of the World

The centennial year of F. Scott Fitzgerald's birth, 1996, is also my father's, and ever since my finding in Matthew J. Bruccoli's biography (titled after his subject's extravagant words, *Some Sort of Epic Grandeur*) a photo of the author at age six captioned "Fitzgerald in Syracuse, New York, 1902," he has become, in my far-fetched thoughts, my father's counterpart.

My father was born on Christmas day, 1896, in Syracuse, New York, and his middle name–Salvatore–was in honor of the heavenly Savior whose birthday he shared, while his Italian surname, Mollica, translated, evokes bread, the staff of earthly life. *Buono come il pane,* good as bread, Italians say, not "good as gold" in the American way.

But my father had his own favorite saying, one which, for him, covered everything and was the one he most repeated:

> *Questo è il mondo,*
> *chi sa navigare*
> *e chi va a fondo.*
>
> *Chi navigare non sa,*
> *presto a fondo va.*

Freely rendered, it means that in the way of the world there are those who know how to sail their course, and those who, through not knowing or disregarding their knowledge, soon sink to the bottom. It is pitiless, realistic, the wisdom of obstinate self-reliance which taught a man not to count on grace, but to pull himself up by his own bootstraps.

For Dante the submerged, *i sommersi,* are the unfortunates whom he places in the fourth ring of Inferno. They also figure in *I sommersi e i salvati*, *The Drowned and the Saved*, the title of Primo Levi's last book, and in references throughout: "the Jews of Europe had been submerged. . . ."

Even without any literary reference, my father knew the difference between those who sink and those who don't. His is the story of the self-made man, of work and perseverance in the old style, of being his own boss. But he also had a fantasy; his Diamond as Big as the Ritz was to settle in California where he would live, work, thrive, raise a family, and play golf in that perfect climate. But that dream was trounced by the duty that cemented him with his recurring bouts of pneumonia to Syracuse and its miserable winters. Before he could leave for California, his dying mother, passing over her husband, made her son promise to stay to take care of his younger siblings.

It meant that I grew up in a home not of expressed affection and encouragement, but of duty discharged. I was disaffected from a sense of joy and personal fulfillment and understood only responsibility. The estrangement from my one remaining grandparent and the mysterious relatives on his side cast a shadow over the family and squashed close relationship. It made me distant from everything except my love of literature, a solitary calling in which the remote author is the one presence to cling to and believe in. The right author will never betray, disappoint, or leave one. Authors can be counted on as mere people cannot.

Fitzgerald, whose name commemorates Francis Scott Key of "The Star-Spangled Banner," was born in St. Paul, Minnesota, on September 24, 1896. The circumstance that F. Scott Fitzgerald and my father shared not only commemorative names and the same birth year, but also early school years in Syracuse, filled me with the same thrill of overlapping lives that Henry James experienced when he learned that he was in Florence at the same time that Clare Claremont, Lord Byron's mistress, was still living and residing there.

In Fitzgerald's diarylike ledger there is an Outline Chart of My Life, in which parodying the nasal inflection of upstate New Yorkers, he noted his parents' move in January 1901 from St. Paul to "Sarycuse" where they occupied an apartment on East Genesee Street. The next year they were at the Kasson Apartments on James Street, a grand, main thoroughfare of stately homes that had been named for Henry James's grandfather, an early real estate investor in the emerging city. Finally the Fitzgeralds took a flat on East Willow Street just off James. This is all familiar territory to me. I grew up at the eastern end of James Street, the less grand part, where my father had bought a two-family house in 1928. I went to school in Syracuse and graduated from the university there, then daily walked the length of James Street to my downtown job without knowing that the street was named for the first William James, whose fortune allowed Henry his comfortable margin as a writer. Perhaps my ignorance was all for the best; I might have been even more overcome with literary tremors and associations.

Scott Fitzgerald's being in Syracuse from 1901 to 1903 meant that he and my father started school at the same time and could well have been classmates, except that Scott was enrolled in Miss Goodyear's classes, a private school in a Victorian residence near the beginning of James Street which still in my day was attended by the daughters of prominent families, and my father went to the old Genesee Public School. Even if circumstances had put young Scott at Genesee Public, he and my father still wouldn't have met. For in those days children with Italian surnames, even though born in the United States, were separated from their "American" classmates and put into what was known off-record as the Dago Room. My father remembered this dispassionately as a curiosity of the times. He and centenarian Carrie Cashier, a onetime schoolmate and then the great-aunt of actor Robert De Niro, used to chuckle about those old days that could no longer hurt them.

In school Pop never got farther than ninth grade because he had to work, but he was impressed for life by his English teacher, Miss Katherine Bell. She called him not Anthony or Tony but Antonio after the character in *The Merchant of Venice*. He referred to her as Kitty Bell. Years and years later, when he was a leading wholesale produce merchant in Syracuse and I was a high school student, I wrote him a birthday poem which ended in a salute to "a sport not all wet like Venice / to Antonio, my father, the Merchant of Lettuce." The poem, printed and framed (and passed out by the hundreds to customers and friends), hung in the sunroom of the house on James Street until first he, then my mother went off to end their lives in nursing homes.

For Miss Bell the young Antonio dutifully memorized lines from Sir Walter Scott's *Lay of the Last Minstrel*–the ones that go, "Breathes there the man, with soul so dead / Who never to himself hath said, / This is my own, my native land!" That was a time when the cadences of certain lines learned in grade school were kept forever in mind without the reciter's necessarily knowing anything of the poet who wrote them. My father spoke the lines to his end.

Fitzgerald knew the poets. He wrote his personal observations on them and their work in the same ledger that served as his book-keeping record, his favorite being Keats's "Ode to a Nightingale" which gave him the title for *Tender Is the Night* and the assurance that anyone who did not know poetry could not be a writer.

If not the same school, still the young Scott Fitzgerald certainly would have attended the same church my father did as a boy. Given the Fitzgerald home addresses in Syracuse, Scott would have gone to mass with his observant Catholic parents at nearby St. John's Church, which is where my father's parents, both immigrants from Sicily, were married—not upstairs, in the church proper where the Irish practiced their Christian devotions, but downstairs in the basement which was the place for Italians.

"The Irish were our worst enemies in those days," my father equitably offered by way of explanation decades later.

I myself have never been fond of St. John's garish pseudo-Gothic decor. And I admit that when I think of those little boys of a century ago entering the church on different, highly symbolic levels, I am still offended even though I understand that it no longer pertains . . . that times have changed . . . that such practices have died. One Easter, visiting my parents in Syracuse, I went to mass at St. John's with them and thought during the service of how the celebrated and the ordinary sometimes touch without recognition, as in E. L. Doctorow's *Ragtime,* then go their different ways navigating through time and life. Some sail, some sink.

My father held his course until his ninetieth year. He lived all his years in the place where he was born; where, in the old days, he swam in the Erie Canal when it still ran through downtown; where he made pocket money reading and writing letters for the immigrants on the North Side; and where, for a dollar saved over the months from his paper route earnings, he could hire a horse and buggy and ride out to Long Branch on Onondaga Lake for a fish fry and ginger brew and feel on top of the world. He also played the clarinet in the marching band of the Società Agostino DePretis. In a time that didn't understand and frequently despised them, the

Italians in Syracuse formed social clubs for pleasure and sense of identity, and named them for the high dignitaries of the Old Country. The members gave banquets and marched in parades and restored their pride in themselves, to the tune, my father remembered, of the triumphal march from *Aida,* or his own favorite, "The Poet and Peasant Overture."

My father had been introduced to the produce business at age thirteen when he worked for his uncle and had to get up at 4 A.M. each day. He learned to hitch the horses and buy hay, timothy, and alfalfa at market for them. He learned to inspect produce, to collect payments, and to keep books. As he told it, he "fell in love with the business" and stayed with it the next fifty years. His college was the bustle and cunning of the marketplace, and it served him so well that he would later be called upon by Syracuse University's School of Business Administration to participate in panel discussions on small business and the economy.

By the time he was sixteen he was able to purchase a Harley-Davidson motorcycle and was photographed leaning jauntily against it at a grape harvest he rode to in the Finger Lakes vineyards; he's wearing a turtleneck sweater and jaunty cap and is smiling widely. When he was nineteen he was president of the Syracuse Fruit Company, having gotten his father to sign the papers of incorporation since he was underage. It was then he started driving a customized Hudson car. Around the same time, Fitzgerald, after a promising beginning, withdrew from Princeton, noting "a year of terrible disappointments and the end of all college dreams." That of course would soon enough be reversed.

In the earliest days of my father's business, wholesale fruit was bought through brokers in New York City—boxes of lemons from Sicily, say, or barrels of Almeria grapes packed in cork sawdust and shipped from Spain. But motorization and California agriculture revolutionized produce buying, and it was then he decided that his future, too, would be in California. But it never happened.

A business trip to Utica brought him the acquaintance of my mother who, as she tells it, first noticed the Hudson before she did the driver. He waited to marry her until the 1923 grape season was over, for the shipments meant big profits in that time of home wine making, and with the $5,000 profit made on the grapes, he took her to Europe for their honeymoon.

They got there the year before Scott and Zelda settled in Paris. In

1920 Fitzgerald published his first novel, gathering his fame and $18,850 from words, not grapes; he married Zelda (who had first broken their engagement because he seemed unable to earn a living), named the Jazz Age, lived the Life. In 1924 in Paris the Fitzgeralds were, indeed, the golden pair. His novel writing was interspersed with an outpouring of stories, and his ledger shows a canny businessman who knew how to keep recycling those stories in order to produce continual income.

Like my father the merchant, Fitzgerald kept meticulous accounts. But hard times hit them both. My father had to weather a disastrous fire, then the Depression and repayment of loans. Again he thought of California. In the late thirties, with Zelda hospitalized and his own life on the skids, it was Scott Fitzgerald who got to California. He was in Hollywood writing film scripts when he died there in 1940, age forty-four.

Instead of going west my father subscribed to the *National Geographic* magazine. Half a century of its issues were kept on specially built shelves in the basement of the house on James Street. He was seventy when he and my mother finally made the trip to California with Syracuse friends, a retired bank president and his wife. In Los Angeles they were met by a shipper my family had done business with on credit during the hard Depression years. "Well, Tony," the shipper said, "you must have done all right. I see you now travel with your own banker."

"Yes," Pop replied, "and an Irish one at that."

Some of his grandchildren are part Irish. "That's what this country is all about," he often reflected philosophically, the old enmity gone.

Fitzgerald's cardinal tenets sound like the numbered bits of wisdom my father once found printed on a paper placemat in a diner, brought home and framed, and made part of his philosophy. Fitzgerald stressed four virtues: Industry, Discipline, Responsibility, and Maturity (i.e., learning to regard failure as inevitable, and yet making one's best efforts always). Ditto for Pop.

My father finally retired from getting up at four in the morning and going to work in the dark, but never from life. He continued to golf in the summer at a country club which named its Senior Men's Tournament for him; he bowled in the winter, and lunched every Friday with the Syracuse Rotary Club. He steamed at the Y, attended to things like getting his hearing aid adjusted or his car washed, began to help my mother with the dishes, called to ask how my finances were ("Bad," I'd say, but he couldn't hear), and continued to pick out his own grapefruit at the market where a few old-timers still remembered him as the Banana King of upstate New York.

His last years were spent in a benign haze at the nursing home where he thought he was waiting to tee up on the golf course, other times repeating, Well, it's time to go home now. When he died, age ninety-five, he, too, though in a way different from Fitzgerald's, had brought forth his fruits in his season.

And yet, as I tell the tale of the two boys from Syracuse, something rings false. Do I really mean that my father sailed while Fitzgerald sank just because Pop mostly stayed sober and outlived him? No. Pop's life was more fraught than my simple story of it says. He didn't, in fact, change his destiny. He was shadowed by his mother's revenge on an adulterous husband which she had delegated to him; he was bound by his word to her not to leave Syracuse. His life was set. Is that a success story? Fitzgerald we still read and remember. Is that a failure?

So what do I mean? Perhaps that the happy life successfully lived is as much a fantasy as "The Diamond as Big as the Ritz."

Another Convent Story

The story went in my high school crowd that I left Nottingham High and transferred to The Convent School because of the two-cent soup. I was the pinchpenny stock figure in those broad characterizations schoolgirls make of each other. We defined ourselves in large, caricatural strokes, the better, I suppose, to get past the real questions of who we were becoming and what we wanted.

It was during the years of World War II. And, according to the story, I was won over to The Convent School by hearing my friend MaryAnn Sheed's accounts of what the nuns prepared for lunch: soup was two cents, a wonderful hot-dog roll stuffed with crisp bacon was seven cents, for ten cents you got a lot of hamburger gravy swilled over mashed potatoes. By changing schools and joining MaryAnn at the Convent I would be way ahead on my weekly lunch-money allowance, which meant I could buy more Glenn Miller and Jimmy Dorsey records in our after-school shopping forays downtown.

The story survived, with embellishments, because it amused everyone, including myself.

I thought at the time that my transfer had to do with shorter walking distance to school, and being with MaryAnn again. We had started kindergarten together in the public school and been best friends from childhood. Then, in fifth or sixth grade, upon the advice of her Uncle Pat, a priest, MaryAnn's parents took her out of Lincoln School and sent her for a Catholic education to Blessed Sacrament. My parents weren't concerned about Catholic education. My mother went to Sunday mass as if she were making insurance payments on the afterlife; my father, like the other Italian American family men I remember, was vociferously anticlerical. I had a cousin who was a nun, but she was regarded benevolently as a simple soul.

10

Her vocation was not the mark of distinction that it was in an Irish Catholic family like the Sheeds, who greatly revered their Uncle Pat.

It was a great surprise to my parents when I told them that I wanted to finish high school at the Convent. "I have to pay *them* and *they* don't pay taxes!" my father said, clamping down on his cigar angrily. "How will you meet boys?" my mother worried. Still, I went. But it was for neither the soup nor the shorter walk.

Now I know. It was for sanctuary.

At Nottingham (where, at football games, the opposing side jeered "Nottin' but ham" at our team, a crude racial slur since so many students were Jewish), I was not only with the scholastically ambitious children of professors from the university who lived in that part of town, but also with a waspy social elite. There were no black students at Nottingham, no Italians, Poles, Armenians, or other exotics like some of my classmates at Lincoln who all went on to Central High. When I entered Nottingham, I said goodby to the likes of Helen Sobieski, Gennaro Cacciacavallo, and Angel Bedrossian who had been my classmates since kindergarten—the real mix in the romanticized melting pot of American wishful thinking. We were the American dream: all creeds and colors and races coming together to mingle in friendly and childish innocence, Huck Finn and Jim on the raft. That multi-ethnic composition worked in the elementary grades, but the real world began to impinge when the students from Salem-Hyde finished there and joined us for junior high at Lincoln.

Salem-Hyde School served a noticeably different residential area than did Lincoln. Salem-Hyde children lived in single-family Tudor-type homes; their fathers had gone to college and were professional or businessmen, not tradespeople. Salem-Hyde children had "American" names: Shipton, Northrup, Hamilton, Yarwood, Barth, Stewart, Graham. They went to Protestant churches and never got excused from class for religious instruction as Catholic children did.

I lived in a two-family house. Every Saturday MaryAnn Sheed and I walked to Blessed Sacrament Church, stopping first at Woolworth's to look at things or snitch a root-beer barrel from the seductive bins of penny candy, and then on to confession. She was Irish and I was Italian. Of course we were both American, but I sensed that she was somewhat more American than I was. For one thing, MaryAnn's grandparents spoke English, mine did not. For another, her name was easy, mine was not. Yet neither of us was as American as the Salem-Hyde kids. We tacitly understood and accepted this because of the prototypes who filled our eyes and minds: Andy Hardy in films; Nancy Drew and her crowd in books; Jack Armstrong, all-American, on radio. Whoever heard of a hero or heroine with an unpronounceable name or with an uncle who was a priest?

What we didn't know growing up, we know now. It wasn't that we weren't really American, it was that we weren't Anglo-American and Protestant, and in those days the test of one's Americanness was how well one compared to the anglicized model. MaryAnn might have passed when her father became vice-president of a bank; my surname excluded me. But we were Catholic, and that didn't fit the requirements of the best high school sororities.

I could tell, even then, that anyone Irish was more Catholic than I was. MaryAnn, in fact, took her uncle the priest very seriously; she took Holy Days of Obligation and fasts very seriously; she did her penance devotedly; and she could recite the "laws" of the church with absolute certainty to tell me when I was afoul of them. I was much looser than strict interpretation permitted, and certainly more irreverent toward the clergy.

I also looked down on parochial schools. I was smart in school and I wanted a real education. I also wanted to be with kids who weren't all Catholic. At Lincoln, from seventh grade on, I aspired to the company of the Salem-Hyde crowd. They kept together once they got to Lincoln and ate together in the cafeteria. I remember the day I walked past the table with my old friends and made my way to the table where Sally Stewart and Betty Howard sat. I admired their looks, their sandwiches, their names, their small noses. Sally Stewart, who had mentioned once that her ancestors could be traced to William the Conqueror, awed me the most. I didn't know anything of the great world, but I knew that in my world it would be something to be accepted by her. I didn't want to go to Helen Sobieski's place anymore—that basement apartment of the building where her father was janitor. I didn't want to go to Annette Schlosser's birthday parties. I lost interest in Saturday afternoon confession.

I knew that Sally and Betty and their crowd were going to Nottingham High School after we all finished at Lincoln. That's where I decided to go, too. I lasted a year. Sally and the others got absorbed into sororities and the Junior League-sponsored holiday dances called Assemblies. As far as I could see, elitism was already established: socially, it was the Salem-Hyders; scholastically, it was my new Jewish classmates.

I began to feel out of place because I *was* out of place. My old friends from Lincoln were at Central High. I was the odd ball at Nottingham. Without the right name I could be neither Wasp nor Jew; I wasn't Irish Catholic; and I didn't want to be Italian. I was nowhere, tossed by the uncertainty of who I could ever conveniently be in a society which, at that time, prized variation and difference not at all.

So I went to the Convent where there was MaryAnn Sheed, my friend from a childhood when things were simpler and I didn't know one could grow up alien in one's own world.

In a sense it was a right move. At the Convent we all wore the same uniform and a blazer with the same insignia, and were nominally all alike. I was rushed for a Catholic sorority and became one of two or three exotic surnames in a sea of Healy, Murphy, Farley, O'Donnell, Dolan, Sheed, and the like. But it was also a wrong move: I was still out of place. I wasn't the kind of Catholic the Irish were; I was skeptical, questioning, detached from ritual except in its aesthetic function. And, paradoxically, I was too spiritually ambitious for the Convent. I was interested in the search and skirmish for faith, not in being an unthinking follower of set dogma.

The Convent School was run and staffed by Franciscan nuns for female day pupils and boarders. It was situated on the beautiful walled grounds of a former orchard, set back from the century-old brick Motherhouse of the worldwide order, the chapel and novitiate. Except for a beautiful, fine-featured, remote superior named Mother Carmela who was of Italian birth, who never appeared before us but whose picture we saw in our principal's office, and whom we heard mentioned in reverent tones and knew of as the world head of the order and thus like a royal personage whom we would never lay eyes on because the weight of her duties and the height of her position put her beyond us—except for this fabled nun, the others, the ones who ran the school and taught us, were Irish.

And the students were Irish. Or so it seemed. Certainly there were girls of other backgrounds in the Convent, but the *tone* was Irish. There was a moral priggishness, an obsession with observances, a preoccupation with shrines and chapel that were at odds with my notion of what was the good and the true.

I would sometimes discuss my reservations with MaryAnn as we walked home from school. She was staunch in her faith. She also said her Uncle Pat had warned her against me but she had told him I didn't really know what I was talking about. She believed that.

At the Convent two students weren't Catholic at all. One was Renee, a Jewish girl, who was enrolled by her mother because of the school's social amenities: Arthur Murray dance lessons on Friday afternoons, instruction on the harp and in archery, classes in etiquette and fine needlework. But the main reason, according the Renee, was what she was supposed to avoid: wearing lipstick, being clothes crazy, the company of boys. Renee was very likable; she was witty and smart, and amiably tolerant of our customs which she politely observed except for going to chapel. She went to the library instead.

Abbie Garrett was Protestant. She was a boarder at the Convent because her parents were often traveling and it was the safest place for her to be. The strange thing was that Renee's Jewishness and Abbie's Calvinism were closer to the puritanism of the nuns who taught us than my own Catholicism which was so full of relativism, doubt, and humanist references. My first notion of being "Italian" was of being less strict and more skeptical. I was uncertain if this were good or bad. The nuns had no doubts: they said it was a sign of intellectual pride, one of the seven deadly sins.

Though I came to the Convent to be among my own, to escape from being an outsider, it was only by hanging onto my contrariness that I found my true place there.

The Convent provided both a haven for me and a focus for my rebellions.

The one thing my parents concurred in concerning my going to the Convent was that, since I was getting out of hand, the school's emphasis on deportment (an area of education in which one was then graded) would calm me down and teach me to value manners as well as I did a critical outspokenness that had become hard to live with.

Of course they were wrong, just as all parents are wrong.

The Convent merely gave me a more visible target for everything I said I detested: authority, conformity, mindless obedience. It also gave me a supreme opportunity to show off. From the day I arrived in the principal's office for my enrollment interview with

Sister Anna and startled her by being dressed to go skiing, I was the instrument of the good nuns' penance, the cross they had to bear.

Soon enough I rebelled against the lunchtime hamburger gravy and mashed potatoes. It was not only dreary and daily, but I had read that mashed potatoes were often served as an institutional food because they were easily laced with saltpeter, a sexual depressant. I drew up a petition to replace that dish with a hamburger on a bun and potato chips. This led to my being summoned to Sister Anna's office.

"What is this fuss about lunch?" the nun asked, smiling her Cheshire cat smile, trying to appear friendly and amused as if at a childish prank.

"We are having gravy and mashed potatoes too often," I replied, not amused, but not at all ready to tell her that our sexuality should not be tampered with. "Too much will dull our senses," I said in what seemed clever circumlocution.

"Nonsense!" said Sister Anna, not at all taken in.

"It's very fattening," I persisted.

"It's also wartime," she answered, dismissing me.

That wasn't the only occasion we met in her office. I was also called in for failing religion, for organizing a cancan chorus line on the assembly hall stage during lunch recess, and for being found smoking in the grotto behind the statue of the Blessed Virgin. By spring I was reported for not wearing stockings as required, for having tried, instead, a tanning lotion on my bare legs. These were all matters, I was told, not only damaging to the well-being and morale of the school community, but personally offensive to Our Lady.

And while I constantly remarked that our uniforms were the outward signs of fascist regimentation, that our school was segregated by sex and religion and therefore undemocratic, that there should be less emphasis on prayer and more on a better library—the truth is, I relished my Convent days.

Being there appealed to my imagination. Lord Byron had put his love child, Allegra, in a convent in Italy where she had languished and died. If at that time I had known the story of the nun of Monza from Manzoni's novel *I promessi sposi,* I would have adored her tragic story. But my knowledge of Italian language and literature was still in the future; at that period of my life any Italian association was deliberately avoided.

The school was restful sanctuary from the anxiety I had felt at Nottingham and from the war with my parents at home. It was filled with the kind of girls I could easily impress with my heresies as I carried around a copy of Voltaire's *Philosophical Dictionary* (still on the Index of Prohibited Books in those days), which I had found in a cheaply printed edition at the Economy Bookstore for forty-nine cents. At a huge school like Central High I wouldn't even have been noticed. At the Convent, as Sister Anna put it, if my class-mates had numbered twelve like the Apostles, instead of our thir-teen, I would have been Judas Iscariot.

"This place is a prison," I'd grumble to MaryAnn. "And it has no class."

"Who says a prison has to be classy," she'd shrug.

"Some are! Some schools are former millionaires' estates and have Mexican heiresses boarding there, or the children of divorced movie stars and of famous converts like Clare Booth Luce."

"We've got the mayor's daughter," MaryAnn pointed out, "not to mention Eugenia and Eudora."

Eugenia and Eudora were sisters who belonged to the local founding branch of the then notable Schraffts empire of restaurants and quality candies. They were beautiful, sleek, haughty beings who were driven to school each day in a chauffeured limousine and were the most glamorous creatures our school contained. One of Eudora's classmates, a plain girl named Marie, met the car each morning in order to carry Eudora's books to class for her. Rather than the reg-ulation uniform we all wore, Eugenia and Eudora wore two hand-some variations made for them by their family dressmaker—fine wool worsted in winter and silk in spring; and both versions had indented waistlines, trim sleeves, and the all-around pleated skirts that were denied the rest of us. Even the nuns were dazzled by Eugenia and Eudora.

But it was not enough for me. I would have liked a school run by the Sisters of the Sacred Heart, who were intelligent and sophisti-cated and came to their order with dowries provided by their rich or titled European families. Our nuns seemed to me no more than parochial school teachers. For me there were two kinds of nuns. One was the naive, simple kind like my cousin with her demure ways and the tremulous name, Sister Angelica. She was of the same order as the Convent School nuns and, indeed, had gone there as a boarding pupil some years before I did. On her annual home visit she was shielded from unsettling family news and taken out for a chocolate ice cream soda. I remember her squirming nervously when five o'clock approached and she had to be back at the Mother-house. She became visibly apprehensive lest she be late . . . What, I'd wonder, did she think would happen? Would she be stripped of visiting privileges? Defrocked? Dismissed from the order? Sister Angelica was one of a gentle sisterhood who quaked before sin and transgression and spent their lives sheltered against encountering it.

The other kind of nuns I'd never met but knew of just the same. They exist in literature. They are the clever, witty women of Mary McCarthy's Catholic girlhood, the skilled adversaries of sin who meet it on equal terms and make each encounter a thrilling intel-lectual skirmish. They are the educators of girls who become charm-ing, scandalous women like Lady Antonia Fraser. They are the nuns who write concrete poetry and are abstract painters and appear in *Vogue*. But I did not meet them in my school.

The Sisters I knew were plain women with uncomplicated call-ings. Only the names they had taken in religion were expressive of some special view of themselves: Sister Aquiline, the Latin teacher, was a pale, ascetic beauty of refined coolness; Sister Teresita, dimin-utive and round, smiling, playful, and humble, taught the domestic arts; Sister Tarsicia, the grim-faced theologian with that awful name which bespoke martyrs and penitential hermits; Sister Flavia, sweet-tempered and pretty, who played the harp and taught voice; and Sister Matilda, the sharp, beady-eyed harpy of history and senior religion whose medieval namesake, the great Countess of Canossa, had humbled the Holy Roman Emperor.

We were taught French by an ancient Belgian nun, very wrinkled and settled by age into a squat tea-cozy shape. *"Bonjour, ma Soeur,"* we used to greet her as we curtsied before entering her classroom. She detested teaching grammar, and our lessons consisted in repeat-ing our prayers in French (*"Je vous salue, Marie, pleine de grace . . ."*) until our pronunciation wouldn't, as she put it, make frogs in her ears.

She called us by some approximation of our last names. "Shade!" she'd call out to MaryAnn Sheed, holding her left index finger alongside her nose, her eyes rolling in mock horror, her right hand holding up to our view MaryAnn's homework paper with well-marked mistakes. "You make spiders!"

Still, she wished us well and wasn't averse to easing our way through the Regents exams with off-the-record explanations of troublesome words in the *dictée*. In return it was understood that we would give generously to the monthly collection she made among us for the upkeep of the shrine to her patroness, Ste. Marie de Nemours. "I pray for you, *mes petites filles*," she said as she collected our nickels and dimes.

She also advised us. The worst tragedies of our lives—pregnancy or an automobile accident—could be avoided, she told us, by our going out only with the boys of the Christian Brothers Academy, our brother institute. Since scholarship was held of no great account in our school, teaching made little demand on the Sisters and they were thus able to spend their time more profitably warning us against "the world" and "the Fiddler" whom we would certainly have to pay if we weren't careful.

Their main task was not to impart knowledge, or God forbid, a capacity to think for ourselves, but to keep us from sin. And especially the sin of pride. Of all transgressions, it was pride that most troubled them. While the other side of pride, false humility, flourished among the more unctuous boarders, it was I who was regarded with suspicion for being too eager a student.

"We have a shining star in our midst," Sister Matilda would say with a tinge of sarcasm when I volunteered answers or made some relevant point in her history class. It was regarded as unladylike.

With no solid education, I was left with a longing to fill the empty spaces, and this in turn made me a greedy, though often undiscriminating, reader. Dorothy Parker, who also had a convent education, said that convents are like progressive schools but don't know it—they don't teach you how to read or learn; you have to find out for yourself.

In chapel, while everyone else sang the Tantum Ergo from their missals, I read from a little book of modern poetry concealed in mine. In Latin class, I protested Sister Aquiline's efforts to read Christian prophecy into Vergil. And in English I asked why we didn't read Shakespeare.

"We're following our text of *Great Catholic Authors*," Sister Anna replied, her mouth set tightly.

The nuns had no misgivings about the sycophant boarders, or about the Schraffts sisters whom I thought cruel and haughty. They had none about Renee who was treated as an honored guest and were most discreet about not proselytizing in her direction. But they did have doubts about me. I bothered them all the more since my cousin, Sister Angelica, had been so exemplary. The problem couldn't be a family taint but something personally wrong with me. They prayed for my enlightenment.

Real distinction in that school had to do with demeanor, with the right responses, and with highly visible piety. All our behavior was referred to the Virgin Mary as the highest model of decorum. Would Our Lady wear a strapless gown to the Senior Ball? we were asked to consider. Would she commit fouls in basketball games? Or go without stockings?

When school plays were put on they were usually morality dramas about saints. One I remember was "Saint Francis and the Wolf of Gubbio," which I disdained. Years later, living in Italy, I was in Saint Francis' territory; I studied Italian in Perugia and visited nearby Assisi and Gubbio. By then I was charmed with the story of the wolf and could read *I fioretti* in the very language I had once, in Sister Matilda's class, scorned.

Some question had come up about the inventor of the wireless. "Let's have our Italian star pronounce Marconi's first name for us," Sister Matilda said, nodding in my direction.

I was outraged at thus being singled out. How dare she call me Italian in front of the class and thus join me with Mary Ciccio, a heavy-browed classmate with a funny way of talking whom I particularly hated. I couldn't, in fact, pronounce Guglielmo or any other Italian name or word at that time.

"I don't know Italian," I said quickly, eager to disassociate myself from Marconi, Mary Ciccio, and Mussolini who had just stabbed France in the back and was our enemy in war. What was wrong was that I was glad not to know. I was glad to abjure a heritage that was, at that time and place, too painful for me to accept.

I was Italian American and filled with the shame of being something unacceptable. At best Italians were long-nosed buffoons, at worst they were gangsters in movies or pathetic prisoners of war in the news. It was a difficult time to grow up.

With MaryAnn and my sorority sisters I tried to fit in with the Irish crowd. But every day in school, we had current events in which we discussed the ongoing war against the Axis powers of which Italy was one. And Mary Ciccio was there in the flesh to personify all I wanted to distance myself from. I snubbed Mary and, with the others, made fun of her shoes, the thick sandwiches she brought from home, and the little gold earrings in her pierced ears which in those days were considered low class, the mark of a peasant.

The lowest point of my apostasy was the satisfaction I felt when Mary Ciccio lost the French prize to Ann O'Fallon. Usually the French prize was for a written effort, but in our senior year we were to memorize a long passage of poetry by Victor Hugo and recite it to Sister Anna who was then to award the prize for the best delivery. All thirteen of us recited the lines and were winnowed down to two: Mary Ciccio and Ann O'Fallon. Even with my prejudiced ear, I could hear that Mary's pronunciation and fluency with the language were far superior to Ann's.

"Well, that is fine, girls," Sister Anna beamed at the finish. "I think you both did extremely well. But Mary has a bit of an advantage I would say, because she's Italian and can twist her tongue around those French words more easily. Since that's the case, and Ann had to make an extra effort to speak a foreign language, the prize goes to her."

I was pleased at Mary's defeat and even at the aspersion that was cast on her adroit "foreign" tongue. Now I am appalled. Mary, as American born as Ann, was made to seem alien. The fact that her French was so good was held against her. I hadn't yet identified the ugliness of a discrimination so subtle and so generally accepted that even the very strengths of a person could be turned to a disadvantage, into cause for shame. Stupidly, with no understanding that the prejudice against Mary could, in other ways, be used against me or anyone, I basked in her defeat.

Yes, I was Judas; though not for the reasons the nuns thought.

The last part of my senior year I began a calculated recantation.

"I think," I told MaryAnn, "I'll be May Queen."

At our school pious politics were engaged in by nuns as well as students to determine the president of the sodality, Senior Prom Queen, May Day Queen, and finally the valedictorian at graduation. Points were gained by the girls who made novenas, went to mass on the first Fridays of each month, and kept absolute silence during the three-day spiritual retreats. Not brains, nor skills, nor charm, nor family, nor even Schraffts chocolates could prevail against the kind of showy piety that two or three girls in each class, always the boarders, were especially adept at.

"Hah!" MaryAnn scoffed at my announcement. "You've got as much chance of that as Renee has of becoming a nun."

"Not if I change. Sister Matilda will see making me Queen as encouraging me to keep up the good work. What could she gain by rewarding a goody-good? For each soul she wins, she gets years off her term in purgatory."

"But you're failing religion," MaryAnn noted.

"On purpose!–just to show how little I cared. I can catch up. Sister Matilda will *have* to choose me, just for the sake of the teaching that the Good Shepherd will leave his flock of ninety-nine obedient lambs to go after the one who's strayed."

"And you really want to be May Day Queen?" MaryAnn hooted. "That's boarders' stuff!"

"That's why," I told her.

My behavior became exemplary. I stopped painting my legs with tan-gel and wore my hated stockings all through the spring. I stopped disputing the Sisters; I sang out in chapel.

"Now that you are about to leave us, you are showing great promise," Sister Anna commended me with her false smile. Perhaps she thought that the sadness of leaving the school after graduation had changed me. She asked me to prepare the valedictory address.

I received communion during our senior retreat, and I made that retreat (my last) in complete, penitential silence. Everything went well until the day Sister Matilda was to announce the name of the May Day Queen in her religion class.

To start with I was late for that first-period class because it was a clear and beautiful morning and MaryAnn and I roller-skated to school the long way. The bell was already ringing as we stood out on the front steps pulling up our rolled down stockings and hitching them to our garter belts. "I think I'm sunk," I told her.

Not for being late just one morning," she reassured me.

As we walked into religion class, Sister Matilda interrupted what she was saying to greet us with a sarcastic, "Good afternoon, ladies."

We apologized and she resumed. She was speaking that morning of the need for irreproachable conduct in young women. Now, of all the nuns in the Convent, it was Sister Matilda I most loved and hated and wanted to impress and annoy. In religion class her tight-lipped tirades against a corrupting world made me fidget with impatience. "Remember," she'd hiss, her beady eyes implacable, "remember who pays the Fiddler. It's always the girl who pays the Fiddler."

In the Convent the wickedness of the world was sex, and our puritanical strain of Irish Catholicism was geared toward exorcising it. Our deliberately misshapen uniforms, the insistence that we wear stockings even on hot days because the rubbing of bare legs against our desks might be arousing, those daily saltpeter-laced potatoes, all that careful routing of sex only made us that much more aware of it.

A definite undercurrent of sexual morbidness ran through the school, palpable and disturbing. It was there in the words Virgin Mary and Immaculate Conception and the Harlot Magdalen; it resounded in the phrase "fruit of thy womb" which we voiced in everyday prayers. It was evident in the embarrassment of poor Sister Gabriel the day she was asked, regarding the Feast of the Circumcision, what circumcision was. All she could manage to stutter from the depths of her discomfort was, "I really can't say . . . Perhaps a nursing sister . . ."

Only on one other occasion have I experienced that same affluence of sexual morbidness that infused the Convent and firmed the resolve of its chaste Sisters. It happened many years after my Convent School days. I had been twenty years a wife and five a widow. And I was going on a lovers' tryst to a nineteenth-century resort inn in the upper Hudson Valley. The sign, as we wound our way up a mountain road to the inn, said, Slowly and Quietly, Please. Gazebos dotted the place like the Stations of the Cross on the old Convent grounds.

The Victorian lodge loomed up like a vast, wooden version of the red brick Motherhouse and school. Inside I recognized the dark, threadbare rugs; the wide, oak stairways, the genteel sitting areas of wicker and plush arrangements, the bracketed wall light fixtures, the faded wallpaper, and even the prints of Raphael Madonnas and Venetian canals. Silent clandestine couples, honeymooners, single elderly ladies and older gentlemen hovered in the shadows of the ill-lit sitting rooms where bridge tables stood unoccupied and shelves were filled with the untempting brown volumes of long ago. A sign at one sitting room, irreproachable in its lack of allure and sybaritic comforts, read Keep the Door Open Please. I was transported back to the Convent with its God Sees You reminders everywhere.

The inn's dining room was reached through lengthy beige corridors from whose walls hung pictures not of saints but of bewhiskered

Quaker worthies (the old boys at golf, on an outing, at meeting). The feel of the Convent was there, the sense of things repressed or hidden away or not at all what they seem on the surface.

At The Convent School, sex, a constant undertone, came out of hiding at each senior retreat and was openly there in the great themes of Chastity and Physical Purity.

That morning of my senior year, the spring day gleamed glorious and bright through the windows behind Sister Matilda's black habit and veil, past her thin nervous hands which played with the cord of the window shade. I could see golden jets of forsythia, I could smell the sweetness of cut grass, and I was eager for the world which seemed not evil but divine. Shortly we would graduate and be out of the Convent.

Sister Matilda was going on with some balmy story about a young girl traveler being driven by an unscrupulous taxi driver not to her hotel, but, instead, to a house where innocent girls were delivered into prostitution. As the girl was being set upon by a patron of such places, she drew out her rosary and begged him to think of his mother and to desist. The girl's piety touched the man. He reformed on the spot and helped her to get out.

"Remember your faith is your armor," said the nun, "and above all, remember who pays the Fiddler—the girl always pays."

I couldn't keep quiet. "Not necessarily," I said evenly. "There are ways to get around having to pay."

How I managed that assertion that hinted at an expertise I didn't have, I still don't know. It amazed me as much as it startled the class and horrified Sister Matilda.

I did not become May Day Queen, nor class valedictorian. I was expelled from The Convent School. Now as I look back, I see the episode as part of youthful idealism, of wanting to defend life and believe in it; it was my age and my ingenuousness and perhaps the nuns should have known it.

After an interview between my mother and an icy Sister Anna, and my own retraction and apology, I was allowed back in time to graduate. At the ceremony I heard pious Elizabeth, a boarder who was going to enter the novitiate, give the valedictory address. How sanctimoniously she delivered her platitudes; how ingratiatingly she knelt and kissed the bishop's ring; how sickening she was. And how quickly it was over and I was out, for good.

"You know," my mother told me years later, "I was so angry with you when you got expelled from the Convent that I never told you the real reason they took you back and let you graduate."

"What was it," I asked.

"When I went to see the principal, she told me she'd take you back because, based on citywide reports from all the schools, you were going to be a Regents award winner. The Convent School never had a winner before and she did not want the school to lose that honor by your graduating someplace else."

By the time my mother told me that I was living in Rome. I was married to an Italian poet and had long lost the desire to be Irish. I spoke Italian and it gave me no qualms to say Marconi's first name. My children are named Teodolinda, Susanna, and Nicoletta and they speak Italian as well as their mother tongue. I have, among my Italian sayings, a favorite: *Chi paga, balla*. It means, freely rendered, "Whoever pays gets to call the tune"—the Fiddler is understood.

How I Learned
to Speak Italian

He was a patient man. His slopping shoulders curved with a bearing that spoke more of resistance and steadfastness than of resignation; his ruffled hair was graying, his eyes were mild and gray behind the glasses that were the badge of his work–he set type and proofread for *La Gazzetta*. It was because of his job at that weekly Italian-language newspaper in Syracuse that I met Mr. de Mascoli. In my last year at the university I found it wasn't Spanish that interested me, after all, but Italian. However, at that point I couldn't switch my language requirement; I would have to keep Spanish and do Italian on my own. I went to the *Gazzetta* to put in a want ad for a tutor. Instead I found Mr. de Mascoli willing to teach me.

And why Italian? Because during that last year before graduation I had met an Italian student who had come over on a Fulbright grant to study at Syracuse University. Knowing him awakened in me unsuspected longings for that Mediterranean world of his which I suddenly, belatedly, realized could also be mine. I became conscious of an Italian background that had been left deliberately vague and in abeyance by my parents who, though children of Italian immigrants, had so homogenized into standard American that their only trace of identity was an Italian surname, often misspelled and always mispronounced.

I knew nothing of Italian. It was not a popular subject at home. We had just come out of World War II in which Italy had been our enemy, and my father was at once scornful and touchy about Italy's role in that conflict. And even before that we had never been part of the Italian community of the North Side, my parents having

25

selected their first, then second, homes on James Street, a thorough-fare of great mansions receding eastward into large, comfortable homes, then more modest two-families until, finally, it became the commercial area of Eastwood. I did not learn until recently that I had grown up on the street named for Henry James's grandfather, an early developer of the barren tracts from which Syracuse grew and from which Henry enjoyed his income.

My parents' aspirations were away from the old Italian neigh-borhoods and into something better. My father made a significant leap into the American mainstream when he became a member of both the Rotary Club and the Syracuse Yacht and Country Club where he and my mother golfed and I spent aimless summers.

It never occurred to my father to speak his own father's language to my two brothers or to me, and so we grew up never conversing with our only two living grandparents, my father's father and my mother's mother, and so never knowing them. My grandfather came to call each Christmas, my father's birthday; he sat uneasily in the sunroom with his overcoat on, took the shot of scotch he was offered, and addressed the same phrase to me each year: "Youa gooda gehl?" Then he'd hand me a nickel. There was a feeling of strain in the performance. My father was a man of substance, his was not.

With my grandmother there was a brief ritual phrase in her dialect mouthed by us children when we went to the old Queen Anne-style house in Utica where my mother and all her brothers and sis-ters grew up. My grandmother was always in the kitchen, dressed in black, standing at a large black coal range stirring soup or some-thing. My brothers and I, awkward in the presence of her foreign-ness, would be pushed in her direction by our mother during those holiday visits and told, "Go say hello to Gramma."

We'd go to the strange old woman who didn't look like any of the grandmothers of our friends or like any of those on the covers of the *Saturday Evening Post* around Thanksgiving time. Gramma didn't stuff a turkey or make candied sweet potatoes and pumpkin pies. She made chicken soup filled with tiny pale meatballs and a bitter green she grew in her backyard along with broad beans and basil, things that were definitely un-American in those days. Her smell was like that of the cedar closet in our attic. She spoke strange words with a raspy sound.

When we stepped into her kitchen to greet her she smiled

broadly and tweaked our cheeks. We said in a rush the phrase our mother taught us. We didn't know what it meant. I think we never asked. And if we had known it meant "how are you?" what difference would it have made? What further knowledge would we have had of the old woman in the shapeless black garment, with her wisps of gray hair falling out of the thick knob crammed with large old-fashioned tortoiseshell hairpins? None. We were strangers. Yet she is part of my most fundamental sense of who I am.

When on a visit upstate recently I had occasion to drive through Cazenovia, a village on the shores of Lake Cazenovia, it appeared to me as if in a dream. I saw again the lakeshore meadow that has always remained indelibly imprinted on my mind from childhood, but which I had thought must have vanished from the real world. That meadow, now called Gypsy Bay Park, was the site of family picnics to which we and Aunt Mary's family proceeded from Syracuse, while the other contingent (which was by far the greater number, my mother's three brothers, two other sisters and all their families, plus our grandmother) came from Utica. Cazenovia was the approximate halfway point, and there in the meadow on the lake the cars would all pull up and baskets of food would be unloaded for the great summer reunion.

My father drove a car that had a front fold-up seat which I was allowed to stand at and hold onto while looking straight out the window at the roadway, pretending that I was the driver guiding us all to the lake. I always made it, and the weather was always fine.

And so we met in a landscape which, today, I would never have expected to glimpse again in its original state. Whenever, over the years, I would think back to the picnics in Cazenovia, I would imagine the locale filled with new housing developments or fast food chains on the lakeshore. But no, the meadow was still green with grass, still fringed with trees bending toward the water, still free of picnic tables, barbecue grills on metal stands, and overflowing trash cans. It was the same as when I was five years old and the gathering took on the mythic quality that it still retains for me.

It was Gramma who had decreed this annual outing. When two of her daughters married and moved from Utica, she had made known her wish: that the family should meet each summer when travel was easier and eat together *al fresco*. It was her pleasure to have all her children, and their children, convene in the meadow, and spend the day eating, singing, playing cards, gossiping, throw-

ing ball, making jokes and toasts. It was a celebration of her prog-
eny of which she, long widowed, was the visible head, the venerable ancestor, the symbol of the strong-willed adventurer who had
come from the Old World to make a new life and to prosper.

She was monumental. I can see her still, an imposing figure, still
dressed in black although it was summer, seated on a folding camp
chair (just for her) under the shade of a large, leafy elm tree. She sat
there as silently as a Sioux chief and was served food, given babies
to kiss, and paid homage to all day. The others spread around her,
sitting on blankets on the grass, or on the running boards of their
Oldsmobiles and Buicks. What made my grandmother so intriguing was the mystery of her. For, despite its gaiety, the family picnic
was also a time of puzzlement for me. Who was this stranger in
black with whom I could not speak? What was her story? What did
she know?

What I knew of my grandmother I heard from my mother: she
believed in good food on the table and good linens on the bed.
Everything else was fripperies, and she had the greatest scorn for
those who dieted or got their nourishment through pills and potions.
She knew you are what you eat and she loved America for the great
range of foods that it provided to people like her, used to so little,
used to making do. She could not tolerate stinginess; she lived with
her eldest son and his family of eleven and did all the gardening
and cooking, providing a generous table.

She founded the family well-being on food. She had gotten up
early, baked bread, or used the dough for a crusty white pizza sprin-
kled with oil, oregano, and red pepper or with onions and potatoes,
olives and anchovies—but never with tomato sauce for that disguised the taste of good bread dough and made it soggy and soft. She
provided these pizzas, or *panini,* to the mill workers whose wives
were too lazy or too improvident to do it themselves. She kept the
men's orders all in her mind; she had great powers of concentration
and her memory took the place of jotted-down notes. She never got
an order wrong. From workers' lunches, she expanded into a small
grocery store. Soon she was importing foodstuffs from Italy. Eventually, what she turned over to her sons was one of the largest
wholesale food companies in central New York.

At those picnics my cousins were older than I, mostly young
people in their teens and twenties. The boys wore knickerbockers
and played banjos or ukeleles and the girls wore white stockings

and sleeveless frocks. My uncles played cards and joked among themselves; the women arranged and served endless platters of food. Somebody was always taking snapshots, and I have many of them in a large album that has survived a dozen moves.

My grandmother stayed regally under her tree like a tribal queen, and mounds of food were placed around her like offerings. Her daughters and daughters-in-law kept up a steady parade of passing the foods they had been preparing all week: fried chicken, salames, prosciutto, roasted sweet peppers, fresh tomatoes sliced with mozzarella and basil, eggplant fritters, *zucchini imbottiti,* platters of corn, huge tubs of fresh salad greens, caciotto cheese, rounds of fresh, crusty bread, every kind of fruit, and biscotti galore. It was as if my grandmother's Thanksgiving took place not in bleak November, but on a summer day when there would be sun on her shoulders, flowers blooming and cool breezes off the lake, blue skies above and the produce of her backyard garden abundantly present. She lived with the memory of the picnic through the long upstate winter, and by the time spring had come she would go out to plant the salad greens and put in the stakes for the broad beans and tomatoes, planting and planning for the coming picnic.

We were about fifty kin gathered in that meadow, living proof of the family progress. Gramma's sons and daughters vied to offer her their services, goods, and offspring—all that food, those cars, the well-dressed young men who would go to college. And Butch, an older cousin, would take me by the hand to the water's edge and I'd be allowed to wade in Cazenovia's waters which were always tingling cold and made me squeal with delicious shock.

And yet with all that, for all the good times and good food and the happy chattering people who fussed over me and my brothers, I still felt a sense of strangeness, a sense of my parents' tolerating with an edge of disdain this Old World *festa* only for the sake of the old lady. When I asked my mother why Gramma looked so strange and never spoke to us, I was told, she came from the Old Country . . . she doesn't speak our language. She might as well have been from Mars.

I never remember hearing our own mother speak to her mother, although she must have, however briefly. I only recall my astonishment at mother's grief when Gramma died and we went to Utica for the funeral. How could mother really feel so bad about someone she had never really talked to? Was it just because she was expected to cry? Or was she crying for the silence that had lain like a chasm between them?

Mother was a smartly dressed, very American lady, who played golf and bridge and went to dances. She seemed to us to have nothing to do with the old woman in a kitchen where, at one time, a dozen and more people had sat around the long, oilcloth-covered table. Nor did my father, with his downtown meetings and busy manner, seem to have any connection with his own father, who was called the Old Man and wore baggy pants and shuffled like a movie comedian.

There was no reason for me or my brothers to think, as we were growing up, that we were missing anything by not speaking Italian. We knew that our father spoke it, because at Christmas when the Old Man came to call, we'd overhear long streams of it and laugh at the queerness of it in our home. My mother, no, could never have been said to speak or know Italian, only some dialect phrases. But in my father reposed the tongue of his fathers; and it hadn't been important to him (or to us) that we have it.

What had I to do with any of those funny types I'd see on the North Side the few times I accompanied my mother there for shopping? We didn't speak or eat Italian at home with the exception of the loaf of Italian bread my father brought home every day from the Columbus Bakery. Occasionally my mother would prepare an Italian dinner for her mostly Irish friends, and then she'd have to go to the North Side where the Italians lived and had their own pungent grocery stores to find the pasta or the imported cheese and oil she needed. I hated to accompany her, the smell from barrels of dried and salted baccalà or of ripe provolone hanging by cords from the ceiling was as great an affront to my nose as the sound of the raspy Italian dialect spoken in the store was to my ears. That it all seemed crude and degrading was something I had absorbed from my parents in their zeal to advance themselves. It was the rather touching snobbery of second-generation Italian Americans toward those who were, in their view, "just off the boat."

But it was on the North Side that the *Gazzetta* offices were located, so I had to go there. And there I met Mr. de Mascoli. I could have grown up in Syracuse and lived there all my life without ever knowing that the *Gazzetta* existed. It took the Italian student to make me aware of the Italian paper, the beauty of Italian, and a lot of other things, too.

My father, as a Rotary project, had invited the Italian student (and a Colombian and a Venezuelan, also) home for Thanksgiving dinner to give them a taste of real America. What happened during that curious cultural exchange was not so much a forging of ties with America for the Italian and the South Americans, as an awareness in myself of my own Latin bloodline and a longing to see from where and what I originated. At Thanksgiving dinner it wasn't Pilgrims and Plymouth I thought of but Catullus. The Latin poets I read in my college courses connected me to the Italian student who was already a *dottore* from an Italian university and was saying things in a sharply funny, ironic way—a way no American spoke. It was strange that my awakening came at an all-American celebration through the medium of a tall, lean-faced student of forestry who was relating to my father in good English his experience during the war as an interpreter for the British troops pushing up through the Gothic Line to Florence.

Florence! I had never given thought to that fabled place, but in that instant I longed to see it. In my immediate conversion, I who knew nothing of Italy or Italians, not even how to pronounce Marconi's first name, became aligned forever with the Italianness that had lain unplumbed and inert in me. My die was cast, over the native American bird, Yankee creamed onions and Hubbard squash, across parents who would have been horrified to know it.

I was attracted to the Italian student, and he to me. When we started seeing each other, he was critical of my not knowing his language. "I know French and Spanish," I said. He was not impressed.

"Your language should have been Italian," he said sternly.

"I've had Latin, so it shouldn't be so hard to learn," I replied.

"Try this." He handed me his copy of the *Gazzetta*. It was the first time I had seen the paper, seen Italian. I couldn't make any sense of the unfamiliar formations like *gli* and *sgombero,* the double *z*'s and the verb endings. I was filled with dismay, but I decided to learn and I thought it could be done easily, right at home. After all, my father knew Italian.

"No use in learning a language like that," my father said dismissively when I approached him. "Spanish is more useful. Even Portuguese will get you further than Italian."

Further where? Toward the foreign service in Brazil? But that was not my direction.

Learning Italian became something stronger than just pleasing the Italian student. I began to recall things like my mother saying that just before her death Gramma had called for a sip of the mountain spring water near her Calabrian village. That was her last wish, her last memory; she had left Calabria at the age of seventeen with a husband of almost forty and had never gone back. But sixty years later as she lay dying in Utica it was only the water of her native hills that she wanted and called for.

I wanted to go see where she came from. I wanted to be able to talk to the Old Man who still came each Christmas, and to tell him who I really was besides a gooda gehl and to find out who he was.

I went deliberately to the *Gazzetta* on the North Side to find an Italian teacher rather than to the university's Italian department because, when I called the department, I was answered by a professor who said, giving his name twice, "Pay-chay or Pace speaking." As if one could choose between the Italian name and the anglicized version. For me, even then, there was only one way he could have said his name and if he didn't understand that he was not the teacher I wanted. Mr. de Mascoli was.

He was like Pinocchio's stepfather, a gentle Geppetto. And he was genuinely pleased that I should want to learn Italian. He would give me lessons in his home each evening after supper, he said. He wanted no payment. He had come from the hard, mountainous, central part of Italy called the Abruzzo. He arrived in America in the late 1920s, not as an illiterate laborer, but as an idealist, a political emigré out of sympathy with the fascist regime. And he had been educated. He had a profound love for his homeland, and it was love which made him want to give me its language.

I accepted his offer. And I thought of all the fine things I would send him in return when I got to Italy—the finest olive oil and parmesan cheese for his wife; the nougat candy called *torrone* for his children; and for him an elegantly bound volume of Dante. I would send him copies of Italian newspapers and magazines because he had told me confidentially that, yes, *La Gazzetta* was really the *porcheria* everyone said it was. But bad as it was, it kept the language alive among the people on the North Side. When it was gone, what would they have?

I went to Mr. de Mascoli's home each night in the faded old Chevy my father passed on to me for getting to the university. The first night I arrived for my lessons I wore a full-skirted, almost ankle-length black watch tartan skirt my father had brought me from a trip to Chicago. It was topped by a wasp-waisted buttoned to the neck lime-green jacket. It was the New Look that Dior had just introduced to signal the end of wartime restrictions on fabric and style, and I felt very elegant, then too elegant as Mr. de Mascoli led me down a hall to his kitchen. We sat at the table in the clean white kitchen which showed no sign of the meal he and his wife and children had just eaten. Mrs. de Mascoli, a short, pudgy, youngish woman, made a brief appearance and greeted me cordially. I could hear she was American, but she had neither the education nor the ascetic and dedicated air of her husband. She spoke the kind of rough-hewn English one heard on the North Side. In her simple, friendly way she, too, was pleased that I was coming for Italian lessons.

In their clean white kitchen I spent a whole winter conjugating verbs, learning the impure *s* and the polite form of address. I began to speak Mr. de Mascoli's native language. I learned with a startled discomfit that my surname had a meaning and could be declined. *Mollica* was not only a family name but a noun of the feminine gender meaning crumb, or the soft inner part of the loaf as distinct from the good, hard outer crust. The name had always been a bane to me since teachers, salesgirls, or camp counselors were never able to say it. I would always have to repeat it and spell it as they stuttered and stumbled, mangling and mouthing it in ludicrous ways. It was my cross, and then I learned it meant crumb.

I began to fantasize: what if, like the draft that changed Alice's size, I could find a DRINK ME! that would switch me from a hard-to-pronounce crumb to something fine like Miller? Daisy Miller, Maud Miller. Even Henry. I'd be a different person immediately. In fact, for the first time I'd be a person in my own right, not just a target for discriminatory labels and jokes.

From years of Latin I could see how my name was related to all those words meaning "soft": mollify, mollescent (the down side of tumescent), mollusk. (A moll, as in Moll Flanders, was something else!)

The Italian minces no meanings: *mollare,* the verb, means to slacken; from that, the adjective *molle* means not only soft or limber, but flabby, pliant, even wanton. From *molle* comes *mollica,* and then, *mollizia,* that intriguing word meaning effeminacy and suggesting its counterpart, *malizia,* which signifies cunning malice. But I was marked from the start by softness not cunning.

And what must have been the lewd cracks my father was prey to with a name from which so many allusions to soft and limp could be made?

A molleton, or *molletone* in Italian, is literally a swanskin, or a soft skin. Is this, I asked myself, why I was so hypersensitive, and thin-skinned? Because I came from a genetic line that was so incongruously delicate among the smoldering emotions of south Italy that they became identified forever after by a surname that told all? Were my forebears a soft touch, too soft for their own good in a place where basic fiber and guts would have been more pressingly urgent than skin like a swan?

What if I had been not Miss Softbread but, say, Sally Smith of the hard edge, a name evoking the manly English smith at his forge with all the honorable tradition and advantage *that* entailed? How my life might have advanced! I wondered about translating my name to Krumm; being female had an advantage—I could marry a right-sounding name. But then I'd have to abandon my Italian lessons and the plan to go to Italy and the Italian student.

I continued my lessons. At home I practiced singing in Italian with my opera records as I followed words in the libretti. In the high-flown phrases of operatic lingo I began to form myself a language as remote as could be from the grandmother's dialect or the North Side, but, I thought with satisfaction, very grand and eloquent.

"Ardo per voi, forestier innamorato," I sang in the sunroom along with Ezio Pinza. *"Ma perchè così straziarmi,"* I said to Mr. de Mascoli one night, right out of Rossini's *Mosè,* when he plied me with verbs. Or, rhetorically, *"O! Qual portento è questo?"* I expressed no everyday thought but something compounded of extreme yearning, sacrifice, tribulation, or joy. In the speech of grand opera everything becomes grander, and I felt so, too, as I sang all the roles. It was as if I were learning Elizabethan or Chaucerian English to visit contemporary London as I memorized my lines preparatory to leaving for Italy. I had worked and saved for a year to get there.

When I went to say goodbye to Mr. de Mascoli, he seemed sad and stooped. We had often spoken of the harshness many Italians had suffered in their own land and how they had had to emigrate, leaving with nothing, not even a proper language to bolster them. I told him I would write to him in Italian and send him news of his country. He said, "My country is a poor and beautiful place. I do not hate her."

"And I never will!" I answered.

I went to Italy thinking to rejoin the Italian student, who had already returned to his country, but that is another story: he turned out to have always been married. It wasn't the end of the world for me. I was in Italy and everything else was just beginning.

I studied in Perugia, I wrote articles for the Syracuse *Herald-Journal,* I saw Italy. I surpassed my initial Italian lessons and acquired a Veneto accent when I met and married Italian poet and journalist Antonio Barolini. He had courted me reading from a book of his poetry that included an ode to Catullus with the lovely lines (to be put on my gravestone):

> *ora la fanciulla è sogno,*
> *sogno il poeta e l'amore . . .*
>
> (now the girl is a dream,
> a dream the poet and love . . .)

Thus I acquired another Italian surname. Like the wine? some people inquire at introductions. Yes, I say even though they're confusing me with Bardolino. But having been born bread, I like that union with wine.

We lived some years in Italy before Antonio was sent to New York as the U.S. correspondent for *La Stampa.* We found a house outside the city, and it was there, finally, that I thought again of Mr. de Mascoli. The unlikely link to the printer was a May Day pageant given at my children's country day school. As the children frolicked on the lush green lawn, they sang a medley of spring songs, ending with an English May Day carol whose refrain was:

> For the Lord knows when we shall meet again
> To be Maying another year.

It struck me with great sadness. I thought of the Italian student, of my grandmother and the mountain spring she had never returned to, of Mr. de Mascoli and his gentle patience, of all the lost opportunities and combinations of all our lives.

I had never written to Mr. de Mascoli from Italy or sent him the fine gifts I had promised. That night I made a package of the Italian papers and magazines we had at home along with some of my husband's books and sent them to the printer in Syracuse with a letter expressing my regret for the delay and an explanation of what had happened in my life since I had last seen him more than ten years before.

The answer came from his wife. On a floral thank-you note (which I still have) with the printed line, *It was so thoughtful of you,* she had written: "It is almost three years that I lost my husband and a son a year later which I think I will never get over it. I miss them very much . . . it was our wish to go back to Italy for a trip but all in vain. The books you sent will be read by my sister-in-law who reads very good Italian, not like me, I'm trying hard to read but don't understand it as well as her, but she explains to me. Like my husband to you . . ."

I thought of time that passed and the actions that remained forever stopped, undone. The May Day carol kept coming back to me:

For the Lord knows when we shall meet again
To be Maying another year.

And if not Maying, all the other things we'd planned to do for ourselves, for others. And then the others are no longer here. A few years after that May Day, Antonio died suddenly in Rome. He is buried far away in his Vicenza birthplace while I continue to live outside of New York, alone now, since our daughters are married and gone. Life does not permit unrelenting sadness. May goes but comes back each year. And though some shadow of regret remains for all the words left unsaid and acts left undone, there will be other words, other acts . . .

I often think of how my life, my husband's, and the lives of our three daughters were so entwined with the language that Mr. de Mascoli set out to give me so long ago. Despite his efforts and my opera records, I am still the child of my mother tongue. I still speak Italian with an upstate tonality; my daughters do much better. Though Italian couldn't root perfectly in me, it did in them: the eldest is chair of the Italian department at an Ivy League university; the middle one lives and teaches in Italy, a perfect *signora;* and the youngest has classes in Italian for the children of her town.

Occasionally I visit Susanna in Italy, but it's long between trips and each visit is short. The country has changed: Mr. de Mascoli's Italy is no longer a poor country of peasants pushed into war and ruinous defeat by a dictator, but a prosperous industrial nation. Susi married an Italian artist from Urbino and they have two sons, Beni-amino and Anselmo, with whom I speak Italian for they speak no English.

Now I am called *Nonna.* I never knew the word with which to address my own grandmother when I was a child standing mute and embarrassed in front of her. Now, if it weren't too late, I would call her *Nonna,* too. We could speak to each other and I'd hear of the spring in Calabria.

How unexpected it all turned out . . . how long a progress as the seed of a long-ago infatuation found its right ground and produced its bloom. None of it did I foresee when I sat in his tidied white kitchen and learned with Mr. de Mascoli how to speak Italian.

The Finer Things in Life

Even as I saw the rusty, battered little oil lamp in the window of a quasi-antique store near the Italian president's residence and decided to have it, I felt it would be a mistake. Inside the shop I tried to brake myself when the rather smart, busy-aired, cigarette-smoking, and pearly mouthed young woman who ran the place got it out of the window and showed it to me.

"It has no wick," I said breathing easier.

"Oh, you can find a *stoppino* in any *ferramento* of Rome," she said smoothly and, fondling the tin object, added, *"Quanto è carino!"*—how cute it is.

The oil lamp was completely crusted over, but its small size was attractive, and besides, I told myself, in that state it would have to be cheap. Didn't I remember my mother coming home from country auctions in upstate New York with peeling and warped rocking chairs or garden benches for which she had paid ten cents and twenty-five cents? My husband and I could use the oil lamp on the terrace we were fixing up—just hang it on the wall and save the trouble and expense of outdoor wiring and outlets. It needed a wick but the woman in the store said I'd have no trouble finding one in any hardware store.

I bought it for 3,500 lire, uncomfortably aware that my mother could have done better and knowing as I counted out the money for it—too much, too much, I kept thinking—and as the shop woman wrapped it in a piece of yesterday's *Messaggero* that I'd never find the wick. Or whatever else I was looking for in that forlorn relic.

I had come upon the oil lamp because I like going to that store near Piazza Quirinale. And even better than the store is the splendid piazza which is fronted on three sides by palaces whose ensem-

38

ble of umber and tawny tones is matchless in Rome, and in whose center is an obelisk and the two giant figures of Castor and Pollux that even in antiquity were landmarks of this hill site. On the fourth side of the piazza is a kind of balustraded parapet from which to watch the spectacle of sunset over the city or changing of the guard at the Quirinal Palace, originally a papal, then a royal, and now a presidential residence.

Just down the street from this great paved piazza is the store that is neither the usual antique shop nor yet a junk store, but something in between—old things in a state of honest disrepair and tattered abandon that, the woman dealer told me, assured their age and authenticity better than the slick veneers on the restorations of Via del Babuino. The place was full of fine things: cupboards from the Abruzzi, a dilapidated swivel-seat barber's chair with headrest in wine velvet which I tried to picture at my husband's desk, a baptismal font from some country church, eighteenth-century cradles, old hats and spectacles, and pieces of carved marble or stucco decor whose provenance was evasively explained as "curious."

I left with my oil lamp and stopped at all the *ferramenti,* the hardware and paint stores, that I found on the way home. No wicks. Shopping in Rome is not a serious business as it is for my mother in Syracuse, New York, but an art of improvisation. Or total serendipity.

If I were another type I would not have bothered about a wick; I'd have just called my oil lamp an *objet trouvé* and hung it, rust and grime, in the living room or above my bed. But the whole point, for me, was to see it function. Someday I'd attend to the wick, I decided; in the meantime I'd clean it.

During the scraping, then, something extraordinary happened: as the rust gave way, the raised letters which had been stamped on the lamp base as its trade name came into relief reading Selenes III. And that name, so unexpected, immediately called forth another—Climax II—that had appeared on a desktop pencil sharpener my mother had once brought home from a house sale in Syracuse years before.

My mother liked shopping of all kinds, but what she liked best were sales and most particularly house sales, where she could unearth and carry off to her own home those discarded or surviving treasures of other homes that had for her some particular tone of the past, some link with other, finer times. And it could be coin-silver teaspoons or a French-papered hatbox, a piece of yellowing lace or a beautifully illustrated child's book. It hardly mattered. She always came back with something: not to would have made the whole expedition pointless, a waste of time. And she wouldn't be countered with the consideration that it was a waste of money to buy simply not to waste time. "I never waste money," she'd explain, her eyes darting excitedly over her acquisitions, her manner serious. "I only buy bargains, so no matter what they cost, it's always a saving."

She had her own logic, her own rules, her own game, and her own special skill at finding things. She didn't neglect department store sales or visits to thrift shops, auctions, antique fairs, white elephant teas, charity rummage sales, and junkyards. But her favorite was the house sale for the connection the items on sale had with living personages—the elite of Syracuse society. "These came from the Dey mansion," she'd say of a handsome pair of wall sconces in our living room; or, "That fireplace set—it's all solid bronze—was in the Flora T. Smith place on James Street before they demolished it and built a health club on the site."

For me the whole idea of house sales was depressing—those gloomy, sad, ransacked houses whose owners had died and whose heirs, not wanting any part of the accumulations of their past and dividing the profits amongst themselves, sold off all the frying pans and canisters, the bedpans and travel toilet sets, the soiled pillows, limp hand towels, silver-plated réchauffés, 78 rpm opera records, tarnished picture frames, or albums of picture postcards from some aunt's trip abroad.

Once in a while I'd accompany my mother to a house sale (usually she didn't want me, or my father, or my brothers around because our impatience and disapproval ruined her concentration, but sometimes she had to put up with us if she couldn't get Aunt Jay or anyone else to drive her, though in the end she solved the problem by learning how to drive herself, and my father got her a red Rambler to get about in). Those houses, emptied of their own intimate, continuing family life, their contents thrown helter-skelter by the hordes of ladies in bright dresses who sorted and pounced and carried off their booty—those houses were like browned-out, desiccated husks. My one remaining impression of all of them is brownness—sad, lonely, dusty brownness. And the women like vivid jackals.

I might, however, have been more understanding of my mother's part at house sales if I had realized then, as now, that that excitement of hers was not morbid bargain hunting but a passionate search for a past. Her hunt for things was a kind of progress from the limitations of her childhood—from the prejudices of her own parents who had come as possessionless immigrants from Italy and who, having had to work hard to buy all the new and shining objects of America, naturally looked with distaste on the old.

My mother was different from most Italian Americans of her generation who valued sleek, new, Hollywood-looking things and wouldn't have anything in their homes that had been first owned by someone else; when they bought Early American or Louis Quatorze it was the latest Grand Rapids model. They didn't honor the past; the past was misery, and coming to America had meant the chance to start new and buy new.

Yet what explains my mother's difference? For her parents and my father's, too, had come from just as poor and miserable a part of Italy as the other immigrants. My mother's family left Calabria, my father's Sicily; and they left their birthplaces without a stick or a scrap, a memento or photo to recall their life there. But departing from the usual Italian American pattern, not one of my grandparents ever returned to Italy, to the *paese,* to spend their American money among those who had stayed; nor had they retired to ranch houses filled with as many examples of brocaded sofas and modern appliances as they could possibly squeeze in. They stayed what they were, exiles belonging to neither American nor Italian life.

My grandparents' ambivalence, the never healed dichotomy they must have felt between their old and new worlds, was all interior, a continuous nostalgic, tenderly sad monologue I could read in their eyes. (We couldn't speak. I knew no Italian—they, only a few garbled words of English or their regional dialect.) Yet though they, like the others, could neither assume an American identity nor hang onto the old Italian one, they didn't bolster their outward lives with the props of this ambivalence which were so painfully present in other homes we knew of where, in rococco living rooms, gilt-framed pictures of, say, Enrico Caruso, or Dante meeting Beatrice on Ponte Santa Trinità, hung over an American bar. Where in the master bathroom there'd be a mural of the Bay of Naples painted over a tub whose faucets were shaped like dolphins. Where kitchens radiated with chrome and whirred with mixers while the dining room would be a regal state chamber filled with fake Renaissance. So fine, in fact, were such dining rooms that they were never used—just shown, like paintings. On holidays or family occasions everyone gathered in the basements where additional kitchens had been installed, and they dined from long, fold-up aluminum tables set with plastic lace cloths and heaped with all the impossibilities of a week of cooking.

My mother was considered a romantic and often teased for her attitudes. She, especially, didn't care for what was self-consciously Italian, like octopus dinners in the basement or Dante and Beatrice pictures and old-style weddings where the bride sat in front of a plate of money donations. She felt there should be a place in her home for the finer things in life and that these were best represented by the belongings of those old American families who embodied American virtues and ideals and had had the time—the necessary generations on this side of the ocean—to let their possessions be endowed with the patina of the past.

She liked the feeling of a solid, far-reaching family background and a long experience of gentility that the things she bought at house sales gave her. They gave a sense of depth to her life which, otherwise, was all in the foreground, the here and now. Behind her parents, the immigrants, there was only an anonymous, possession-less crowd of progenitors whose faces she would never find in a velvet-covered family album. She couldn't know her grandmothers or grandfathers through a watch chain or a lace cap or an inscribed book, for they had never owned any. So now if she sought old silver and linen it was not only for their own elegance, but for the ties it gave her to a past that was all too short for her.

Usually my mother went antiquing with Aunt Jay, who was her brother Joe's wife and commanded respect for her shrewdness and know-how in getting ahead socially. Aunt Jay and Uncle Joe carried authority in the family for their social and financial primacy—he was a banker and had even once run for the state senate. They were the first to move to a big home on spacious grounds in the fashionable outskirts of their town and to keep live-in help; they were the first to have a dog, a billiard (then TV) room, to send their children to name colleges, to see the children marry into Irish families, to go to Nassau instead of Florida for the winter.

My mother always said she owed a lot to Jay's great knowledge of antiques—a culture acquired when Jay had worked as a young girl in an antiques and gift shop of a high-toned college town. But she didn't share Jay's taste completely—a taste that, in line with Uncle Joe's growing fortune, tended more toward grandeur (bombé side chests, carved bedsteads, immense library tables, epergnes) than my mother's. In any case, it was Aunt Jay who had first showed my mother the little out-of-the-way places and taught her the rules of bidding at auctions, making silent appraisals, and successfully throwing thrift shop owners off guard by showing interest in a decoy rather than the real object of pursuit. And it was Aunt Jay who had impressed that cardinal rule upon her: never dress up when you go out antiquing.

The afternoon my mother brought back Climax II, she and Aunt Jay had gone to Cazenovia to the Hitchcock sale where heirs were disposing of the contents of old Judge Hitchcock's house in that pleasant village on the lake just ten miles from Syracuse. That particular sale, my mother used to declare dramatically ever afterward, changed the whole course of my life—that is, *her* expectations for my life. And the object with which she charged my destiny is an insignificant little Italian phrase book she had picked up for five cents and which, with her flair for melodrama, she blames for having led me to things Italian, for my going off to Italy to study and, consequently, my marrying an Italian and, finally, my living in Rome.

For if my parents didn't want any of folklore Italian American, even less did they feel any atavistic urge toward Italy proper; when they went to Italy on trips it was as tourists and visitors, and they kept a proper distance between themselves and any involvement with Italian life. It was when I had finished college that I first thought seriously of studying in Italy. My parents were perplexed at my idea, though not absolutely unwilling—study was study, after all, even though my wanting to learn Italian seemed impractical since there was little market for it back home.

It was my grandfather who was angry; he had come from Italy with nothing, not even a look back, and he had never wanted to go back. He couldn't understand how his grandchild, born to all the good things of life in the United States, would want to go to a poor country like Italy to study, to a country that didn't have enough schools for its children, to a country where many of the people couldn't read or write and nobody cared. Weren't schools bigger and richer in America? Everything was in America, he said.

My parents, not having been born in Italy, were more detached about it; they had stopped in Rome on their European honeymoon (and decided they liked Paris better), but still they couldn't account for my sentimental wish to see the land of our origins. All I should say is that it wasn't the little book which led me to Italy; I would have gone anyway. This avowal, however, doesn't appeal to my mother; whenever she thinks of the little phrase book–and I've always kept it–she thinks of the premonition she had (she says) the day she picked it up from a table full of odds and ends at the Hitchcock house.

It's a little, green-cloth-covered book that bears on the inside cover and in her own handwriting the name of one of the old Judge's sisters, Jeannette Hitchcock, and the address of her *pensione* in Rome with the year of her stay, 1887. Perversely, perhaps, it might have appealed to my mother because that was just about the same time as her parents were emigrating from Italy to America. And Miss Hitchcock had been in Rome then learning proper Italian and visiting the art galleries while my mother's parents had never seen an Italian painting, did not even speak the Italian of a Miss Hitchcock, would live and die without ever knowing what Italy was outside of their villages.

There was no real reason for my mother to buy the little book–she was the first to admit it. No one spoke Italian at home, my brothers weren't remotely concerned with travel to Italy. So, going against her principle that every purchase should have a function, she bought the book because it only cost a nickel and because it had the authority of having been used by a Hitchcock. But she never did resolve her doubts about it–doubts that were confirmed when I suddenly brought up my wish to study in Italy.

The day she brought home the book I remember picking it up and laughing as I thumbed through it, reading aloud some of its phrases: "Can I offer you some refreshments? Call someone who can speak English. Take my card to the manager. You are very charming. I have a pain here. Where is the W.C.?" But the book in that moment was incidental. What took my major attention was the pencil sharpener named Climax II.

It was certainly handsome: a large, old-fashioned handle-turning, screw-down pencil sharpener. I suppose my mother had been fascinated by the idea of the old Judge using it in his book-lined, oak-paneled study.

"You and your brothers can certainly use this, with all the writing and schoolwork you have to do," she had said as she showed it to me. "Look at this," and she turned it over to show me GREAT BRITAIN and 1900 stamped on the bottom. "That's a country that makes things to last!" We were just a year or so out of the war, England had won, the end of the Empire had not yet come, and my mother still placed full reliance on Britain, her name, and her woolens.

I studied the sharpener in fascination, not so much for its nationality or age as for that jarring name in a flourish of gold script on the domed top. It seemed flighty, somehow, on such a basic, stolid bit of desk accessory. Worse than flighty–irrational. For, being called Climax II, it must have outmoded some earlier model called Climax I, thus negating the absolutism of climax per se. Could relativism go so far?

As a mechanism it was superb; adjustable clamps on springs held the pencil tightly, and by pressing the little levers together openings could be made to fit the size of any pencil exactly. It was a large, capacious sharpener and had a pull-out drawer for emptying the shavings; it looked ample, majestic, and recalled the style and authority of still-living Queen Mary. It had her sternness and no-nonsense air, too, for the instructions on top read: Keep machine oiled. Do not tamper with adjustments.

But there was something more to the machine, something faintly sinister to the grinders, the cutter frame and screws, the sheath of iron on which the clamped pencil rested. I turned to my mother and said in faked awe, "Good lord, it's a Kafka torture machine!" And I shouldn't have.

"What's that? What do you mean?" she asked irritably. "Do you always have to make some funny remark after I've been chasing around all day and bought this because I thought you could use it?"

I knew my saying something of the sort would provoke my mother–it always did; but I persisted in that pretentiousness, deliberately trying to create distances, to savor my difference. I thought myself superior to house sales, to accumulating material possessions, to the need to find pleasure and escapism in senseless buying.

But years have passed, and in Rome I saw myself retracing certain footsteps. Now I shop for old things with a past–preferably when my husband and daughters are not with me–and, like my mother, must rationalize my acquisition, trying to believe in its utility. She ended up with a pencil sharpener that evoked all the strength and durability and class of the then British Empire; I with a rusty oil lamp whose name, to me, suggested the moon goddess of Greek mythology, that Selene who loved the shepherd prince Endymion and enchanted him to eternal, youthful sleep . . . or the moonstone of legend . . . or the selenite windows of the basilica of

Santa Sabina on the Aventine. We both got striking names in her Climax II and my Selenes III, and what coincidence was it that in both cases the name was followed by a Roman numeral—a presage, perhaps, of Rome in my life?

But the better bargain, I know, was hers.

It's strange how that name, emerging from the rust of my oil lamp, reminded me of a pencil sharpener I haven't thought of since the years, long past, when I was in school in Syracuse and used it as I worked on my compositions; strange, too, is the understanding it brought me of my mother, an understanding I never thought in my reach. We were too different.

My husband ridiculed my oil lamp just as I had my mother's Kafka machine. And yet those objects had struck responsive notes in us. The pencil sharpener from Judge Hitchcock's home in Cazenovia spoke of stability and order and precision and purpose and the finer things in life to a woman who believed in them; Selenes III from the secondhand store near the statues of the Dioscuri (who, on Greek vases, attend Selene's horse-drawn chariot and even now attend the moon as the constellation Gemini) was like an augury, a charm, an affirmation of poetry and fantasy, an evocation. All completely different from my mother, and yet all the same.

Shutting the Door
on Someone

It's been a long time since I've cared to remember the day I shut the front door of our Croton house in John Cheever's face.

My weird response to his ring and to seeing him on our porch, dwarfed by the columns of that large, four-square gray stucco house, so dismayed me at the time that I chose to obliterate it. I never mentioned it to anyone. Nor did I ever refer to it on any occasion I ever saw John again, not to apologize, not to explain, not even to laugh it off as I might have since he was forever amused and indulgent at the bizarreness of everything.

And so I have never known what he thought as the door closed. Did he imagine that I might have been sheltering the garbage man? That I was batty? A prude? Maybe he was wise enough to see a young woman thoroughly discomfited and taken aback by the unexpected presence of a well-known writer saying, "I've brought back your stories," as he held out a thick manilla envelope. He had driven over from Scarborough to give me the packet. "Oh!" I gasped, said "Thank you," and immediately shut the door.

I panicked. I was not only taken by surprise, I was also terrified by what John might have said. In a colossal failure of nerve, and in a split second, it must have flashed through my mind that he could— politely, of course—dismiss the stories, wipe out what confidence was burgeoning, turn off those tentative beginnings of mine. He might have said something like, "Look, if you have anything better to do, why don't you." He might, on the other hand, have said, "I think these show promise." But at that point in my life, having receded into the shadowy recesses of translation and camouflaged my voice with another's, I felt my hold on my own work was too fragile to risk losing through any words that might have pushed me into the morass of self-doubt.

All this occurred at mid-morning on a fall day a year or so after my husband and I first met the Cheevers and just before we moved from the stucco house in Croton to a barn house we purchased from Aaron Copland at Shady Lane Farm in Ossining Town. I still remember the acrid odor of faded, once-blooming geraniums from the boxes on the front porch that hit my nostrils when I opened the door. It was the end of summer, sun and light were lower on the earth. There must have been a chill—perhaps a frost?—John was wearing a camel's hair coat. I was alone at home since Antonio had gone off to his office in New York on the commuters' 8:02 from Croton-Harmon as usual; and our two girls were at school.

It was because they were enrolled at Scarborough Country Day School that we met the Cheevers. Ginny Kahn, who was then married to E. J. Kahn, Jr., long of the *New Yorker,* was at a parents function we attended. The minute we were introduced to the Kahns and Antonio opened his mouth, Ginny exclaimed, "You're Italian!" followed by, "You'll have to meet the Cheevers who've just come back from Italy." And so we did. And, in a strange conjunction, when we moved into the Copland house, John and Mary Cheever were about to move into their own new home just over the hill from us which made us neighbors.

In many ways John and Antonio had similar natures. They both had a natural gentleness and fragility from privation in boyhood—Antonio had lost his father, a naval officer, when he was only nine, and John's New England family had begun coming apart when he, too, was young and susceptible. Both had genteel families who had seen better days. Both were natural and hilarious storytellers who embellished with deft embroideries the stories they told. They were also both very religious, and haunted by loss. They communicated in versions of either English or Italian depending on who was using which language. They enjoyed each other's company, and there was that counterpoint of Antonio's ongoing discovery of America and John's just having been in Italy that bound them. At the same time they were worlds apart, and John's suburbia was never Antonio's provinces nor vice versa.

John had just published *The Wapshot Chronicle.* Ever since my girlhood in upstate New York, I had been reading his stories in the *New*

Yorker. Now Antonio's stories, in my translation, were also appearing in its pages. He was pleased, but must less taken by the aura of that publication and of John's name than I was. He simply delighted in the company of an American author who had just come back, enthusiastic, from his country.

So many strands go into this story! It is not just my overwrought and inconsiderate action in closing the door on John Cheever, but all the factors and events that led up to it: from my growing up Italian American in Syracuse to my nourishing, as long as I can remember, an unconfessed and guilty wish to be a writer as were those men and women I revered and whose works I lugged home every Saturday, after confession at the Blessed Sacrament, when I stopped at the Eastwood branch of the public library. How did I, from a family who did not practice reading, become enamored of the written word? Was it the beautiful fairy-tale book my father once brought back from a business trip to Chicago perhaps on the suggestion of a salesperson when he was searching for a gift? Or was it something in school that caught me and led me, ever after, to library after library? Something took, and by high school I had a subscription to the *New Yorker* which, when it arrived, was the highlight of the week for me as *Life* magazine was for my two brothers.

I seemed to be the only student at The Convent School of the Franciscan Sisters Motherhouse in Syracuse who knew and admired those faraway people named John Cheever, John O'Hara, Mary McCarthy, E. J. Kahn, Wolcott Gibbs, William Maxwell, Gênet. They were the most luminous names I could think of. They, and not those old standbys–Columbus, Dante, Verdi (always extolled at annual Columbus Day dinners to help the Italian American community feel better about itself, especially in those war years when Italy was an Axis power and our enemy)–they, Cheever and Company, were the eminences I thought about. To write like that!

I lived a plain, upstate life. My Convent School classmates were simple girls, Irish and German, who took piano lessons and were serious about their religion. I lost mine, age twelve. Though I stopped going to confession I continued to visit the Eastwood branch library. I wanted to read what was missing from the drab and untouched bookstacks in our Convent library. What was missing were the forbidden books on the Index, and when I found them I wondered why Voltaire's wit and good sense seemed so dangerous to the nuns.

Graduating, I said goodbye to my classmates who went on to colleges named for the saints while I went to one named for a businessman: Wells College was endowed with the fortune Henry Wells made through his Wells Fargo express.

At Wells I continued the years of Latin started at the Convent; the light and warmth, beauty and composure of the classical world swept over me, and I felt the power of the Mediterranean locus of my forebears as the lure to an essential part of myself with which I longed to connect. As with the forbidden books (including, effectively, though not specifically, Shakespeare because he was not in our book of Catholic authors), so in my Italian American family, Italy and things Italian were also neglected except for our daily bread. Everything else about Italy was cause for shame and humiliation—those March of Time newsreels featuring Mussolini, the strutting buffoon; the shameful assault on Ethiopia; the treachery against France. It was difficult to live with an Italian name in those days, and, after the war, actually to want to go over and explore my Italian background seemed to my parents—to everybody—like a typical act of contrariness.

I got there with a letter of introduction to a journalist in Milan who, I had been told, might help me get around because it was just after the war and conditions were still chaotic. The journalist read me his poetry. I studied Italian. He said he would learn English. I read his first novel, published in 1943 during the height of the war, when only a few hundred copies survived a bombardment and eventually none, since it had been printed on an ersatz paper that was already yellowed and crumbling. Antonio, the journalist, and I decided to marry. He said we would have a life of art together, two writers. We married and soon had two, then three children.

Life's circumstances are unforeseeable. Our first daughter was born in Syracuse, our second in Milan, and then we were settled in Westchester County where our third was born. We lived in a big old stucco house in Croton about which Antonio wrote a series of poems collected into a volume called *Elegie di Croton* that was to win a literary award in Italy. Before that, however, he had already begun to publish quite regularly in the *New Yorker*. His stories, which I loved, were evocations of the prewar Veneto region he grew up in and where his family roots were. I was his translator (unacknowledged in those years before the *New Yorker* credited translations), and that was the only work of mine I saw in print for a long while. I had the home, the children, the satisfaction of helping my husband and seeing him published in a prestigious magazine—I had even gotten to know John Cheever because I was married to Antonio!

It should have all been enough. But it wasn't. I was a writer, too. Unpublished but undaunted. I wrote stories, too.

I don't know how John Cheever got my story manuscripts, but I have often thought it was Antonio who, sensing my discontent, might have asked John to have a look at them and see if they were publishable. That's what I imagine because I can remember what I felt when a suburban woman whose name I long ago forgot invited us to dinner and, ingratiatingly, I thought, served chicken tetrazzini which is not an Italian dish but the pasta equivalent of what Wonder bread is to a freshly baked crusty Italian loaf. Over espresso she produced a sheaf of her own stories with the suggestion that Antonio might introduce her to his editor at the *New Yorker*.

I was shocked at her boldness. More, I was frustrated and angry at myself that the years had passed without my becoming a writer in my own right. "We were to be artists together!" I said on the way home as if Antonio, and not I, were responsible for the silence.

All this led up to the morning when John Cheever appeared in Croton with my stories. Why didn't I ask him in for coffee? Why didn't I ask him how he got the stories, what he thought of them? Antonio died without my ever having asked if he had had any part in it, as I suspect he did. John is gone now, too. I think that years ago I must have feared that John would think of me as I did the woman who served chicken tetrazzini and then asked for a favor; he'd think we valued him only for what he could do for me.

But even more, I now realize, it was the moment of total self-illumination in which I repeated to myself that self-chastising and self-effacing phrase of my convent education, *domine, non sum dignus*— correcting it mentally, in the intellectual pride the nuns accused me of, to *domine, non sum digna*. It was not just The Convent School that taught me to efface myself before the male partner who was surely more important, worthier, better. It was also my Italian American education which upheld the eternal sacrificial position of the woman. We were the uprights of the home; we were there to give of ourselves for our men and for our children. We were not there for ourselves.

John had his own moments of self-doubt; did he recognize the reflex of my anxiety when I closed the door and so, in charity and graciousness, refrain from ever mentioning the episode to me? That is the only explanation I have, for we continued to see John until we went to live in Italy and he never spoke of the incident. Nor did Antonio. Not even when the three of us were together in Antonio's room at the hospital in North Tarrytown where Antonio was recovering from his first heart attack and where three years earlier our third daughter had been born.

We and the Cheevers had been neighbors a few years on lands that had belonged to the Acker brothers in pre-Revolutionary times. John and one of his dogs often walked over the hill and down past our house to the aqueduct trailway which led to Croton Dam. John's *Wapshot Scandal* had followed his first novel and won him the National Book Award. His picture had appeared on the cover of *Time*. He told about being stopped on Main Street of Ossining by a man who looked at him quizzically and said, "Aren't you someone?" No, John answered. You're someone, said the man, you're David Wayne the actor.

Antonio's stories had been collected and published in a volume, and, in my translation, Pantheon was to publish his novel with imposing endorsements on the book jacket. As for me, I had gone to library school.

When Antonio was stricken, I was the acting director of Briarcliff Manor Public Library, and each day I would go from the library to the hospital to visit him. One day I brought him a bright yellowy-orange silk tie. John was in the room when I got there. *Auguri!* I said as I bent over and kissed Antonio. He unwrapped the gift package, beamed, and extended the tie at arm's length to gaze at it: *"Bellissima!"* he smiled. John was amused: "Will you wear that?" he asked Antonio.

"Of course," Antonio said, noticeably cheered. He recognized the augury, knew that it was a symbol of light and the summer to come.

In fact, in the summer after his hospitalization he was back in Italy, looking for a place in Rome where we would join him while I, saddened, sold the house at Shady Lane Farm and got the children ready to leave. We lived in Rome for eight years and I began to write there and to see my work published. I started a novel. Just before it was finished Antonio had his second, fatal, heart attack.

I moved back to Ossining. John and Mary came to see me, and I went to visit them at the lovely old house where they still lived, adjoining Shady Lane Farm. Maybe John had forgotten the shut door. I hadn't.

I think he understood about pain and loneliness and self-doubt and all the self-tormenting things that assail us, even on sunny days and days filled with comely children and a devoted spouse. I think he understood about the longings of the heart, about irrational and eccentric behavior cloaking our fear and terror. I think he knew of the colossal failure of nerve that sometimes comes to all of us. With me it was the mirror side of that unbridled pride that had wafted me through my Convent School years and had taken me to Italy. I think John knew that that door hadn't closed on him as much as it had sheltered me from what, then, I couldn't bear to know.

John is gone now, too. On occasion when I go into New York, I stand on the station platform with the late commuters waiting for the 9:37 local. It is always preceded by a fast Amtrak train going in the other direction, north. That fast train has named cars: De Witt Clinton, Manitoba, James Fenimore Cooper, Hudson Valley . . . and then, there it is, the silver-gray coach named the John Cheever. *Ciao,* John, I whisper. The car whizzes by, a glimmer of quick recognition and remembrance, then gone in a flash.

Looking for Mari Tomasi

One summer I drove to Vermont to find the flesh and blood memory of Mari Tomasi, a relatively little known author who died in 1965 and who is most remembered for her novel of the Italian granite workers of Barre. I was interested in her background as a writer, and wanted to find out why, after a notable beginning, her literary output remained so slight: two novels, a few stories and poems in local magazines, and a brief history of Italians in Vermont are all she published.

What I found, instead, was that it was not Mari Tomasi alone I was looking for, but an answer to how she, I, and other Italian American women of our generations had become authors at all–an improbability to begin with.

Was Tomasi, I wondered, emblematic of the aspiring woman writer of Italian American background who, if not altogether silent, is still not perceived in any appreciable way; who has been closeted in the shadowy recesses of the national literature, a known presence to very few? It is typical of our situation that in the *Harvard Encyclopedia of American Ethnic Groups* no woman author is mentioned in the entry dedicated to the literary accomplishments of Italian Americans. This oversight repeats what regularly occurs in bibliographies, conferences, and written histories.

I knew that in Tomasi's time, as in our own, the way to literary expression was filled with rebuffs; there were the internal conflicts one faced in being creative in defiance of a family code which discouraged apartness and self-expression; there were external barriers in a surrounding culture which valued and fostered in literature Anglo-American themes, attitudes, and personages; and there were the mind-racking doubts as to the worth of one's own experience because of the lack of related models in the readings our schooling provided. We are what we read, but, in the case of Italian Americans, we can seldom read who we are.

Unraveling the story of Mari Tomasi might, I thought, unravel the larger enigma of the Italian American woman writer.

Tomasi was born in 1907 in Montpelier, Vermont, the third of five children of Northern Italian immigrant parents. She was crippled as a child, never married, and after two years away at college, she returned to the family home where she remained, working as a journalist and writing, for the rest of her life. She died at the age of fifty-eight.

Good connections in established literary circles helped launch Tomasi. She was a protegée of Arthur Wallace Peach, a writer, editor, and founder of the Poetry Society of Vermont of which Tomasi was a very active lifelong member. Copies of Tomasi's correspondence in the archives of the Vermont Historical Society show that she wrote novelist Faith Baldwin for an endorsement of her own soon to be published first novel. At that time, Tomasi was employed by the Vermont Writers Project, a member of whose advisory board was the widely known author Dorothy Canfield Fisher.

Mari Tomasi's first novel, *Deep Grow the Roots,* depicts the tragedy brought to the life of a young peasant in the Piedmont region of Italy by the growth of fascist militarism in the thirties. Tomasi's father had taken her as a young girl to that area of Italy for a prolonged stay to recuperate from an operation, and the land and its people had remained forever impressed in her mind. Her book appeared in October of 1940, published by the major firm of Lippincott and bearing on its jacket the influential endorsements of well-known, contemporary authors Dorothy Canfield Fisher, Mary Ellen Chase, and Faith Baldwin.

With newspaper headlines of the day reporting on Italy's invasion of Greece and an alliance with Nazi Germany, the time seemed to be right for Tomasi's story of Italian peasant skepticism of Mussolini's Ethiopian war; it provided a corrective to the idea of all Italians as enthusiastic fascist followers of Il Duce. The book was quickly reviewed, and Tomasi became one of ten new novelists selected by the American Booksellers Association and the *New York Herald Tribune* to be honored at a luncheon at the Hotel Astor on November 26, 1940. In a unique show of Italian American literary presence, not only Mari Tomasi was honored that day, but also Guido

D'Agostino for his *Olives on the Apple Tree*. The 1,250 attendees were told they were meeting the "Hemingways, Steinbecks and Ferbers of the future."

What becomes interesting about *Deep Grow the Roots* is the degree to which the critics misread it by describing it as a simply told tale of peasant folk—"quaint," "unpretentious," "pastoral." The story is, instead, tougher than that.

There is the buildup of gradual menace as the shadow of Il Duce's Ethiopian war comes ever closer to the peasants of the Piedmont, co-involving them in the affairs of a land and people remote from their lives and prenoting a compelling parallel to American involvement in Vietnam. So, too, the Ethiopian war against a far-off people in a strange land is perceived as unjust, wasteful, irrelevant, and wrong. Nor does Tomasi allow any concession to happy endings in her so-called pastoral tale. Nina's selfishness does her in; Luigi compounds superstition with foolishness and dies of a self-inflicted wound trying to avoid conscription in a futile war.

There are scenes and characters of unusual boldness, including a scene of forthright sexuality between the peasant Luigi and Nina, the village girl he loves, which is unusual for someone of Mari Tomasi's time and place. The freeness with which Nina is drawn is striking. Her character is more complex, certainly sharper than Luigi's.

Another striking female character is La Tonietta, the village midwife, who manifests qualities recognizable today as those of a liberated woman. Sickened by her father's brutal treatment of her mother, she determines at an early age that she'll never marry and let herself be dependent upon any man. But neither will she deny her nature and her love for children. Very deliberately she has three children out of wedlock, refuses to marry their father, and raises them by herself. She not only surmounts the disapproval of the villagers, but even makes herself a respected and important figure among them by her nursing skills. It is well to remember, at the time Tomasi was writing, that women as nonconformist as La Tonietta, both in fiction and in life, were made to end up badly and that Tomasi was breaking with convention in more than one way.

Although *Deep Grow the Roots* was mostly well received as a first novel, the reviewers seemed to have either sentimentalized it or to have been without any real discernment of what Tomasi's real strengths were as a writer.

In an entry on Mari Tomasi in the 1941 issue of *Current Biography*, she is reported working on "a new novel revolving around Italian American stonecutters in Vermont." She was at the time interviewing Barre granite workers and their families for the Federal Writers Project in Vermont, and she made use in her subsequent novel, *Like Lesser Gods,* of the material she gathered. That novel appeared an unaccountable eight years later, in 1949, brought out not by the prestigious Lippincott, but by Bruce, a small Catholic publisher in Milwaukee which had awarded Tomasi a financial fellowship the previous year, enabling her to complete the novel-in-progress. The book was then chosen by the Catholic Literary Foundation as its Book of the Month. At publication, Bruce publishing company feted Tomasi at a New York reception and dinner attended by representatives of the literary and publishing worlds.

Her two novels are similar only in their favorable reception. Otherwise, there are not only different publishers for her two books, but completely different backgrounds and personages as well as stylistic differences. The slow-paced, descriptive evocation of Italian peasant life in *Deep Grow the Roots* has evolved into the brisker realism of *Like Lesser Gods.* The former novel was based on impressions recalled from childhood and worked on when Tomasi was under the guidance of Sister Mary Baptista Lenhart, a poet and teacher at Trinity College in Burlington; and the second novel reflected the quite different immediacy of firsthand interviewing and the directives of the Federal Writers Project which exacted straightfoward, clear detail, eschewing anything "flowery and gaudy." The models of style which Director Roaldus Richmond held out to his staff to emulate are interesting: they included excerpts from Zola and Pietro Di Donato's *Christ in Concrete.* Tomasi seems to have adapted stylistically to the prevailing influence in each of her novels.

Like Lesser Gods developed from a short story entitled "Stone" which was first published in the spring 1942 issue of *Common Ground.* The story has since been reprinted in a collection called *The Literature of Vermont,* and the novel itself has been reprinted.

In the story, as, indeed, again in the novel, Maria Dalli, like a jealous rival struggling to wrest her husband Pietro, a granite carver, from a deadly mistress, rises from their bed in the middle of the night to go to the shed where Pietro's newly carved masterpiece, a granite tombstone, awaits consignment. Wrathfully, Maria takes a tool and mutilates the work irreparably, hoping it will cost Pietro his job. She has begged him for years to leave the shed with its lung-destroying granite dust and to open a grocery store with her in the front of their home. Her scheme does not work; she is found out, though her secret is not disclosed to Pietro, and, in expiation of her failed attempt to pry Pietro from his stonework, she accepts that his creativity and his desire to leave his eternal mark in stone are, in essence, above his family ties. This she accepts not in passive resignation, but with a stolid strength as hard as the stone which is her enemy. She does not weep when Pietro lies dying of silicosis, and his final thoughts are a tribute to her: "As strong, as unflinching as granite she was, he reflected, in his last earthly flicker of humor. The same qualities in these two he loved. . . ." Except that, as a man, an artist, he loved his work, his art, the more. He is allowed that. Maria, the wife and mother, the family pillar must embody the traditional womanly traits—she must be stolid, enduring, silent, sacrificial. It is a powerful contrast that Tomasi implicitly makes between the choices available to men and to women of the Dallis' background. Could Tomasi have felt in her own life that, as a woman, she could not, as Pietro did, give everything to her art?

In a talk sometime after publication of her second novel, Mari Tomasi referred to being at work on a new novel and to having reached chapter 5 in it. No trace of that work-in-progress has been found—not in the Mari Tomasi papers of the Vermont Historical Society in Montpelier, nor in the author's papers located in Bailey Library of the University of Vermont, nor in the family house on Barre Street where Marguerite Tomasi still lives.

I wonder what subject matter Mari Tomasi was dealing with in her new work. Was she beginning to express some of the real conflicts that existed, perhaps, in her personal life as well as in the society around her? In *Like Lesser Gods* she had curiously avoided the reality of labor's bitter strikes against management; there is no depiction of the slights and humiliations felt by the Italian community in an area dominated by Scots and English descendants; nor did Tomasi delve into the political radicalism and antichurch feelings of many of the Northern Italian anarchists who were strong in Barre. Rather, she depicted in her Italian characters a religious acceptance of destiny that is clearly at odds with the activist situation. And she provided the perfect gloss by having the daughter of the Italian granite worker (who dies of stonecutters' silicosis) marry the son of the Scottish quarry owner at the end of the novel.

Self-censorship in writers, as a form of silencing, is even more pernicious than the outward forms of silencing. Tomasi's lived reality was of being "other" in New England; her mentors were all impeccable New England Yankees. Could she afford to come to terms with her own inner feelings, and those of other Italian Americans in an often hostile society, and express them in writing? Was her work-in-progress perhaps so sensitive or controversial for her time and place that she could not continue it and preferred to destroy what had been written?

Tomasi's only other significant writing was a researched piece, "The Italian Story in Vermont," which appeared in the January 1960 issue of *Vermont History*. There she pointedly shows the contributions of Italian Americans to Vermont life. More telling is the author's foreword to *Like Lesser Gods,* which was omitted from the book in both editions, but is among her papers at the University of Vermont. Tomasi had written, "This story could not have been created were it not for these sculptors, artisans, and quarrymen who have contributed to the country in as great a measure, at least, as they have taken from it." It is a proud statement, indicating, I feel, her awareness of many aspects of Italian American life that had still to be acknowledged by society at large.

Her fictional attempts to exonerate both Italy from the crime of fascism, and America from the fault of xenophobia, reflect, I think, her own tensions of ambivalence in being Italian American.

In his essay "The Novels of Mari Tomasi," Prof. Alfred Rosa put it this way: "It appears as if Miss Tomasi's hopes for America get in the way of her material. . . . She wished to actualize the union of positives (i.e., the positive Italian and the positive American character traits) for her readers, and perhaps for herself. . . ."

Very much for herself, I think.

Mari Tomasi was singled out as a notable first novelist in 1940; just a decade later her trail grows cold. Cold as the granite in the hills above her Montpelier home. What happened in her artistic growth? What was the thematic line of her unpublished material? Did she leave diaries? Notes?

These were some of the questions which I set out to answer.

Looking for Mari Tomasi, the author, I started with her curious first name. "I always called her Mary," said her sister, Marguerite Tomasi, whom I met in Montpelier, in the brown shingled family home on Barre Street where Mari lived, worked, and died. But it was "Marie" she was baptized at St. Augustine's Church just down the block. In college she was Mary Margaret. As an author she chose to be Mari, perhaps in the style of a contemporary fellow author, Jerre Mangione, who was born Gerlando. That was a generation, of course, bent on Americanizing.

Interviewed in 1941 in Middlebury, Vermont, at the Bread Loaf Writers Conference to which she had won a fellowship, Tomasi explained that her first name, Mari, was pronounced like the "Mary" to which she had changed at school because her real name was "too foreign." The compromise of Mari (neither Mary, nor Marie) is a striking clue in documenting her feeling of ambivalence at being caught between two cultures.

Mari Tomasi is the name on the family tombstone which Marguerite Tomasi took me to see in the Catholic cemetery overlooking Montpelier. There Mari's birth date is 1907, though in life she adjusted it to 1910.

In the old-fashioned house where I was made welcome with iced tea and Vermont cheddar cheese, I sat with Marguerite Tomasi in the parlor and my eyes were drawn to two pieces of granite in a small adjoining room: one, a polished slab, like a fallen tombstone, was a coffee-table top; the other, set on the floor against an armchair, was the replica book cover of *Like Lesser Gods*. Chiseled into eternity was the book title and author's name. She had achieved for herself Pietro Dalli's desire of immortality.

On the wall of the small room hung an oil portrait of Mari in a red suit, her nails painted red, her lipstick the vivid red slash of the forties, her hair in an upsweep. She had a look of self-importance, and I imagined her, in that modest, small-town family, as the celebrity and centerpiece, the one who was different, the writer. I imagined the family—a close-knit household of Piedmontese parents who came to Vermont at the turn of the century and brought with them the qualities of their Northern Italian provenance: frugal, independent, self-reliant, taciturn, hardworking.

I asked questions but Marguerite and the other family members present could not answer them: only that Mari had not discussed her writing in the family, had not kept a diary, had left no material for other novels.

The family was mute, Mari was mute.

And then I knew that that very silence was a key to the puzzle. So much had remained unsaid in her writings; it's as if she had used up the two safe themes available to her. "Safe," I say, because one book exonerated Italian Americans from the associated guilt of fascism by showing that not all Italians were of that persuasion even during the height of the regime, and the second book absolved Italian Americans from the shame of their actual status by depicting Italians who became good, assimilated Americans in an aura of benevolent religiosity, thus downplaying the bitter discrimination, racism, and resentment that actually existed in the locale of Tomasi's Vermont novel.

Then, too, stone being impersonal and mute, was safe to write about; as, being distant, the peasants in Piedmont were also safe to write about. What would not have been as safe was facing up to the inner conflicts and denials of being "foreign" in Yankeeland—being Marie instead of Mari.

In the writing of hers that we have, Mari Tomasi did not choose to look inward at personal conflict for her material. I think the fact alone that she was an artistically ambitious person living all her life in the family home in a small New England town must have created the tensions that might well have been expressed in novels of personal growth, and frustrated desires, and an unmarried woman's acceptance or denial of sexuality. Italian American lives are full of the drama and high tension of living astride two cultures—the internal family-oriented Italian one, and the external one of American pressures of self-realization. Mari Tomasi did not, in the work we know, choose to confront the dichotomy of a life spent conforming to an Anglo-American norm while still feeling ties to an Italian heritage.

The need to sidestep controversy could have hindered her writing and created the long silences between works. That it was difficult for someone like Tomasi to confront painful social issues is more than likely. It was a more guarded time. Had that difficulty anything further to do with being a woman in an Italian American family?

I believe it to be so. I believe that the presumed dilemma of Mari Tomasi is still the actual dilemma of many women of Italian American background who are novelists, playwrights, writers of any kind.

It is a truth universally acknowledged that Italian Americans and family are synonymous. It is also true that the family structure, brought over intact as the one institution from the Old Country that worked and the one cultural possession which was common to all regions, could not make peace with the Anglo-American ideal of Rugged Individualist and Self-made Man, not to mention the Autonomous Woman. Thoreau as loner and Emily Dickinson as gifted recluse were not Italian cultural ideals. Cornelia, mother of the Gracchi, is closer. It follows, then, that the American descendants of the immigrant culture would be conflicted between the restrictive family tradition and what the American school system fostered—that is, the notion of each one as an individual able to aspire to whatever he or she wants, independently. Not choosing decisively between the old ways and the new creates an ambivalence that debilitates one's focus and perseverance. Choosing decisively means betrayal of that not chosen—and what do you choose, allegiance to your family or to yourself?

It was natural that the focus of their greatest tension, the family and the wider surrounding culture that put it to the test, would be the source of Italian American literary and dramatic writing. The sense of isolation in an alienating society, conflicts between Italian parents and American children, the strain between the sexes in their quest for new roles, the search for unequivocal identity, and the trials of self-actualization—these are all themes for the author of this background.

Predictably, until recently, it has been the women whose forebears came from the North of Italy who were more quickly open to the literary experience than those from a Southern Italian provenance. Mari Tomasi's characters are of Piedmontese origin, like the author herself. In *Who Can Buy the Stars?* Antonia Pola wrote of a Piedmontese immigrant woman who, through bootlegging during Prohibition days, became financially successful in the best American tradition though at enormous cost to herself. Authors Marion Benasutti and Dorothy Bryant are also of Northern Italian background. In Italy, Northern women were less restricted than their Southern counterparts, more independent and more educated, factors which accelerated their debuts as writers.

Women create and maintain the family; and if family bequeathes its blessings, it also demands loyalty. Yet women's old allegiance, maintained through their silence, is now dissolving. They are finding their voices. It was the push, finally, of the times: both feminist consciousness and ethnicity have, in a sense, given permission to the young women of today to look deeply and closely at the family, to examine its values and its limitations, to detach themselves from it in order to write.

It is a vantage point that Mari Tomasi, writing fifty years ago, did not have.

Tillie Olsen's *Silences* pertains to the condition of all women whose expressivity and literary creativity are strongly curtailed by the conditions of their ethnic background, social class, color, and the preconceptions of the life role into which they are born. Bring into literature, she says, what is not there now. And for Italian American women that is the whole range of their lives: the experience, from their souls, of what it means to be who they were and are.

Is it something Mari Tomasi might have tried to do in the unfinished novel she was working on that is lost to us?

I can, in my own mind, then, settle the case of Mari Tomasi: she was of her time and accepted the limitations the culture at large imposed on her, while still trying to honor her heritage. She left no diary to tell us of any internal dilemma, of the cost to herself and her writing of her guardedness. On the other hand, she used well the materials available to her and wrote a story of the Italian granite workers in Vermont which is still unique and still lives in print.

But just as revealing as the writings Mari Tomasi left are her silences.

Buried Alive by Language

I remembered two seemingly incongruous things when I first heard about the racial murder of the Black youth Yusuf Hawkins in August 1989 in the Bensonhurst section of Brooklyn by a gang of mostly Italian American young men. I remembered a friend telling me of being in Louisiana and finding "Wop Salad" featured on a menu. What was that? I asked. He laughed and said, salad with Italian dressing."Didn't anyone care about the language," I wondered. No, he said, it was a joke. But language is no joke. And racial murder starts with racial intolerance that arises and spreads from such apparently innocuous jokes.

The second thing I remembered was hearing Lynn Samuels' talk show on radio WOR when a listener called in and said, "How come I'm called anti-Semitic if I make a remark, but Jews can get away with calling the rest of us goyim, schwartzer, wop, or whatever it is?"

Samuels, who is Jewish herself, answered unhesitatingly, "They're politically organized."

And that, I told myself, is why there'll never be a kike salad on any menu.

I think that Italian Americans are too easily used as objects of ridicule and scorn. It has been said that anti-Catholicism is the prejudice of choice of the liberal intellectual. That could be expanded to include Italian Americans, as reflected in the reportage of the Bensonhurst affair in the *New York Times*. What happened was a tragedy of far greater ramifications than reported in the news media. What also is tragic is the insularity and backwardness of the Italian Americans. "Niggers, stay out of our neighborhoods!" they shouted to Black marchers protesting the Hawkins murder. Their language was shocking, arresting. Worst, it was uninformed and unformed.

Listen to their voices, as quoted on the murder in their neighborhood, by the *Times* reporter: "This wasn't racial and I've never been racial in my life. But white people should stick together for ourselves," says a young woman. And an old woman in a Bensonhurst candy store speaking of the murdering gang, adds, "These were good boys . . . they were defending the neighborhood."

"We don't go to Harlem; the kids were in the wrong spot," says an eighteen-year-old youth. "This is Bensonhurst. It's all Italian. We don't need these niggers."

These Americans of Italian descent spoke haltingly when interviewed on television; they groped for words to express themselves, their constructions were ear-grating, their words defamatory, racist, pathetically ignorant. They were people imprisoned by being closed off from education, from wide social interaction, from knowledge of broader values than those of their Old World village. As their pastor, Father Fermeglia of St. Dominic's Church in Bensonhurst, explains, "This is a very provincial neighborhood . . . everyone knows each other. . . . People get the meaning of their lives from their relationships."

What they also get is an inbred, self-perpetuating inability to think, and hence to speak in an informed way; they are buried alive in the low language of insularity.

Like illiterates using picture language, they hold up emblems of their intolerance, watermelons are raised as a racial taunt against the Blacks marching in protest of the Yusuf Hawkins murder. Ludicrously, they hold up an Italian flag. What they can't express verbally, they show. Show and Tell: that is the level of a people in a linguistic backwater, in a backwater of old outdated attitudes; of a people uneducated in values beyond the blatant materialistic one that seduces so many newcomers to America: get rich and make good, defend your property values.

"It is an old truth that if we do not have mastery over our language, language itself will master us . . . it is through language that we control and create the world. We discover life through language, and that—as all great writers have told us—is why we must master it," Malcolm Bradbury wrote in another context.

Language *is* relevant. The racial outbursts that have taken place in Howard Beach, Staten Island, Bensonhurst are committed by young white men who are both poorly educated and socially marginal. They are feeling what it is to be outcasts in a society which promised them that if they made it materially, that would be what mattered. They are outraged because society lied; they are looking for scapegoats to take their rage out on, they are responsible for the reprehensible attacks on Blacks (and more recently, Jews). As the anthropologist and writer Thomas Belmonte has said, "We ignore their yearning and waste their fierce energies at our peril."

Along with the tragedy of the murdered Yusuf Hawkins is the tragedy of a whole community locked in extreme xenophobia and doing, wrongfully, to others what was done to them. It is useful to review the discrimination perpetrated against Italian Americans themselves in order to put into context some of the motivation for their current antisocial behavior. They, too, were once victimized by those who got here before they did and so "owned" their neighborhoods and didn't want the wops in them. Did Italian Americans learn another American lesson as well as materialism—that violence is a means of expression, and the last one in gets it? They got it, now they'll give it to the Blacks who move into "the Italian neighborhood."

In an ironic synchronization, Black filmmaker Spike Lee's film *Do the Right Thing,* about Blacks in Brooklyn hanging out at Sal's pizza parlor, came out just at the time of the Bensonhurst murders, and addressed racial violence. What, in fact, is the right thing to do? Is it, as in the film, for Blacks to take out resentments and rage on white society by attacking and destroying their pizza parlor? Is it, as the last scene of the film shows, for the Black pillagers to remove from Sal's ruined walls the photographic totems of his Italian American allegiance—Sinatra, DiMaggio, Perry Como, et al.—and to replace them with photos of Martin Luther King, Jr., and Malcolm X?

Symbolically that is a masterful statement. The leaders of the Black movement, who have powerfully and eloquently spoken for their people and have had broad social influence, will in the end replace the meager idols of Italian Americans, for whom the inadequate message has been: make a pile, keep it in the family, aim for material satisfactions. What do the "famous" Italian Americans stand for? Money and celebrity status. Not much uplift there, not much for the soul of an alienated and ambivalent people to feed on. No gut nourishment.

Take this exchange between Sal's son Vinnie and Moukie, the Black youth who works as a delivery boy at the pizza parlor. When Moukie says, "Hey Vinnie, how come you're always talking of Black baseball stars and singers? I think you want to be Black," Vinnie, who is imprisoned as much by inadequate language (the reflection of inadequate thought) as by his restrictive social attitudes, gropes to express what he has never thought out. "They're not Black," he finally mumbles, "they're famous."

Vinnie thus not only unconciously identifies the unillustrious (including himself) with the to him demeaning connotation of Black, but must painfully grasp for words and meaning in order to speak at all. The scene is a graphic illustration of what it is to be without articulation because the language of thought has never been fully absorbed or respected, only the language of money.

Thus, "Black" is code for poor, deprived, ignorant, the dregs; it's nigger and wop all over again. And that includes all who have believed only in the commercial opportunities of this country and haven't educated themselves in the language of other values or in what America most hopefully signifies.

It's the triumph of materialist views and Sal's narrow sense of property rights (not exclusively an Italian American attitude, as we recall the actions of Southern Anglo-Americans) that contribute to racial tensions. Rather than recognize the interdependence between his business and the exclusively Black clientele who eat his pizza, Sal insists on making his place a fortress of his Italian background. And the Blacks, too, like Moukie, look for the differences, not the commonality between them. Just as the Power Structure intends.

"Break the Power" is the theme song of the film which is dedicated to the Black or Hispanic victims of police brutality. It is powerful music, and the words are aimed at the structure of a society that abuses people, makes them violent and filled with rage, makes them drown each other out with shouts and curses and shrieking radio music, and ultimately causes them to turn on each other in their frustration.

The police in their patrol car who go up and down the streets of the Black neighborhood where Sal's pizza parlor is located look malevolent as they view the scene through cold, suspicious slit-eyes. Their counterpart is the striking arrangement of three Black men under a bright umbrella against a red wall who are laid-back, benevolent, and the wise commentators on what they observe. They spurn a boycott against Sal, as do others in the neighborhood ("I was born and brought up on Sal's pizza" says a Black girl). And yet in the anguish of their powerlessness, the Blacks will, reacting to police violence, vent their fury against Sal rather than against the societal attitudes that keep the *all* down.

With two eloquent and effective metaphors, *Do the Right Thing* depicts the futility of racial war. One is the wall of photos that provokes one Black youth to ask why, since all of Sal's customers are Black, he doesn't have Martin Luther King and Malcolm X up there, too. Sal says it's his place and he's Italian and he'll have who he wants, showing remarkable insensitivity and stupidity all at once.

The other symbolic device used by director Spike Lee is the shrieking radio music that prevents spoken communication between people as talk becomes a duel of shouts and curses, each attempting to drown the other out. The blaring music is the final provocation that incites Sal to throw a Black kid and his radio out of his place. This precipitates a police action that ends in the youth's death at the hands of the police. Moukie then leads a riot destroying not only Sal's place but his own livelihood and something of value to the neighborhood. The Blacks will be as much kept down by their more overt and mindless violence as Sal and sons by their impoverished social attitudes and lack of self-knowledge.

Blindly, not even noticing the friction between them, Sal had extolled to his sons the money that can be made in a business when families are in it together. He tells them (to their horror) that he'll pass the business on to them. Feeling trapped in the alien territory of a Black neighborhood, all the sons want to do is get out.

But what will get them out? Sal is blind in his defense of a lost cause: his family, his business, his property rights, his pathetic Italian pride, as manifested on his wall by Sinatra & Co., none of whom has the stature of the Black leaders. Sal has not awakened to reality, he lives in a time warp of old, played-out, irrelevant allegiances and chauvinism. He's a decent, hardworking guy, and his sense of responsibility and kindness are well contrasted with the fecklessness of Moukie who has fathered a son and left him, and seems to have no aim in life. But Sal has not evolved with the times. He is harboring a narrow, limited mentality in a time and place that urgently call for more expansiveness. Are the Koreans across the street, whose place is spared by the rioting Blacks, meant to be Sal's smart counterpart? At least they understand the reality of their situation and are not spinning pipe dreams based on spurious values.

Chauvinistically, Sal has defended a wall of false images. In the end, the photos of Martin Luther King, Jr., and Malcolm X, with their two different messages, get pinned to Sal's burned-out wall which no longer can mark the bounds of narrow territoriality. That, Spike Lee's film seems to say, is the right thing to do. It's a lesson, like language, still to be learned in some insular Italian American city enclaves.

A young man in Bensonhurst, again quoted in the *Times,* spoke an American fact of life that many harbor, few speak: "No one likes no one if they don't look the same. Everybody's prejudiced. And that's the way it is."

He is confirmed, sadly, by Adele Dutton Terrell, program director of the National Institute against Prejudice and Violence, who adds, "Every day we have incidents . . . the sad lesson is that in America we have neighborhoods where people do and don't belong."

But *Do the Right Thing* tells clearly that such narrow territoriality is doomed.

"Go home," call the Italian American taunters of Bensonhurst to the protestors who march through their blocks. "We are home," the Black marchers call back.

Rome, 1981

In 1981, just before Christmas, I returned to Rome. The plane from New York landed at Leonardo da Vinci airport during a deluge and the skies poured forth torrents in the mild 10 degrees centigrade (about 50 degrees Fahrenheit) temperature.

It was my first visit back since I had lived there.

As a young woman I had studied in Italy; I wrote my first published work in Italy; I married poet Antonio Barolini in Italy. We lived both in Rome and in the States when he was the United States correspondent for *La Stampa* of Turin. After his death in Rome, harrowed by bureaucracy, loneliness, and the expense and difficulty of a divided family (for our eldest daughter was already in college in the States), I began to dissolve my Italian ties of more than twenty-five years.

The feelings of delight and discovery that first bound me to my ancestral land as it disclosed both its marvels and also the hard truths of my origins had subsided in the press of trying to survive. My parents, in tones reserved for the unspeakable, used to warn me about Italy when I first raised questions about who we were. But no dread warnings of strangeness, backwardness, or *la miseria* had kept me from my voyage of discovery. Then everything changed. I wanted to get out.

I first sold the little farmhouse in the Marche region that had been restored as a summer place and planted with a thousand pine trees on the rolling slopes beyond which lay the Adriatic Sea. Then I rented out the Rome penthouse, a delicious two-room apartment (called an *attico* there) with fireplace, a window which framed the dome of St. Peter's, and a large terrace overlooking the pines of the Janiculum hill; it had been intended as the retirement place for

70

Antonio and me. It was where my youngest daughter and I lived after he died, and before we moved back to the States. Then I decided to sell the *attico,* too.

The apartment was in Antonio's name and mine. His half went both to me and to our daughters at his death. That meant we all had to be present in Rome for the closing of the sale, and that could be accomplished only during their Christmas school vacations. Just before the closing the lira was devaluated, and overnight I saw my proceeds vanish by 30 percent; in addition to that loss, there was difficulty with absurd and arbitrary taxes, there was the bother of establishing that I was the rightful guardian of my minor children, and there was the final obstacle of getting my money out of the country. My leave-taking of Rome in 1975 had not been a happy one. I regarded it as permanent.

Yet though we were resettled in the States, it became apparent that one way or another my daughters and I retained an Italian connection: I found work translating books from Italian; Teodolinda Lucia, the eldest, lived up to her medieval name and became a Dante scholar; Susanna dropped out of college, returned to Italy, and married an artist in Urbino; and Niki, who had lived in Rome from age two and thought of herself as *romana di Roma,* got herself back there in 1981, in her college's Junior Year Abroad program. Italy was still in our lives; I could no more banish it than my parents could.

It became time for me to go back. I had a grandson in Urbino to visit, and two out of three daughters were in Italy that Christmas. I could even justify the trip as a research project: while there I would collect material for an Italian holiday cookbook I was interested in doing.

The cookbook project made it all right again to admit that I loved Italy, that I had lived a fundamental and important part of my life there, that I was forever connected to it because my husband, my children, and now my grandchild were Italian, and because, in fact, it was my own blood.

Thus my return to Rome that rainy December 22, 1981. Taking a taxi from the airport I could see dozens of small cars flooded by the downpour and abandoned on the sides of the road. I reminded myself of the precariousness of Italian life; as my father years ago had harped on the communist threat in Italy, so I reminded myself of the new terrorism on left and right, of the flight of well-off Italians to open businesses in New York, and of the expatriate Americans who had given up on Italian life and returned home.

As we passed through an outlying section of the city called Magliana the taxi driver told me it was the center of Rome's underworld. "You can't come into this area at night," he said. I was remembering a Rome where one could go anyplace at night—one of the pleasures of life had been strolling through old Rome late on a summer evening, dining *al fresco,* stopping at a caffè for hours of talk. But what the driver was showing me was another of the city's expanding peripheries, the areas which have sprung up as high prices force Romans to vacate their historic center to the rich foreigners who can afford it. Everyone else is emarginated to the increasingly built up outskirts. No more carriage rides out into the *campagna* beyond the city gates to stop at a roadside *osteria* for a glass of wine and a view of the sunset over vistas broken only by vestiges of the ancient aqueduct as Margaret Fuller described it in her accounts of Rome in 1846–48; and, indeed, as I had still been able somewhat to replicate a century later in 1948. In that year, as if in a dream, I had seen a flock of sheep being herded through the great gate of Piazza del Popolo toward Via Flaminia.

The cab got into the city proper by way of Viale Trastevere with its swirl of cars, streetcars, buses. On the side of the number 75 bus I saw an ad for Fiat's new compact car called *Ritmo* (Rhythm) with the slogan: *È bella nella vita avere una Ritmo,* It's great to have a Rhythm in life.

Yes, I thought, but my rhythm is American once again, I no longer sway to that of Rome. Had I once dared to drive in the maelstrom I saw all around me? Yes, and as boldly as the drivers who now shocked me.

I kept looking avidly around me, filling my eyes with the Roman shapes and colors I remembered so well. The parked cars that once filled Piazza Venezia were gone—a hopeful sign, I thought. New to the square was a tall, skinny pine (an imitation of the Christmas giant in Rockefeller Center?) in the middle of a grassy parterre. "A tree!" I exclaimed.

"It's always been there," the driver answered untruly, perhaps not recognizing through my American accent a former resident of Rome. But, in fact, the Nordic Christmas symbol *was* new, as new as the discomfiting information that the Italian Parliament had just abolished the feast of Epiphany, popularly known as Befana, from the calendar of observed holidays. January 6 had always been the gifts-giving day in remembrance of the arrival of the Magi at the Child's crib on the Twelfth Night after the birth. An Americanized Christmas had taken over Rome. I saw clumps of white plastic ferns affixed to storefronts on Via Quattro Novembre, and styrofoam angels dangling above Via Giulia. The city had started adopting Nordic trappings for Christmas in the early seventies; now the holiday had become the same orgy of consumerism that it was in the States. The sweet, soberly observed religious occasion announced by the sounds of the Abruzzi bagpipers come down from the mountains to the streets of Rome, in sheepskins and leather foot wrappings, to play those whining, moaning Christmas tunes and pick up some money during their slow season, seemed to have vanished in a tawdry display of commercialism.

I had only just arrived in Rome and already I sensed a new urgency to my holiday cookbook—I had to record the old *feste* before they were all gone. I thought of the great fanfare ending of Respighi's tone poem "Roman Festivals," which ends with the Befana segment in a great sounding and clashing of instruments to mark the unbridled joyousness of that holiday. Yet here I was face to face with how easily, in reality, the Befana witch could be banished. Santa Claus, or *Babbo Natale,* had dethroned her, and the incongruous "I'm Dreaming of a White Christmas" was everyplace. I thought of how the goddesses of antiquity had themselves been transformed into various Virgin Marys and female saints. Rome has always had the agility to change its skin.

I met Niki at the central post office and we headed for Piazza Navona, the site of traditional holiday stands of crèche figures and props, torrone and other sweets, but disappointingly empty of people when we got there. It was two nights before Christmas. A few raggle-taggle Santas stood about aimlessly ogling the women shoppers; a gussied-up pony carriage for hire, lined in "ermine" and decked out in lights and tinsel, waited for a passenger. It all looked wrong to my eye. Niki seemed not to notice. She was elated to be living her junior year in Rome, and everything in the city was all right with her. She was charmed by the fixtures for the manger scene which, originated by Saint Francis of Assisi seven hundred and fifty years ago, is, thankfully, still part of an Italian Christmas. All the parts of the scene could still be bought in Piazza Navona, everything from an exquisite miniature tray of all kinds of breads for $2.50 and a vibrant marketplace vendor's stand at $18, to a magnificent model of a whole hill town with bridges, streets, and houses for a million and a half lire, about $1,500.

That was the real center of Christmas for me—the perennial celebration of life on every level, from the well-dressed figures of *signori,* to the chestnut roaster, storekeepers, shepherds, peasants, and priests. Christmas came to everybody, and everybody was depicted, from the wine drinkers in the tavern to the Holy Family itself, in the miniatures created for crèche scenes.

Other new things had crowded in: an arts and crafts fair of dubious quality had taken over the classic proportions of Piazza Farnese where, on the far side, stood the finest palace of the high Renaissance in Rome, diminished now by the conglomerate stalls and tents in front of it, the two beautiful fountains from the baths of Caracalla canceled out by the clutter.

Nearby, Via Giubbonari was thronged with a sideshow of street peddlers displaying their stuff on the paving stones of the narrow street. People stepped between the chestnut and candy vendors, in and out of shops and by stalls of plastic nonsense. Jewelry, fake flowers, and lots of East Indian scarves and blouses were featured. Scraping against pedestrians, cars made their way down narrow Via Pettinari, the Street of the Comb Sellers, another old Rome street named for the craftspeople who once made it theirs. Shop girls now had a punk look and the rude manners to go with it. Entering a bookstore I asked a defiant-looking salesgirl if there were something on Italian festivals. No, she shrugged, only fairs. What kind of book would that be? I asked. Would it have holidays? "What do I know?" she said impatiently. "It's potatoes, vegetables, beefsteak—that kind of stuff."

I came upon remembered scenes . . . Piazza Quercia, named for the oak tree that still grows there . . . my old workroom with its view of the stunning facade of Palazzo Spada . . . Via Sistina, up which I had walked Niki to school every morning . . . the magnificent Triton fountain in my old neighborhood of Piazza Barberini, now newly surrounded by a paved pedestrian island where a sculptor was making a small replica of Bernini's masterpiece.

Old memories did not flood in on tides of nostalgia or homesickness, or feelings of loss or regret. I was comfortable with a familiar sense of place even though I was not in step with this Rome—felt, actually, a resistance to its pace, to the visible Americanizing of its life. I had changed, too.

I had become a spectator, not a participant, and the scene was different. Gone were the days when Rome was a good buy and one could put up with certain absurdities in exchange for its pleasures: the deep humanity and tolerance of the people, the joy of walking at any hour through a magnificent and monumental city, eating well and living well, having a sense of latitude with time rather than pressure.

Even though there was a favorable 1,200 lire for a dollar exchange, a few chestnuts in a paper cone now cost 1,000 lire, tea for two at Babbington's was 11,000 lire, and a haircut 35,000. Still, the traffic-freed streets in the shopping center, from Piazza di Spagna to the Corso and Via della Croce to Via Frattina, were thronged with shoppers taking advantage of unbroken hours in the shopping day; gone was the closing from 1 to 4 P.M. when the center of Rome was deserted. Maxim's of Paris had opened a luxury food shop on Via di Propaganda. Furriers abounded, and even in December's balmy weather, Roman women paraded their furs. Windows were filled with the china, silver, crystal, hand-worked linens and silks of the high style, while the streets were full of people in punk-rock or late-hippy attire.

I noticed more beggars interspersed with the shoppers than at any other time since I first arrived in the battered and struggling postwar Italy of the late forties. I witnessed a scene which seemed to capture the long familiarity of an old civilization with all the ways of human existence: everything had been seen, known, accepted. It was Terence, after all, a Roman, who wrote, "I am human, therefore nothing human is alien to me." In Via del Gambero, where people pass from Piazza San Silvestro to the elegant shopping areas of Via Frattina and Via Condotti, a legless man sat in the street calling out, "Don't abandon me!" He singled out a smart young woman strolling by with her friends and called, *"Signorina!"* She glanced over, said *"Ciao"* as if greeting a child, and walked on as a bystander snickered. It reminded me of the film *Caligula* where the spectators laughed as heads of prisoners were severed by a chopping machine in the Colosseum. Nearby, children in Piazza San

Silvestro stood gawking at a ragged woman huddled in a doorway asking for help in a voice that screeched on and off as if with a faulty battery.

When I mentioned this to Cecilia Barbieri, who headed the Italian committee to observe the United Nations Year of the Handicapped and was herself the mother of a spastic daughter in her twenties, she responded strongly: "Italian barbarism! This country is still in the dark ages as far as civility toward the afflicted is concerned! How they laugh and pass remarks when I take *la bambina* for a walk—and the government is no better!" She feared that the meager subsidies granted to the handicapped would be rescinded. She remembered the care she received from American friends of mine when she took her daughter to the States for consultation on physical therapy methods which she said had helped but which everyone in Italy viewed negatively.

Rome buses were still plentiful, efficient, and a bargain—only 200 lire a ticket, about 20 cents. Even so I noticed many people getting on buses by the central exit door rather than the back door where, on an honor system enforced by the sporadic appearance of inspectors, the passengers were supposed to insert tickets (purchased at a newsstand or *tabacchi*) into a date-stamping machine. This procedure eliminated the patient ticket man who once sat on a raised platform at the back door and gave out the tissuey 50-lire paper slips. It was said to be more efficient this way; even if a certain percentage of people cheated, it was already calculated in the fare and still cheaper for the transit system than paying salaries.

I saw a woman with a small child trying to leave from the proper center exit door, but being pushed back by a press of people illegally trying to get on there. A man in the bus began to shout with rage that the oncomers were harming a child while they tried to get on free. "Are you the father to care so much?" someone retorted. This called forth further comments, and sides were taken pro and con. Feeling is warm and on the surface in a Rome bus, not silenced by indifference as in the carefully arranged blankness of faces to be seen on a New York subway. Italians do not quickly turn their eyes away, embarrassed, from confrontations or ugliness—they participate in everything. It is all part of life. Even the young woman's callous greeting to the legless beggar in Via del Gambero was an awareness and an acknowledgment of him; she didn't, as New

Yorkers do with the homeless, pretend he wasn't there. She greeted him on her terms, cynical and tough as they were.

Human contacts and exchanges are as much the daily stuff of Rome life as their fresh-baked daily bread. Some people still sang in the streets, like one young man with a jovial refrain in Via dei Pettinari that translated as, "Drop dead to you, and to you . . . and to you."

Everything is expressed—not only compliments but barbs, ironies, sarcasms, expressions of love, jealousy, anger, flirtation. Here, indeed, is freedom of speech. The curtailment of insult or offense is not debated in Parliament, nor do assertiveness training centers have to be instituted to teach Romans the art of the stinging rebuttal.

Niki and I took the number 52 bus to the Parioli section to visit playwright Luciano Codignola, his wife Tea, and any of their children who were still home. I learned that former classmates of one daughter were among terrorists captured in Rome a year or so ago. Tea was truly shocked that these "children of the middle class," as she called them, could have gone so wrong. Silvia, the youngest daughter, Niki's age, was just recovering from a deep depression that came upon her at the Aldo Moro assassination when Rome life suddenly was wrenched out of comfortable indifference *(menefregismo)* had become disturbingly precarious. For the Italian prime minister to be kidnapped and assassinated and dumped near Via Botteghe Oscure in the center of Rome was a horror that affected everyone.

But terrorism wasn't all; there was also a newly visible drug culture in Italy. I thought of how, in the late sixties and early seventies when we were living in Rome, American friends would write to say how fortunate we were to be bringing up children so far from the drugs and violence which then dominated American life.

Ten years later the drug and dropout scene was in Rome, as it was everywhere. There has always been a time lag before what is current in the States catches on in Rome. But time lags and distances are shrinking. I felt a mirror effect. In Rome I seemed to be back in the America of protest; in the States, where it was Reagan country, we seemed, by contrast, to have regressed to the mentality of Italy's law and order fascist past.

The next evening, with friends in a Chinese restaurant (itself a novelty to me who had only frequented Rome's *trattorie*), I met a latter-day Ippolito Nievo, named for his grandfather's uncle, the author of the classic *Confessioni di un italiano,* who died in 1861 at age thirty after an adventuresome life in which he participated in Garibaldi's Sicilian campaign. The present-day Nievo was eating only white rice; he had, he said, an ulcer from the tensions and stress that life in the capital gave him. Later, walking from the restaurant, he pointed out a horrifying sight—a cluster of bedraggled people waiting at the all-night pharmacy to get plastic syringes and distilled water for shooting up heroin. I was appalled. Signora Nievo said it had become usual. She told of being pushed aside in a pharmacy by a young man who ran in calling, "Emergency—a crisis is coming!" She thought he had some aged person who needed care; instead, he wanted a syringe to shoot up before he went into withdrawal. Without batting an eyelash the pharmacist simply left Signora Nievo and got the addict his equipment. This, she pointed out in a dramatic conclusion, happened in a good neighborhood.

After that, I began noticing the evidence everywhere. I saw crumpled boxes of distilled water and disposable needles littering the ground in Trastevere, in Campo dei Fiori, near the Spanish Steps. There is no class, no section of the city that is free from addicts, my friend Daniela Colombo, editor of a feminist journal, told me. Her pocketbook had been snatched in broad daylight, and she said it was simply a fact of life now that one would, sooner or later, be mugged.

Everything reinforced her words. On Via Condotti, in front of the fashionable Caffè Greco where artists and writers have for two centuries at least held court, a large table of leaflets and placards had been set up to solicit contributions from the Christmas crowd for the rehabilitation of drug addicts. The volunteers also wanted funds to campaign for the defeat of a proposed law in Parliament which would legalize drugs. Daniela's husband, Giuseppe Sacco, a professor of economics and development, said drugs should be legalized; only criminals would profit from their not being so.

"But people are less alienated from each other in Italy than in our society," I said, unable to explain to myself the shocking evidence of drug use. "Why are Italians turning to drugs?"

"There is as much hopelessness in society over here as anywhere else," he replied. "We're all in the same world."

And the signs were everywhere: graffiti couched in a hybrid drug culture lingo: *morte ai pusher,* death to the pushers, was scrawled on a wall. A newspaper headline reported a death as *Morto di Overdose*. And the school notebook I bought to record my observations was called the dropouts' notebook—*il quaderno dei Dropouts*.

Just before Christmas the leftist newspaper *Paese Sera* carried a story announcing the return of the popular TV program "Drug Addiction: What to Do about It." The show would be aired every Thursday beginning after the holidays on the official Channel One, a recognition, said the paper, of the social problem. It further estimated more than 100,000 addicts in Italy, four-fifths of whom had no contact with social services. There were 232 deaths from overdose in 1981, and another 800 or so deaths from drug-related causes. Niki told me of her visit to a former classmate in school and seeing drugs there, too.

On the day of Christmas Eve, Niki and I got up in the dark and walked down refuse-strewn Trastevere streets to get the tram for Piazza Esedra where we'd find the 7 A.M. bus that would take us to Urbino for Christmas with Susi and her family. The tram sped through the empty streets—a different rhythm from that of the daytime crawl through clogged traffic. I noted a woman in the tram, alone, wearing a mink coat. Daniela had told me of furs being stripped right off their wearers' backs. I wondered at the woman's bravery. Then I wondered at my own new thinking.

Niki remarked on the fascist look to Rome in the dark. She was right. When Rome is deserted, the monuments take over: the heroic-size palazzi, the gigantic portals, the huge grilled window spaces. Everything is built on a scale to make people feel insignificant. By day, however, when people fill the streets, their bravado and their numbers attenuate the powerful stance of the buildings that house ministries or bear the names of the old ruling families.

It was a different look in Urbino. Surrounded by the soothing green of hilly countryside where sheep still pasture, even the famous Ducal Palace, epitome of Renaissance culture, takes on a homey air as it presides benevolently over the compact brick-walled town. Urbino is set on two hills, unified into a tight cluster of tile-roofed, brick buildings on steep streets, all radiating toward the dip between the two hills where the central square, Piazza della Republica, is located. A frenetically blinking Christmas tree flashed its holiday signals to the clusters of chatting men—hundred of them, and all the more noticeable for the few women among them—who thronged the piazza.

Urbino is a university town. It attracts thousands of students, many of them from foreign countries. And yet it was almost as difficult of access as in the days when Duke Federico, of the fortified palace, wanted it that way. Other than the 7 A.M. bus from Rome or driving oneself over the Apennines, the only alternative was a train that arrived at Fano on the Adriatic coast, connected to the train for Pesaro, which connected to the Pesaro-Urbino bus. And yet the town was bustling with an old-time market outside the walls and building extending into the outskirts. The commune ran an exemplary day-care center named for Pablo Neruda. No beggars or desperately poor were to be seen anywhere.

When the snow came punctually on Christmas, it came in flakes so big they looked like pieces of torn paper being scattered about– a ticker-tape blizzard for our arrival. The countryside around Urbino, blanketed in deep snow, was soon filled with children sledding. In town, people strolled around in fashionable sports attire. Some cars were buried in snow, and those that weren't progressed slowly with chains on their tires. Walking was dubious, especially on the very steep principal street, Via Raffaello, where Raphael, the town's most famous native son, was said to have lived in a dwelling that can be visited. Everyone was fuel conscious, heat was kept at a minimum despite the frigid weather. Families stuck to the kitchen where, country style, the fireplace is located; there they ate, read, mended, looked at the television set often perched on top of the refrigerator, played cards, kept warm.

The place Susi and her husband Nevio rented was three kilometers from the town walls. By spring it would be beautiful there where vineyards terrace the hills and sheep graze, and Susi would garden in a landscape that seems lifted from a painting by Giotto. Nevio told me he spent a quarter of his salary just to pay for gas (about $4 a gallon) for driving to his teaching job a half hour away over the hills in the region of Emilia. When I suggested they live where his work was, he replied, "No, never."

The *Urbinati* are extreme boosters of their town, and they are enamored of their past. Urbino has the indigenous narcissism of a walled town used to looking inward and suspicious of what's outside the walls. Despite the coming and going of students, its geographic isolation has kept it determinedly insular.

Who then, I wondered, scrawled *cività stronza* (shit city) on the side of a building? That rudeness appeared next to posters proclaiming Urbino's top seasonal attraction, the replaying of a 1924 film that recreates the pageantry attending the nuptials of Ubaldo della Rovere, duke of Urbino, and Claudia dei Medici in 1624. Naturally, the *prominenti* of the town had the featured roles of the nobles and courtiers.

Susi had become completely acclimated to Urbino life. Her father-in-law, Peppino, helped her in the garden; her mother-in-law, Cleofe, helped with the baby. Nevio and his brother were firmly attached to their parents' home, and both their wives were absorbed into the very fabric of the family, visiting there often. There were three floors of family in the parents' house, representing three different households. They liked to come together, eating and drinking and watching TV in the tiny combination living and dining room off Cleofe's kitchen in the bottom-floor apartment.

We gathered there Christmas Eve for the fast-night meal. Instead of the traditional smoked eel which I had half-fearfully, half-curiously expected, Susi's sister-in-law Maria, a sprightly young woman originally from Bari who had come to Urbino for her studies in Greek and Latin, explained that no one stuck to the old ways anymore. "Everyone works now," she said gaily, "no one has time."

I thought of my mother's Italian American Christmas Eve dinner in Syracuse, New York, some three thousand miles from the homeland. It would be far more traditional with its calamari sauce for pasta and *merluzzo a lesso,* plus other fish dishes, than the caviar and smoked salmon hors d'oeuvres we were having in Urbino.

Yet on Christmas Day Cleofe's hundreds of handmade meat-filled cappelletti in broth were the real, rare thing. When the capon was served, it brought on the usual ribald table talk without which no Italian home meal seems complete. The capon's neutered condition led Peppino into an explanation of why November 11, Saint Martin's day, is the feast of cuckolds. "It was the birthday of the little king," he said, "you know, Vittorio Emmanuele III. Since he was married to a very tall and attractive woman, Elena of Montenegro, no one could believe that he wasn't being replaced. In fact, the king's heir, Prince Umberto, is a tall handsome man whose real father, it's said, was one of the Household Guards." November 11 as the feast of the cuckolds! I wondered if I could use it in my diminishing list of Italian holidays.

When the chocolate-covered yule-log pastry dessert was being served with spumante, the upstairs families came down to join us.

The *marchigiani* (so named for their region, the Marche) are a blunt, outspoken people: Margherita, a cousin from the top floor, bounded in to ask abruptly, "So, did you eat well?" And Nevio's eighty-nine-year-old grandfather, named Washington (pronounced Vasinto), and smelling of the garlic to which he attributed his health, came down from the second floor, he said, especially to greet us.

Television has become a powerful presence in Italian life. But the screen was mercifully quiet during most of Christmas Day, and Peppino waxed philosophic over brandy. He was a simple man of seventy, retired but still active in his garden and Susi's. He loved to cultivate the soil and bring forth crops, and he retained a firm faith in nature. All the badness and corruption in the world, he said thoughtfully, could be solved by people going back to nature. "Everything has its season," he said solemnly, unaware, perhaps, of speaking biblically.

I told him of the ad I had seen in yesterday's paper for Findus frozen peas: a full page telling Italians that tender spring peas were now without season, thanks to Findus products. It had been two decades since an unprecedented boom transformed agrarian Italy into an industrial society, and most Italian families had easily admitted convenience foods into their lives. But Peppino thought the old ways—waiting for the fruits of each season in their own time—were still the best. He thought of nature as good, benevolent.

But nature, I said, is indifferent. Moral judgments can't be made about it; and it is people, anyway, who now control nature. He looked skeptical and Susi looked thoughtful.

Susi was attuned to Peppino's simple life concept, and later that evening, in her own kitchen, with the fire and TV going, she read to me from her book of natural food remedies and recommended compresses of cabbage leaves for the pain in my shoulder, chestnuts for depression.

If I hadn't found my rhythm in sophisticated Rome, I found it even less in the elemental Urbino environs. Susi was living the pastoral life I had passed through years ago when I was tending my own babies in a country village in the Piedmont. That was no longer my rhythm, and not Niki's either. Just before New Year's, we left Urbino on the early morning bus by way of the old consular road, the Via Flaminia, one of the many leading to Rome. Traveling on twisting roads through craggy gray mountains was like being in the papier-mâché crèche settings we had seen in Piazza Navona.

By the time we got over the Apennines and into the Spoleto area, the snow was gone and the hills were brown with dried oak leaves.

Rome was thick with an outbreak of Burberry scarves and caps— they must have been the number one Christmas item that season. I went to visit Adele Cambria, a journalist, author, feminist, polemicist, friend. To get to her flat I had to pass by the Ministry of Justice, which was cordoned off and patrolled by guards with machine guns because of terrorist threats. Terrorism had become part of the fabric of life in Rome and other cities. And feminism, too. Certainly, Italian women, by organizing, had been instrumental in bringing about profound social change. To have established divorce and abortion in a Catholic country, right under the Pope's nose and his expressed prohibition, was an enormous feat. Now there was agitation for salaries for housewives, pensions, generous maternity leaves, and more day-care facilities.

At Adele's I met two feminists of a radical group called *Nemesiache,* devotees of Nemesis, the goddess of vengeance. They had just come from a lesbian conference that I had seen announced by poster all over Rome. They were unhappy about what they called violence among women. The conferees had witnessed confrontations between women who didn't want to be photographed because they hadn't come out publicly as lesbians, and those who insisted they take a political stand. "They have to come out publicly or not come to these meetings at all," said one of the women at Adele's place.

Adele took a more conciliatory position: the women in question can learn from association; they don't have, at this moment, to jeopardize their jobs and family situation, too, she thought. Education is a question of time.

But the followers of Nemesis were upset, irritated, disillusioned; above all, they were not feeling well after having slept in cold quarters at feminist headquarters and having eaten badly. The angrier one was dressed in a monkey-fur coat, top hat, gold boots, short black miniskirt, poet's blouse with billowing sleeves, and wore purple scalloped harlequin glasses. Her hair was red and wild. The other woman was more modish, in a thirties kind of style with large plumes sprouting from her over-the-eyes hat.

The *Nemesiache,* Adele told me when they left, are deliberately provocative in their dress. Their tenet was to have nothing to do with men, even though they were not necessarily lesbians. They had adopted celibacy as the only way of not collaborating with a wrongful society. One of the women was a theater director, the other an actress, and they were all going to the country after New Year's to work on the script from Adele's feminist novel *Dopo Didone* (After Dido).

"So, do you miss your old life in Rome?" Adele asked. I told her the old life was good while it was happening, but *that* life in *that* Rome was gone and it was useless to think of refinding it. I found I had no nostalgia for the past per se, but retained a strong sense of place: I found myself instantly in streets I knew, stores I remembered, familiar caffès. I walked into the trattoria Archimede and the proprietor beamed, "*Signora, benvenuta* . . . welcome." I knew him, he knew me; it was as if I had last been there a week ago.

I began to understand: the lack of focus and the lack of direction I felt in Rome were natural. It was no longer enough to wander the streets of Rome looking at its marvels. It was no longer enough to pick up impressions, be dispersive. What I lacked in Rome was what I had, finally, in America—a direction for work. Rome, I found, squandered one's energies with posters which incite and seduce by making immediately known all the temptations a large city offers. I could not walk anywhere without being visually attracted by announcements of this or that exhibit, show, theatrical performance, movie, conference, demonstration, rally, or special event. But even the stores no longer endlessly tempted me. When I was a signora in Rome, yes, everything in store windows beckoned me. The whole city was a sensual trap.

On this return trip, strangely, I found myself rather critical even of the fabulous apartments with superb views where I was invited. I perceived beyond the aesthetics that they were often uncomfortable to live or work in; the heat was not reliable, lighting was poor, telephones badly connected, there was frequently no hot water, and the noise from the streets was always present.

Yes, it *is* good to have rhythm in one's life, as the ad said, but rhythm perhaps means having a rhyme and a reason in life, too; that, for me, was no longer in Rome.

I was no longer a resident of Rome, but I was hardly a tourist there either. I was visiting again a city where I had lived at a peak time of its contemporary story; a city where we had attended events as part of the literary and artistic world such as Luigi Barzini's dinners, and garden parties at the president's Quirinal residence on

the June 2 anniversary of the founding of the republic. As if to sym-
bolize the end of that era, the June 2 holiday was no longer observed. Times change.

I was changed; I came back as a single woman and a writer pos-
sessing a different, personal rhythm, no longer totally absorbed in
my husband's. I was no longer trying to be the Italian he was. I was
American, Italian descended and not conflicted any longer between
the two cultures, but enriched by both. It was no longer a strain to
wonder where I really belonged because my bridge went in both
directions.

It was enough that Rome was there, and always would be. The
weather was temperate, there were marvelous shows to see—de
Chirico, and Jean Louis David at Villa Medici next to the Convent
of the Sacred Heart on top of the Spanish Steps where Niki had
been a student.

There was, of course, also Rome rainy and Rome everlastingly a
maze of bureaucracy. I engaged in some jousting with the bureau-
crats over my husband's pension which kept me running from office to office for two or three days, but the best story of stalemate
that I heard was from my friend Shirley Herbert who had been living in Rome for twenty-three years.

Shirley had an Italian employer and so was enrolled in one of the
obligatory medical plans for employees. Though she distrusted the
plan on principle (as any Roman would), she decided one day to
put it to the test when she had to get new glasses. She was told to
go, with the paid receipt of her eye exam, to the office of reimbursement in Via Santa Croce in Gerusalemme. Nothing could be
done by phone or by mail, one had to go in person. She resisted
taking a cab the considerable distance, she said, because she wanted
to experience in full what was involved in getting the reimbursement
to which she was entitled. It took her two buses to get to the office
where she felt as if only she and the maids from Somalia were left
to stand in such prewar lines. She waited it out and got to the window just before it closed for good at 1 P.M., as all government offices
do. She presented her claim, and was told shortly by the functionary as he started to close that it was the wrong day for *that* claim,
she had to come back on an odd day. Desperate, she made a quick
mental calculation and called out, "Today's the twenty-seventh—it *is*
odd!" No, no, the functionary said dismissively, gesturing her away,
Monday, Wednesday, or Friday.

During the long bus rides back, Shirley figured out the reasoning: since the week begins with Monday, that is day one of the week, and one is an odd number. That must have been what the clerk meant by odd days. That's life in Rome, she told me gamely. It equals out.

For, she went on to demonstrate, she had a television set on which she could get nineteen channels between government and private ones, Italian, French, or Swiss. It's common to have sets that get thirty-six channels, she said, and there are those who could, if they wanted, get ninety-nine channels from all over Europe. Everyone with a set had a remote control device which was used like a calculator to get combinations of channels. That explained, somewhat, the intense participation I had noted among Italian families with their televisions.

Shirley had another explanation. "No one goes out anymore. It's too dangerous. It all happened after the Moro assassination—the city went into shock. It's guaranteed that some time or other your bag will be snatched, so I don't carry one anymore." And she showed me the individual pockets (sent by her mother in the States) that she sews inside her garments. Even worse than the bag snatching is the violence—"I've seen women with bloodied heads, right around here." You learn to live with it, you make up your own defenses, she said.

Many pleasures remained: a chief one was the Roman hairdresser. I stopped by Signor Pino's place where I used to get my hair done, have a body massage or facial with Signora Marisa, have a pedicure or my legs waxed. It was all reasonable, all that luxury, during the sixties. I found Signor Pino still on Via Ludovisi, but his shop looked a lot less elegant than I remembered it.

I learned he was about to move from the premises and into partnership with someone on Via Veneto. "Ah, *signora*," he told me excitedly, his high color due to medication, not a vacation sun, "you who knew the seriousness of my enterprise, how could I survive anymore without going into partnership? I have to ask 10,000 lire for a hair setting, but a pair of shoes will cost me 100,000 lire. How can it work?"

He cut my hair with ferocity as he declaimed with passion on the situation. Yes, one could still save oneself in the provinces, he thought, but city life, especially in Rome, was finished. The family was finished—one couldn't even legally denounce an eighteen-year-old who left home anymore.

"Too much copying of America," said Pino, shaking his head. "But where America is large and has natural resources and the ability to take sudden change, Italy hasn't the resources nor the agility of the younger country. So Italy has fallen into an imitation that will be self-destructive."

Look at the question of absenteeism. People, he said, get salaries without working. He talked with an anguish that was genuine even though it sprang from allegiances to another era; he seemed literally heartbroken at the prospects for his country. "Italy, yes, it could even get along all right, but it's got a fatal disease controlled by trade unions. Everyone wants a guaranteed salary, but no one wants to fulfill his work obligation."

He stopped cutting to step around and face me. "You, *signora,* were here in the best years. Now it's gone."

I saw what he saw, too, all around me, the frantic imitation of American fads and styles. The dress, the food, the music, the slang. Journalist Sergio Maldini had a piece about the Americanization phenomenon in *La Nazione* of Florence. "It would almost seem," he wrote, "that, forced by fascism to embrace a provincial culture and refurbish a highly elusive spirit of ancient Rome . . . Italy now, thirty-five years after the end of the war, is still trying to vaccinate itself against this danger. . . . The result has been a concentration on the international cultural circuit which has taken the extreme form of focus on the United States. It is not just the Italian press that is full of news about the USA . . . but Italian society is itself profoundly Americanized . . . much more so than France or Germany."

In fact, American literature had been thriving in Italy ever since the end of the fascist regime when writer-translators like Elio Vittorini and Cesare Pavese brought a whole range of American contemporary authors (previously interdicted) to an eager Italian audience. American books were everywhere to be seen in translation, attesting to what Maldini called the "omnivorous curiosity of Italy's intellectual culture."

As for music, an Italian musician who had lived for many years in the States and was back in Italy during the holidays told me he felt acutely embarrassed when he went to the Rome opera to hear *Tosca,* that quintessential Roman opera. It was poor, very poor, and the whole country depressed him to the point where he felt he could no longer be there. Yes, I agreed: it took me years to get up the courage to return to Italy. We are afraid that it will no longer be what we loved.

Audiences at the theater, as at the opera, no longer dressed. Standards were down, it was anything goes. When I went to see Dario Fo's rock music interpretation of *The Three-Penny Opera,* the men were dressed in windbreakers and Hush Puppy shoes and the women in motley. The presentation itself was a paradigm for Italy—heavy borrowing from American productions with moments of imaginative creativity that were purely Italian, but so violently loud as to be unintelligible much of the time.

Still, let me count the pleasures: flower stands seemed to have just discovered the beauty of the cabbage. I saw gorgeous ones with centers of purple, pink, or yellow leaves that looked like giant, baroque blossoms. *"Vuole, signori?"* the women vendors in Campo dei Fiori called out as always, and they hit it just right: Do you want it? they asked. Yes, of course! Who wouldn't? On Via del Noro, the old Valzani confectioner's store still produced wonderful holiday confections; further down the street a man on a stationary bicycle busily pedaled the wheels to sharpen knives for the housewives in the neighborhood. That one could still find these services was a blessing not to be lightly ignored.

I kept coming up against the brash, smart-alecky directness of the Romans, their toughness audible in the *romanaccia* they speak. I got a sample even from the well-dressed woman I sat next to at the Mr. Minit (*sic*) shoe repair counter in the Standa ten-cent store where I was getting my boots reheeled. The woman kept after the shoe repairmen to do their work right since her boots, which were also being reheeled, were handmade. She kept mentioning it so often that, courteously, I admired her boots and asked if she had had them made in Rome.

"I'm a Roman of Rome," she shot back brusquely. "Where do you think I'd have them made!"

Following the New Year's Eve custom I brought Daniela and Giuseppe Sacco a bunch of mistletoe to hang in their apartment for good luck during the year. She was preparing lentils for New Year's Eve, but when I asked her about other traditional foods for the holidays, she shook her head. No more time-consuming specialities for her. *Non vale la pena:* it's not worth the pain. Even at Christmas, everyone buys a panettone and that's it. Again I thought of my mother in upstate New York who, in her eighties, painstakingly went through the making of her own mother's Calabrian Christmas cookies every year. They were always delicious, better than any I'd had in Italy. They were, in fact, no longer Italian but a true transplant.

New Year's Eve began with the Saccos' friends in Palestrina, a town outside Rome which, approached at night from the *autostrada,* displayed a wonderful illuminated outline of its triangular layout on the old ruins of the Temple of Minerva in ancient Praeneste. We went to a country estate whose owners had redone the magnificent former stables into a charming country house, complete with beams, hearth, rustic good food, and local wine. We had Daniela's lentils with sausage, roast baby lamb, salad, fruit, and a crunchy short-bread called *sbriciolona.* At midnight, punctually, there were fire-works and sparklers outside in the cold, crisp, starry night, with children applauding and dogs barking.

This was the simple country life scene of New Year's Eve; returning to the city we did what everyone else was doing, we went to find another party. At 1:30 A.M. we landed in a chichi apartment, over-looking the Capitoline, of a many-times-married, rich woman writer. The place was filled with people in all kinds of fantasy dress, and remnants of high feasting were scattered through the rooms. In the large salon, rock music was blaring and a few people dancing; in the dining room, a group of gamblers played chemin de fer; people wandered through corridors and onto terraces, dazed and deca-dent. The women wore a lot of glitter on their face and in their hair; miniskirts had returned, and blowsy blouses. It was a scene remi-niscent of Fellini's *La Dolce Vita.* Outside there was an ongoing on-slaught of cars circling into Piazza Venezia as they raced from place to place, trying to extend the evening. Nightclubs and restaurants, the next day's papers were to report, were filled to capacity as if there were no tomorrow. Life in Rome, once thought to be provin-cial, hadn't always been lived that way.

I noticed that there was little or no throwing out of old stuff from windows, ridding the house of the old to get ready for the new, as custom used to have it in Italy. I could remember when Rome streets were littered with everything including the kitchen sink and one walked out at one's peril on New Year's Eve. Now times are more difficult, people said, everyone's holding onto their things.

In fact, I found that resale dress shops run by well-to-do women had discreetly sprung up in a country which had scorned the idea, not so long ago, of buying anyone's discarded clothing. Many women, newly divorced or separated, now made their living in re-selling fashion. They did it without advertising, letting the word be known among friends, like speakeasies of old, and those who bought resale clothes called it "amusing" to shop for "rags."

New Year's Day heralded the annual plunge into the Tiber of an elderly gentleman who was known as Mr. OK in my Rome years. This year, diving into a yellow, muddy river swirling madly from the recent rains, two male successors, known as O and K, carried on the ritual before a small crowd while most Romans were home sleeping off their *notte brava*. In a bar where I got cappuccino and a brioche, I heard two cops discussing their New Year's Eve. One said he had spent his time very well dining in company where each had a chicken apiece to eat. You know, he explained, the small French kind.

Years ago, when Cecilia Barbieri had gone to Philadelphia to get medical treatment for her spastic daughter, she was invited to an American home and remained forever impressed at seeing each person at table served a chicken. Overhearing the cops in that Rome bar it suddenly dawned on me that those "small French chickens" must have been Cornish game hens. Cecilia always remained con-vinced that a chicken apiece could only happen in America.

From the bar I walked over Ponte Sisto, down Via Pettinari into Campo dei Fiori and across the Corso to look at Palazzo Massimo. The facade is admirable, but it's the backside I prefer. I like the lone column that remains in the tiny piazza behind Palazzo Massimo and the subtle gray frescoes that festoon the building's rear wall. The palace housed Conrad Sweynheim and Arnold Pannartz in the fifteenth century when they brought the first newfangled printing press to Rome. In 1467, the first book printed in Rome issued from that palace. These are the resonances of Rome, where buildings and places awaken ideas and connections, where humanist traces abound.

In a corner of the secluded square, a marble plaque of 1758 af-fixed to the wall is, in effect, a Don't Litter sign, protecting the area from dumping by order of the President of the Streets under penalty of a twenty-five scudi fine. Nowadays, rather than marble plaques, or public lampoons posted on the bust of Pasquino (whence our word pasquinades), there are the city's posters. The continually changing posters were exciting and pleasing. Was there a Roman rhythm in me after all? I wondered.

One who had been here for years and was well synchronized with the city's beat was a former colleague of mine from St. Stephen's School, Edward Steinberg. He had come to Rome to teach history while working on his Ph.D. at Harvard and just stayed on. He married Marya, a beautiful Finnish flautist, and became a founder of the Forum School. Edward lived in old Rome, summered in Finland, visited the States, and was always startled when American friends asked him when he was going to "settle down." As he pointed out to me, it's he who's lived in the same place and has been married to the same wife all these years while his friends in the academic rat race in the States have been changing universities, wives, cities, and careers. What they mean is, when is he going to give up living in Rome and come back and get into step with them. No sense of a different rhythm, I replied.

Some people can take Rome in the right way, and Edward was one of them; others never catch on—can never do their work and get to use the city without it's using them up. At one time I left Rome almost like a refugee, having to remake my life. The good times had left me unprepared and I had awakened to the reckoning. Still, I began to suspect that given more than a two-week Christmas holiday, I might get back the Italian beat.

Daniela Colombo, a name among the established feminists, was at ideological odds with Adele who was more radical. There was a split between those feminists who felt that the time was right to consolidate their gains by institutionalizing them and entering the social mainstream, and those more bellicose feminists who stood outside established society and wanted more radical changes in basic structure. One group saw ten years of progress, the other battles still to be won.

I went to visit the former prefecture in Via Governo Vecchio which, after the prefect's offices were moved out, was occupied by the more radical feminists. It was an old palace, completed in 1480 for Cardinal Stefano Nardini di Forli, and the site of the recent lesbian conference. ("It's better not to set foot there," Daniela warned me, "or you'll end up being a former feminist.") It was January 6, the feast of the Epiphany, and the place was deserted—only a few stray cats roamed the littered stairways. Graffiti were scratched or painted all over and I copied down some of them: our wishes are remembrances for the future . . . Free Abortion . . . Giovanna loves Monica . . . Enough silence!

The place looked dreadful and I could understand Daniela's repugnance. On the other hand, the announcement sheet in the carriage entrance attested to a wonderful variety and number of courses or services offered at this feminist center: cinema, children's playroom, documentation center, theater, art studios, committee for instituting laws, bazaar-market, self-help clinic, birth control instruction, radio station Lillith, psychiatry studio, Rolfing, dance studio, women and work center, editorial offices of a weekly paper called *Quotidiana Donna,* rooms for collectives concerning housewives, women in prison, salaried domestic work, divorced and separated women; unspecified meeting rooms, the Lysistrata bar and cafeteria, and the Pink Panther hostel.

Viewing the littered, abandoned premises I remembered Adele's friends, the two followers of Nemesis, who had stayed there and all their complaints. Though the programs were impressive, the state of things was disastrous. Only the ground floor rooms of the Virginia Woolf Cultural Center, which met on alternate days from 4 to 7 P.M., had the look of being kept clean and ready. There is a fascination among Italian feminists with Virginia Woolf; even radicals, who might have looked among the ranks of Italian partisans or progressive writers for a woman to name their center for, accepted an English aristocrat as their emblem.

Daniela had some good words for the Virginia Woolf Cultural Center. It was serious, staffed by eminent woman teachers, and offered courses for credit that ranged from "The Narrative of Gertrude Stein" to "Women Workers in the Strikes of 1848." I peered in at the empty classroom off the courtyard and felt hopeful about all the enterprises going on. After the holidays, I told myself, the women would come back, clean up the place, repaint and restore, get it moving again. That's what women do. Its rhythm would resume.

From Via Governo Vecchio I walked through the old neighborhood near the Pantheon where I had once lived. I passed by the store of my old butcher with his compelling name, Angelo Feroce (ferocious angel), in big gold lettering above the display window. Meat in that window had now reached an unprecedented high—five dollars a pound and more. But it was even higher in the haute mode butcher shop on Via della Croce called "Star" which looked like a disco both in its decor and extravagantly dressed clientele.

Since Christmas and New Year's Day both came on Friday, the holidays were extended over the entire weekends and people had filled streets and squares in the pleasant weather. New Year's Day everyone was out–throngs crowded into Villa Medici for the David exhibit; throngs stood on the Spanish Steps listening to the pipers at the crèche scene; throngs strolled up and down the Corso and Via del Babuino taking in the art galleries, bookshops, antique stores, or heading for the caffès in Piazza del Popolo.

I was getting into the swing; yes, a new rhythm. *È bella nella vita avere una Ritmo.* I began to feel that I must not let the new ties to Italy become undone; Italy had been an important part of my life and still was.

I thought of this as I, too, headed toward Piazza del Popolo to wait for a friend at Rosati's. It was still a central meeting place and it reminded me of old times . . . long ago romantic meetings at Rosati's, summer nights spent there looking up at the gardens of the Pincio and off toward the triumphal gate raised to greet Christina, the abdicated queen of Sweden. I had written a poem called "At Rosati's" after seeing Sartre and Simone de Beauvoir ensconced there at a table against the wall one summer night. It was still the same.

Bunches of young people were hanging around, and a transvestite walked up, very slim, dressed in skin-tight black leather, her hair cut in a dutch bob of glistening black, her lips shiny red. She waited, leaning against a parked car until approached by a young man; they went off into the evening, down Via Ripetta, smiling.

My friend arrived. She was an American married to a retired Italian army officer and they now lived mainly out of Rome in the very countryside of the Marche region which I had pioneered a dozen years earlier. By dint of bringing visitors across the Apennines to my farmhouse near Monterubbiano, I had introduced that little-known part of Italy to those who had since bought farmhouses for themselves. I had to sell and leave, but they had stayed and had now become a kind of summer colony: besides Alice and the colonel they now came from London, Virginia, Switzerland, Connecticut, and Rome. Unbelievable! Alice said they sometimes speak of me as the founding Mother. Alice gave me an account of her place and the crops that she and the colonel produced. They were semipermanent in the country and had neighbors to look out for them, so they were safe from thieves. The colonel tilled the soil, Alice took long-distance photos of hills and valleys and cloud formations. She showed me some of her pictures. The country was beautiful, yes, but I now knew that beauty wasn't everything.

I thought of the Marche countryside where thousands of peasants had left the land, abandoning their old homes and fields to me and other Americans for a few thousand dollars.They left for the city. We, in nostalgic backlash, wanted to go back to the land. Was it possible we could only do it as perpetual tourists in a land not ours? No, I saw it as a continuum of human life: we are always moving, always migrating; there is a flow to human affairs whereby some leave, others come to take their place. It is an exchange. It is good. We have our different rhythms.

Just when I began to feel relaxed about Rome, once more accepting of her gifts, I heard on the radio that the very streets I had so recently walked had been the scene of an attempted terrorist raid. On January 4, suspicious of a parked Ritmo with Turin license plates in Via della Vite, the police investigated and intercepted a kidnap plot aimed at a FIAT executive in Rome on a business trip.

The night before, television had carried the account of four women terrorists who escaped from a prison in Rovigo after friends left a car with timed explosives near the wall of the exercise yard. The bombs went off at the precise time the women were exercising, making a breech in the wall through which they escaped to another getaway car.

The holidays were over, it was time for me to go, time to leave Rome.

The day I left I read in the paper of an attempted assassination of the deputy chief of the Italian antiterrorist police organization. A terrorist, disguised as a mailman, rang the doorbell of Nicola Simone's apartment claiming to be delivering a telegram. When Simone, gun in hand, opened the door, the terrorist shot but did not kill him, and was wounded himself. Again a Ritmo figured in the getaway.

Weeks later, back in the States, I learned that it was from that bungled attempt—from clues found in the telegram which was dropped when the would-be assassin fled—that police came to crack the kidnapping case of American general Dozier and released him from where he was being kept in Padua. It was a good ending.

I said goodbye to Niki and flew home to the States, back to my present different rhythm but somehow still keeping the beat of Rome.

Bianca, the Gulf War, Saroyan and Me

A shaft of light . . . focus on the light.

I sit cross-legged on the floor, a cushion under the sitzbones, my eyes closed softly, hands on thighs, thumb and index finger lightly touching. The yoga tape is soothing, lulling, focusing; thoughts converge, are blanched by the light. Focus on the light, the smooth voice says. I see a tall column, its capital ionic, a pure white shaft against the blue of the Mediterranean. It is an Italian scene, a classical scene. My call to light is Italy. The column stands for beauty, serenity, for classical balance. I wish, in a difficult time, for the equanimity it promises.

Revelation: the white column evokes Bianca. She has not been in my thoughts for many years. Her name is the whiteness of the column, and I think of Baudelaire's poem *Les correspondances;* in life, he said, we pass through a forest of symbols. Like the war just unleashed and so cunningly named Desert Storm to make it the symbol of a wild force of nature, or a scourge from God out of our control. But neither nature nor God brought the war into being, only human endeavor.

In the column's light I see the correspondence between Bianca and the war: it is violence. The personal violence done against her stems from patriarchal traditions in families like hers, mine, or Virginia Woolf's. The personal *is* political: in private acts the ground is laid for the incremental progression of violence that becomes part of society. The brutal underpinning of aggression starts from what is familiar, therefore acceptable.

From the core of the primitive reptilian brain comes the call to action; what evolves out of reason is slower, undramatic, not geared to change the image of someone who's been termed a wimp.

The President prevails. He has willed us to war.

I see the war start around six-thirty on January 16, 1991, when I turn on television for the news; after that first glimpse of rocket streaks in the sky over Baghdad I stop watching the news. The war is a week old and it's two days past the twentieth anniversary of my husband's death. It is almost eight years since Bianca died. Death is much in my thoughts.

I am on the brink of old now, and there is no turning back, nor–surprise!–is there any rest. There is only to go on and I am filled in this new year with anger and distress at the hideousness of another useless war. (The guru says, You can't control events; keep your own peace, don't wage war yourself.)

The opening-night bombing raids (politely referred to as sorties, like an outing) make me think of the dead in the towns where those bombs will fall. Are those people our enemy? No, in official lingo they are not people but collateral damage. It could be George Orwell's doublespeak being used. Long ago in college, when I read Lucretius' *De Rerum Natura,* it was with little understanding and much impatience at his starkness: "Life is one long struggle in the dark." Now I believe him. The war shows me how little of human affairs has been lifted from the dark.

During the summer and fall of 1990 the greatest number of Americans supported sanctions, not war, to force Iraq to withdraw from Kuwait. Who can forget that summer image, as the Gulf crisis unfolded, of vacationing George Bush tooting around the bays of Maine in his two-miles-to-the-gallon motorboat saying that we would defend our "interests" in the Middle East to insure the American way of life? By September he would make sure that the Fuel Economy Bill was defeated in Congress.

But the Peace Movement is in place. People call their representatives with the message to negotiate, GIVE PEACE A CHANCE! My exercise teacher sends out her fall schedule with a sheet that reads VISUALIZE A PEACEFUL SETTLEMENT IN THE MIDDLE EAST and requests that copies be posted, be sent near and far.

Bush keeps snapping, "This isn't about oil," with the same credibility as Nixon saying, "I am not a crook." Soon a flyer appears in my youngest daughter's office showing President Bush giving a speech, parts of which are highlighted: "We SHELL not EXXONerate Saddam Hussein for his actions. We will MOBILize to meet this threat to vital interests in the Persian GULF until an AMOCOble solution is reached. Our best strategy is to BPrepared. Failing that, we ARCOming to kick your ass.

From August on I compulsively compose no-war letters to the *New York Times*. I know they won't be published, as none of my letters ever have been over years of writing them, for I sign with an Italian name. Although I have no hard evidence of bias, I can't help noting the paucity of *Times* bylines with Italian names (half a dozen out of a roster of several hundred!) and remembering the slanted coverage on the Italian communities of Howard Beach and Bensonhurst and the great propensity of the paper to Mafia references; I know through my gut that crypto-bias exists. Still I write, filling scraps of paper day after day as my outrage grows.

I listen to commentators, read other opinions. Everyone seems so calm! They simply report without any personal edge of horror as Bush's momentum for war grows. Once the November elections are safely over, our Wasp president with the raspy voice and preppy slang quickly orders another four hundred thousand men and women of the volunteer army to the desert half a world away. The "volunteers" are mainly underclass, minority enlistees who are in the armed services because the domestic war has never been waged to get them educated out of poverty and into employment, and ROTC scholarship students who joined for an education, not for combat.

Awesome are the logistics and the astronomical cost of such an operation. Had it been ordered in dozens of wasted American cities, urban blight and its social consequences would have been obliterated, deserts would have bloomed, the drug traffic would have died in its tracks, the AIDS plague would have been addressed. I know in November that there will be war: that amount of manpower and materiel is deployed for only one reason, to be used. Now the majority of Americans for peace have a quandary—how can they oppose war without seeming to oppose American troops? By creating that diabolical dilemma, Bush has secured the base for his war.

Even so, voices of reason are heard in the land. At a Denver town forum, a man with good common sense observes that no war lasts forever; at some point, the combatants stop and begin to talk. Why not talk first?

Neither side seems to hear the other. Hussein holds out; Bush won't negotiate. Bush says no to every Iraqi offer: no compromise, no face-saving, no preconditions, no concessions, no linkage to the Palestine question. There is even a no to Gorbachev's offer to mediate in the interests of peace. Bush hasn't alternate plans, only his ultimatum. Yet in his doublespeak he talks of going the extra mile for peace, of putting all his cards on the table–though he holds only one card, the wild one that's meant, by his rules, to trump everything else.

I am horrified and helpless. This is a country easily addicted to violence. This gun-toting, shoot-it-out country lives in a nightmare of its own conjuring. It has made itself into its darkest image: manly, tough cowboy going to square off against the bad Others (Injun, or Arab), propelled by some perverted, inner mindset about what constitutes the right stuff.

I have sudden flashes of other correspondences: I think of old Freud, stuffed into his patriarchal notions, shaking his head and muttering, "But *what* do women want?" And all the time it's so clear! And in our day, there's the Bush question: "Why can't Saddam Hussein be reasonable and just do what we tell him?" It's the same failure, from Freud to Bush, to understand the *other*. All people want their dignity as human beings to be recognized. Neither a woman, nor an Iraqi, is less human than the empowered men who pose the questions.

Bianca, too, was unheard. No one listened to her wants, her objections to being pressed into line against her own convictions.

Over Christmas of 1990 the plot thickens. The President coerces the UN Security Council by bribes and threats to support military action against Iraq despite evidence from his own agencies that sanctions, given time, will work. There is a concerted psychological assault on the public wherein all counterproposals to war are deemed unworthy of consideration, even suspect. This is prelude to the final brutality of force. American hides seem to thicken. Right through the holidays you can feel in the air how Bush is piping us to war as if it were a football match, a cattle roundup, a hootenanny–good for our morale because it will relieve the Vietnam syndrome once and for all. Barbarism makes its gain over civilization.

My middle daughter in Italy writes on a Christmas card: "Who is the *real* enemy? What will war win?" I reply that Virginia Woolf in a bomb shelter in 1940, as German bombers plastered London, wrote *Thoughts on Peace in an Air Raid:* "Unless we can think peace into existence we . . . will lie in the same darkness and hear the same death rattle overhead." She quoted poet Blake's resolve never to cease from *the mental fight* which, for her, meant "thinking against the current, not with it."

Americans are swept up in the current, then mesmerized by the TV war into the worst kind of jingoism, becoming intolerant and abusive of dissent. It will be a quick war, Bush promises, with few casualties. Why are two hundred American deaths acceptable? No one calculates the Other dead. Now the country is awash in the silliness of yellow ribbons and flags on every tree; we have reached a new moral low and the real peril is the perversion of First Amendment rights. By focusing frustration and fear elsewhere, away from home problems, Bush got his war.

George Bush's words as he lashes out at his former friend, Saddam Hussein, are excessively simplistic—more typical of what is supposed to be the fury of a woman scorned than of a statesman. Bush personalizes Evil in the figure of Hussein, rather than in world greed for oil and drugs profits, or in world indifference and cynicism to other aggressions—Lebanon, for example, or Panama.

I read *Conflicts and Contradictions* by the Israeli author Meron Benvenisti, who sees Palestinians as human beings, not abstracted embodiments of Evil. His warning that "dehumanization is a contagious disease that comes in the aftermath of conflict" applies not only to Palestinians by to all Others.

Dehumanization—not seeing or hearing each of us as a human being—is what happened to Bianca.

She is a person I never met. I know only her story as she sent it to me—fragmentary, almost incoherent, not a story at all but a trying, a striving to write. It was about a young woman feeling out of place, out of focus, out of sympathy with her surroundings. Italian American. Fated not to be taken seriously as herself, but only as part of a family unit first as a dutiful daughter, then as wife and mother. (*La sacra famiglia,* they put it ironically in Italian to refer to individual family members meshed together and presented to the world as a holy entity unto itself).

I was at that time compiling a collection of writings by Italian American women and Bianca had answered my call for submissions.

Her story opened strongly: "Bianca Viglioni, that's your name and don't you ever forget it!"

How, it continued, could she ever forget the name that marked her place in life–a mean and narrow place limited in vision and possibility, where menarche and a developing bosom marked a girl's most prized achievement. Bianca, her mother said, thought too much, read too many books, and was different from the rest of them. But what good was being different? "A fisherman's daughter would become a fisherman's wife." Restless, Bianca walked the beach, searched for colored glass, looked out to sea and questioned: Why am I different? Why do I to want to be more than my mother, my grandmother? Bianca vowed to hold on until she could leave "to be who she was to be." But in the end she did what was expected. She married for love and bore a child for happiness, but all that came of it was that she missed being a human being in her own right. All that was left was the "same old struggle of becoming."

I was touched and held onto Bianca's submission for some time before writing back that what she had sent me was not yet story nor memoir, but a sketch that could be developed. It was the seed of something that I hoped she would work on and resubmit.

Her reply was immediate, a long, revealing letter which threw open her story completely: though she was from an Italian American working-class family, she had married "up and out" of her origins. Born into a female legacy of early marriage and childbearing, she had followed her mother and grandmother in that pattern only to fall into a heavy depression. For she had always longed to be something else–a writer. It was a longing that put her under tremendous psychological stress, for her tradition told her she was wrong to think of herself before family. Now, ten years after high school, she was enrolled in a nearby college working for a degree in English. Her first story was the one sent to me; before that she had written poetry, and her one publication was a poem in the college literary magazine.

"Most of what I do," her letter said, "is groping in the dark. I know that I will be a good writer because that dream has always been with me as long as I can remember. It is the only thing that has stayed with me throughout my life. It took me many years to realize it. I had to muster up the courage to admit to myself that that was what I wanted to do. It is something that my grandmother started in me, she being a rebel. Writers are rebels too. When I graduate I will be the first woman in my family to have had a formal education and the first woman writer."

I heard the pain. In the dashed-off fervor of her letter was her true voice. There Bianca had let herself go and written from the bare bone, from her knotted guts, from anguish. It was unmistakable: she was a person against whom violence had been—was being—done. Not with weapons or physical force, but through an onslaught against mind and spirit, a dehumanization, a wearing away of one's sense of self, of worth, of what one is and does in the world. Bianca was suffering a sense of dislocation and ambivalence, for on the one hand, her still-enduring birthright told her she was valuable as part of the family and she couldn't relinquish her place there; but on the other hand, she was awakened to the possibilities within herself by the message of her times. Bianca, despite her name, struggled in the dark.

I remembered myself as a young woman, uncertain, aspiring, but lacking directives and the inner compass of assurance that would guide me on the path I wanted to travel.

It takes the Gulf War to bring me back the image of Bianca and to make the connection of the violence done against her to the wider violence being done in the world.

Some things ripen late.

Only now do I discover what might have helped me as a young girl with ambitions like Bianca. On one of those long Saturday walks to the Eastwood library for books, why, then, did I never reach for Saroyan's book of stories, *The Daring Young Man on the Flying Trapeze?* I knew the title, it intrigued me. But did it also daunt me because it combined "daring" with being a "young man"? Yes, I suppose subliminally I read the same message that, decades later, Bianca would get: you cannot be daring because you are not a man; your woman's role has been defined for you already and it is not through books that you'll learn your place—it's by not wanting to dare.

What I know is that in those formative years I read books about people not like me, and could never place myself in the lives I read about. If *I* had been daring, I might have read Saroyan and responded to his world, his style. I might have had an inkling of modernism, the personalization of emotion, the cogency of literature, the warmth of a non-Anglo voice. I might have grasped how he,

Armenian, was an American outsider and how it related to me, Italian. But most of all, there would have been the incredible discovery of seeing my own family name in Saroyan's story.

At Christmas I receive a gift subscription to *Story* magazine from a friend. How does it happen that at the start of the war and my recall of Bianca, there arrives like a sign the winter 1991 issue with its reprint of "The Daring Young Man on the Flying Trapeze"? It is, like Bianca's, the story of desperation. The young man is starving, desperate for work, but just as desperately attached to his writing. He thinks, "there was still no end of books he ought to read before he died. He remembered the young Italian in a Brooklyn hospital, a small sick clerk named Mollica, who had said desperately, I would like to see California once before I die."

There it was, a stunning epiphany—*my family name Mollica,* miraculously, astonishingly in print! The name I grew up with and had seen only as an impediment; my difficult, shameful, hard to pronounce, so-called maiden name. It was there in Saroyan's story identified with longing, with a condition of sickness and wishing.

Bianca was right, names do mark one's place in life. To be identified with an Italian surname was to operate under a handicap all the more onerous for being unvoiced and unstated but still tremendously present. It was known in the twenties by young Francesca Vinciguerra who was told by an editor to get rid of her unwieldly name, which would be death on a book spine, and get an American name. And so she translated herself into Frances Winwar.

Would changing my name have made a difference? Yes. In a positive way I would not have felt so isolated in my aspirations to be a writer, so without literary forebears. Negatively, in assuming an anglicized surname, I would have forever falsified myself. Now my name no longer seems to matter . . . except when I write to the *Times*.

Bianca's letter to me completed her story and I decided I would use both in the collection. I mailed her an agreement form to be signed and returned to me. When time passed without my hearing from her, I called. A terse male voice—her husband's—told me that Bianca was not there. And when I pressed for when or how to reach her, saying I had good news, he replied that Bianca was dead. I didn't understand. He explained: she had taken her life just before Christmas. He sounded angry. She was thirty years old. She left him and a young daughter.

There was difficulty securing permission so I did not include Bianca's work in *The Dream Book*. It would have been her first published story, and it still haunts me. It is in part my story and the story of many of us women of Italian American background.

Any violence, psychic or physical, is a terrible thing whether against a person or against a people. Both the violence of this willed war and the psychic violence inflicted on Bianca are devastating because so apparently out of one's control. In this desolate time of the waste of lives, a wasted land, I think of Bianca.

I think of a column of white rising from the darkness, of light and peace.

Difference, Identity,
and Saint Augustine

I was thinking of the early church father Saint Augustine as I set out for Bordeaux, a place I imagined as a center of equanimity (unlike Augustine's Hippo) for its association with Michel de Montaigne, famous son and once mayor.

I admired the tolerant long view of Montaigne as much as I did not the constrictive one of the saint. I thought of Augustine as having given classicism the final push over the edge as the fifth-century world hovered on the brink of transition. After roistering through life the natural way, sated, he found later and more exquisite enjoyment in penitence and conjured up the dogma of original sin to inflict on his contemporaries and all Christendom for millennia to come. He gave the Western psyche guilt and remorse. Harsh he was after his conversion. Antifemale, antinature, antipleasure.

Is it now sign of my own abandonment of a certain recklessness of thought that in coming of age I have come home to Augustine? Not to his church or its dogma, nor to any church or dogma, but to the wide sweep of Augustine's prospect of life and our place in it as individuals.

In a world beset by ethnic divisions and hostility and unspeakable cleansings, it seemed problematic at best, in November of 1992, to attend a conference entitled "Interculturalism and the Writing of Difference" at the University of Bordeaux. I had been invited to participate in the section addressing Italian American literature. I liked the fact that writers from the so-called ethnic or minor groups were being perceived and studied as writers of difference—that opened a range of interest quite overlooked in American criticism where difference is often interpreted as simply making writers marginal.

"Common sense," says literary scholar Henry Louis Gates, Jr., "reminds us that we're all ethnics." Another truth should be just as obvious—that the relevant standard by which to judge writing is excellence, not national origin or gender.

My own belief is that any writer from a marginalized position is writing in the most American of traditions—that of the Outsider. So the conference was enticing, at the same time that it was troubling. Should there be such an emphasis on difference at a moment in history when traditional unities of nations are coming apart on the basis of ethnic differences? The French playwright Bernard-Henri Lévy has decried nationalism that deteriorates into tribal passions and produces opposition to all "Others" save one's own tribe. Speaking of a united Europe, he feels the best hope for Europe's future is integration. "But Europe is exactly what people don't seem to want today. They want identities. The great modern and murderous delirium in Europe is the folly of ethnic identity."

Stories of confusion and conflict proliferate, in Europe and in the United States, indeed in the world. "Catholic Indians Try to Reconcile 2 Traditions" reads a newspaper headline on a story of Native Americans trying to retain their native traditions as well as a religious identity. The son of slain radical Jewish leader Meir Kahane is reported as saying that killing Arabs is natural. The PEN American Center holds a symposium on how authors write through their cultural backgrounds, in which the question of ethnic identity as opposed to some notion of "universality" keeps popping up. Letty Cottin Pogrebin speaks poignantly as both female and Jew of her feeling of "Otherness" in America as she examines her entwined background, attempting to integrate an identity that will be enabling rather than restrictive.

My own persuasion is that I can be no other than an American writer since I was born here and write in English; that I write also of Americans of Italian origin should not keep me from being a strand—thin perhaps and less brilliantly colored than others—but nonetheless a strand in the total pattern of a many-hued national literature.

Along the way, I embraced my heritage, married an Italian writer, lived in Italy, learned the language, and intensified my writing and thinking as an American. Because she had never had the experience of living abroad for an extended time, I could understand Toni Morrison saying at the 1986 International PEN conference in New York City that at no moment of her life did she ever feel as though she were an American. On the other hand, no matter how out of place in the culture one might feel as a disaffected American, sooner or later there comes to the expatriate—even James Baldwin!—the inevitable realization that the language and the culture of birth constitute the homeland after all.

Thinking back, I am transported to my childhood, growing up in Syracuse in a house on James Street named for the land-buying grandfather of xenophobic Henry James. When the question of nationality came up on forms we children had to fill in for school, or for the YWCA, or for going to summer camp (and there were such forms in those days), I never knew what to put: was I American or Italian? My name certainly had a foreign sound, but there was no doubt that I had been born in the state of New York, and my parents, too. Though the records said I was American, from the start my soul wasn't persuaded.

I was a bookish child and my ambition to be a writer was at odds with my family. I did not live in a household of books being thoroughly read and then discussed and everyone keeping diaries like most American writers of my generation. I was not, say, a Eudora Welty who was read to "in every room of the house," whose fantasy was fostered by book-loving parents, and whose goals were not only praised but also obtainable in the Anglo-American context of who she was.

Names are powerful signals. Fifty years ago author John Fante, in his classic story "Odyssey of a Wop," wrote that when still a schoolboy he matched the sound of his surname against that of other Italian names only to be relieved that people could think he was French. Here is what Dorothy Bryant, novelist and author of *Miss Giardino,* wrote me when I was compiling *The Dream Book:* "Calvetti is my maiden name, and the childhood of Miss Giardino is my mother's childhood. I had another Italian name [Ungaretti in a first marriage] after that one. Under neither of those names was I accepted as an artist . . . I wonder if one of the reasons so many Latin women's "identity" is veiled by a WASP name is the necessity of escaping from everything else that may be imposed upon a woman along with that Italian name."

An Italian American surname sets up, I am still learning, barriers of prejudice in those circles of American literature that are hard to penetrate under the best of circumstances. Our names are an immediate signal of difference; Francesca Vinciguerra's strategic move to Frances Winwar was an ethnic change of identity rather than the gender one of George Sand, the Brontës, and George Eliot.

As black skin is what Henry Louis Gates, Jr., terms the "epidermal contingency" of African American writers, so Italian Americans seem to have a nomenclatural contingency. In my own life I went from one signaling surname to another when I married an Italian author and he and Italy became my education.

I began to understand that I could not be as centered in national identity as Antonio Barolini surely was. His name did not marginalize him or make him prone to labels; he was supremely at ease with the fact of his calling as a literary person without having to question his right to be, or whether he was odd to be. Italian literature was his unquestioned patrimony; and when he practiced it, he was automatically part of it. I began to see that American literature was not automatically mine; at best, perhaps, I could belong to a subgroup, as in being picked for a second-best sorority because of my background.

I was left with questions: How does one gain the attention of an excluding publishing world? Can Italian American women become writers out of the intercultural tensions of their lives? How do they use their individual selves narratively to oppose or understand the Otherness not only of the dominant society but of their gender opposite and even their family? What are the strategies to free the self and yet retain a rich tradition?

The price for admittance into our literature was to become a facsimile Wasp, a pact entered into by those past writer-critics Lionel Trilling and John Ciardi, both from ethnic backgrounds they wanted to get beyond. Lionel Trilling, a writer and professor of English literature at Columbia University, well assimilated into a world removed from his Jewish origins, personified the passage from "ethnic" to "in." It was he who objected that writers like Alfred Kazin were "too Jewish," too full of lower-class vitality and experience. It was Trilling to whom Saul Bellow successfully gave the lie when he created the Jewish novel, opening the way for the rest of us.

John Ciardi was of the Trilling persuasion that a homogenized "universal" American voice in the literature was preferable to a rich mix of diversity. Ciardi, the one token Italian American in the

American Academy of Arts and Letters, was reticent about his background until after the ethnic awakening. Then he rediscovered it in himself to the extent of being on the editorial board of several short-lived Italian American magazines, even though he discouraged authenticity in other Italian American writers.

In my own youthful lack of inner fortitude it hadn't occurred to me that they–Trilling, Ciardi, and the real Wasps–were wrong. The burden was made mine: either take on an ersatz Wasp veneer and become one of a whole nation of Huck Finns and Daisy Millers no matter what the blood said, or form a strong enough personal identity with which to oppose the blandishments.

But what was *my* identity? In Italy I was American, but here in the States I never was sure.

Now in a world fraught with many more drastic problems of identity than a literary one, we have to ask the question, What is Identity, after all? And does it matter? Don't we all, as in James Baldwin's panhumanistic view, contain each other: the male in the female, the female in the male; white in black, and black in white? Is it really our life mission to stalk, to hunt down, to try to catch what is only a will-o'-the-wisp–that elusive notion of who we are that keeps beckoning us like a lure?

For if the journey through life is to maturation, then it is toward becoming a self, a distinct individual: realizing an identity. The main obstacle to overcome is dependence on authority in whatever guise–parental, religious, societal, political, literary. Such strength requires a buildup of one's inner core–that personal sense of and confidence in one's very identity.

This is in a way the tragic catch-22 of life. We have our mandate, but it is a vexed one: we cannot ever claim to have reached a perfect identity.

Idem, the same, is the Latin root for Identity. *Identidem = idem et idem,* again and again the same. Identity, thus, is the fixed sameness and stillness that Saint Augustine attributes only to God, the eternal nonchanging: "who art not another in another place, nor otherwise in another place: but the same and very same, and the very selfsame."

Is it not hubris of the most extreme to fixate on a personal Identity, a tribal Identity, a national identity? Perfect sameness can only be an attribute of God.

A fixed sameness is not meant for us, the evolving.

Living in the world with each other, in time and space, we change, move, diversify, put our Self up against the Other to know ourselves and know we are *all* the Other. Just by living we impinge on each other. We invent each other, are part of each other's transformation.

Our humanness is based on our difference. That was Montaigne's paradox when he said the most universal quality is diversity. Some four hundred years later, American scholars like Noam Chomsky suggest that "diversity might be structured into the human experience," that unity through homogenization—or universality—"betrayed a profound misunderstanding of the human condition." But just because we are human, we fret against that condition and covet what is God's—perfect stillness and repose and sameness in Identity. Only death gives that. Life is not a realization of identity after all, but always alterity.

Recognizing difference might, at least for Americans, soften the impact of the so-called Identity Crisis which we are supposed to transit in adolescence. It would sort out the problems inherent in too strict a reading of "ethnic identity." Ideally it would eliminate ethnic conflict and cleansing in the world if the reality is diversity and there can be no fixed Identity in a temporal world where all is flux and change and re-formation.

And *that*, perhaps, frustrates us the most—i.e., *never* completing the quest for Identity, which is sameness, which is God—and so we rage at Difference which is ourselves.

As the Spanish poet Antonio Machado put it, there is a rational faith, an incurable belief of humankind that Identity = reality, as if everything must necessarily and absolutely be one and the same. "But the other refuses to disappear . . . it is the hard bone on which reason breaks its teeth."

Only partially, at a great remove, can the still, calm center which is the God within be experienced through the deep meditation practiced by Yogis. But that is precisely a relinquishing of self-identity, a stopping of reflexes and processes and cognitive thought.

What we could instead be working for and toward, with all the creative tension at play in differences and similarities, is an Ecology of Opposites. Indeed, without contraries there is no progression. Ecology as a network of interdependent relationships. Creativity is the force that deals with a changing reality as an individual emerges from a family or national or religious identity into the newness of self. Creative ethnicity uses one's background as a point of departure and is outward facing, evolving, tolerant, adaptable. Above all, it allows for self-definition, yet is not exclusive of relationships with other groups.

For me, the seeds of doubt regarding identity that had been planted in America evolved and bloomed in Italy. When I stood at the full-length windows of our Rome apartment, I looked down into the gardens of Palazzo Barberini where fierce Puritan John Milton (who in England inveighed against Catholics) had been the gracious guest of Cardinal Barberini; and I thought about the lesson of accommodation, easing myself out of being just this or just that and letting myself drop into the humanist perspective which was Milton's in Rome.

Finally, with my youngest daughter, namesake of the mysterious "foreign" grandmother of my childhood with whom I had never been able to speak, I drove to Calabria. It was mid-August; while my Northern Italian husband and Roman friends shuddered at the unchicness and discomfort of such an undertaking, I went to find where my immigrant forebears had come from. Years later the figure of my grandmother emerged in *Umbertina,* my first published novel. I thought of my work as in the tradition of that most American of literary tropes, the Outsider theme. The Outsider, whether Hester Prynne or Huck Finn or Lily Bart or even the bleak and uneasy surburban characters in Cheever stories, makes up the strongest part of our literature. *Umbertina,* I felt, was an American novel about what it is to become an uneasy American, first by physical transplantation and then by spiritual birth, but in any case American.

My surprise was in my book's being received as ethnic. Did ethnic mean not American, or was it code for "marginal," out of the mainstream? It is important to me as a writer that the name on the spine of my book *is* Italian, and that I am writing something different from the stereotypes of Italian Americans. But does that make me marginal?

Toni Morrison has said that unlike some Jewish or Southern authors who despise being labeled, she does not mind being called a Black writer, or a Black woman writer. "I've decided to define that, rather than having it be defined for me," Morrison said. "I understand that they were trying to suggest that I was 'bigger' than [Black woman writer], or better than that. I simply refused to accept their view of bigger and better." And I refuse marginal.

It's the strategy adopted by Ralph Ellison when he says in *Invis-*

ible Man, " I am invisible because people refuse to see me . . . I myself did not become alive until I discovered my invisibility."

I know now that it's the premise of an exclusionary mainstream in American literature that's faulty. So-called mainstream critics (a kind of self-determined genus of judges), scorning what they call ethnic, marginal, minor, or exotic writing, and claiming standardized "universal themes" as the proper realm of literature, can distort the question of archetypal human feelings and establish barriers of class and elitism and insider hegemony in the name of universality. That kind of standardized universality as established by presumed literary judges of what is right and what isn't is very suspect. It begets the painful process of self-censorship as writers block themselves from their specific material and try for mainstream and what has been described as "the flattest possible characters in the flattest possible landscape rendered in the flattest possible diction."

The reverse of universal is not ethnic, but parochial.

The false hurdle presented to so-called ethnic writers is the charge of not writing universally if they use their own material. Maxine Hong Kingston, asked by Bill Moyers in a television interview to account for the popularity of "exotic" books such as hers, replied, "They are not exotic, they are about human beings. When you take a raw, human event and put it through the process of art, then it speaks to all people." Just before that interview, at a writers' conference, Maxine Hong Kingston had identified herself with minority writers and said how they all had to fight against the term Universal. Margaret Atwood immediately rescued Kingston (and rankled some others) by exclaiming: "Oh, Maxine, no one would think of *you* as a minority writer!" (Echoes of Toni Morrison's comments on how "they" decide who's bigger and better!)

Minority or ethnic or exotic writers explore a fundamental theme: how to create oneself anew in an alien world. It is a restatement of the dialectics of identity. And that is a quest that speaks to everyone.

Nonetheless, I came to a personal recognition that as a writer I would always bear a vexed identity—either I would deny the part of myself that my name signaled, or I would integrate it fully and write off the material only to find myself marginalized.

Yet to be a writer is enough. I agree with what I sensed long ago and what Gabriel Garcia Marquez put into words: "The duty of a writer—the revolutionary duty if you like, is simply to write well." We do not have to carry banners, sprout labels of identity. And yet, as Isaac Bashevis Singer has said, when he looks in the mirror in the morning, who looks back at him is a man of Polish-Jewish origin in whose skin he lives and writes. And so I, too, live in my Italianate, female skin and write from it.

That was the approach of the Bordeaux panel: by focusing on literary works by writers from so-called *minority* or *ethnic* groups in the United States (their italics), they would be better able to appreciate writing that was not per se marginal, but "of difference." How, they asked, can these literatures provide a symbolic locus for the specific emergence of a new, conflictual, and multifaceted self? How does work produced in a context of intercultural conflict and exchange take on an additional degree of complexity with regard to the formation of a literary self caught between alienation and alterity? How does the narrative self come to terms with the threatening presence of the (cultural) "Other" through a dialectical process of rejection and integration? Such questioning gives a thoughtful status to much American writing called "ethnic" that has hitherto been ignored, forgotten, or thought unworthy of appraisal.

This panel gave me the opportunity to ask what, in fact, *is* ethnic in a nation which is wholly composed of a multiplicity of national origins, including the Britannic one of the founding fathers who bequeathed not only their language but the power that goes with it.

Because of the past stigma of being identified "ethnic," earlier Italian American authors either anglicized their names or kept their names but used material that did not at all touch their background, as, for example, Hamilton Basso and Don DeLillo. One wonders what would result if writers like DeLillo or Gilbert Sorrentino or Frederick Tuten did deal with their Italian Americanness; or if an esteemed literary critic like Matthew Bruccoli had examined the writings derived from the great Italian exodus to America as well as those of Scott Fitzgerald.

In my own question of Identity I think of Nobel laureate poet and immigrant Czeslaw Milosz who said for all of us: Language is the Homeland. I cannot ever doubt what I feel so deeply—that I was formed in the English language and its literature and that is my homeland.

I think of my letter exchange with John Ciardi who asked me rhetorically why I do not write like Eudora Welty—why I am not Eudora Welty. I am still taken by surprise. With Black writers triumphant and cultural pluralism in writing creating a new dynamism in the national literature, Ciardi was implying that I was still sup-posed to be a facsimile Wasp! And of the Southern school!

The ring of his words (though Ciardi's ears were stopped against the sound) was of the old assimilationist mentality which would have us all cast off our particular shadings and voice and put on the cov-ering cloak of Waspness. To cover Ciardi's regressive advice there is Jean Cocteau's: "Listen carefully to first criticisms of your work. Note just what it is about your work that critics don't like—then cul-tivate it. That's the part of your work that's individual and worth keeping."

If Ciardi's questions proved spurious, those worth answering were put to me by Professor Jean Béranger of the University of Bor-deaux: What is it you want, he asked, meaning perhaps all Italian American writers collectively: to disappear into the mainstream? to keep your distinct identity and not be absorbed? to be coequal and as American as the Anglos, or dissident, a different voice?

I can only answer for myself. I want to be considered as what I am, a part of American writing undivided by the mainstream or mi-nority rankings imposed not by literary standards but by ethnic ori-gins. I will keep my material, my particular referencing and voice, confident that it can convey values from difference as well as from conformity.

As I left for the Bordeaux conference a welcome piece of news accompanied me: the announcement that the Nobel Prize in Liter-ature had been awarded to Derek Walcott, the Black writer from the West Indies, citing his "multicultural vision and commitment." The validity and vitality of what was previously spurned as ethnic writing were being recognized.

Despite the nostalgic laments from apologists for the exclusivity of "mainstream" work as *the* literary canon, the widening and open-ing of American literature is happening. In the great republic of let-ters are writers of all sorts: each caught in the paradox of striving for the fixed sameness of Identity while claiming complexity, yet never achieving it until repose comes in the fixity of Saint Augus-tine's selfsame God.

Umbertina
and the Universe

With such a weighted title, I clearly have taken on more than I can deliver. So what follows is not so much an explication of *Umbertina,* my first novel, as it is the unraveling of how that particular book became an ethnic novel and what an ethnic novel is, and what literary universals are, anyway.

When I was writing *Umbertina* I wrote it as an American novel about what it is to become an uneasy American, first by physical transplantation and then by spiritual birth, but in any case American. I did this through the particular stories of several Italian American women. I thought of my work as a thread in the fabric of the whole national literature. When it was written in the late 1970s, that fabric seemed receptive to new designs and figures, it held the promise of becoming a splendidly variegated tapestry of many strands and colors. The dominant Wasp figure was receding.

My surprise with the publication of *Umbertina* was that, although a first of its kind–i.e., a transgenerational novel of the Italian American experience from the perspective of the women who lived it, sans Mafia and mob–it was not reviewed in the *New York Times,* and where noticed, it was mainly as an ethnic novel. Is that not a way to sidetrack a work from the mainstream? Is not the category "ethnic" a signal that a book is not to be given critical attention, neither discussed nor written about, and not, therefore, likely to be included in curricula, anthologized, or considered for reprinting and permanence? Is "ethnic" the euphemism to separate main from minor? The term "mainstream writing" has the ring of conformity but it is that against which all other writing is measured and judged as only, at best, a tributary.

With the silence that attended *Umbertina,* I kept hearing xenophobic echoes: of Horace Greeley's cranky old-fashioned quarrel with newcomers to this country, when he said, "Why can't they be like us?" Or the ghost of old Madison Grant who in 1916 wrote "The Passing of the Great Race" to bemoan that pure Anglo-Saxons would no longer be dominant in America, but would have to share it with other, lesser, races. Both could be heard in John Ciardi's chiding words to me that not until Italian American women writers became more like Eudora Welty, Elizabeth Bishop, Hortense Calisher or Flannery O'Connor could they be considered writers of any stature. Why, I wondered, could we not be ourselves?

I got an inadvertent echo from a contributor to *The Dream Book:* "I write only rarely of my ethnic background, and have dealt, mostly, with universal themes," she wrote me. To me that meant she had internalized the message that "universal themes" in this society can only be modeled on Anglo-American characters and values, thus made acceptable to a literary elite which decides what is right and what isn't. It is little wonder with the prevailing canonization system that she has learned to doubt the worth in wider human terms of her own experience and to term it in a demeaning way, "ethnic."

She is not alone.

On the same issue, Bruce Jay Friedman reflected: "All the fine Jewish writers insist that their writing is not Jewish. They are commenting on the *human* condition, not the Jewish one. They can't help it if it comes out sounding Jewish."

But it is absurd to think, first, that Anglo-Americans are not themselves an ethnic group, and second, that one can universalize only from their models and not Italian American ones. Black Americans have shown us how. The Jewish American novel has shown us how.

Yet there are those who think that writing as an Italian American makes one's work ethnic, with themes that cannot be universal. The premise is faulty, and it was devastatingly turned upside down by the irony of theorist Terry Eagleton: "Since literature, as we know, deals in universal human values rather than in such historical trivia as civil wars, the oppression of women, or the dispossession of the English peasantry, it could serve to place in cosmic perspective the petty demands of working people for decent living conditions . . . It would communicate to them the moral riches of bourgeois civilization [and] impress on them a reverence for middle-class achievements."

Eagleton implies that critics, by scorning the realism of the ethnic world and claiming middle-class "universal themes" as the proper realm of literature, can distort our notions of archetypal human feelings and establish barriers of class and elitism and Wasp hegemony in the name of universality.

I do not accept that an ethnic subject is a less human one, any more than would be a feminist subject, or a proletarian one, or a regional one or any other particular dimension that speaks to the human condition. The particularity merely accentuates and details the larger frame to which we all refer. It is the realization of the subject, not the subject itself, which lifts it from the narrow to the general. Behaviors and fashions may come and go but the human soul has not changed since the Greeks dramatized our passions and conflicts.

These days we speak of a pluralistic society and literature; there are encouraging signs of recognition that the aim and tradition of literature is to give the WHOLE experience of life. James Atlas has descried a new Battle of the Book, and says, "It's a struggle among contending factions for the right to be represented in the picture America draws of itself."

But I think it is more than a literary matter. When the Reagan administration, in the person of Secretary of Education William Bennett, tried to censure curriculum innovation at Stanford, it was constriction and provincialism (or the old American isolationism in a new guise?) rearing their heads. Bennett's equating of Stanford's new core readings with the Decline of the West is an echo of Madison Grant's Passing of the Great Race.

I have discussed this with the writer Joseph Papaleo. He once studied with Henry Steele Commager at Columbia, who said that in return for our religious freedom and lack of religious wars, societal conflict and intolerance have taken a racial and ethnic focus. This happens because of the heterogenous makeup of American society. If we were homogenous, as European nations are, the intolerance would be focused on religious deviation. The ethnic and racial bigotry often apparent in American life was captured in Michael De-Capite's novel *No Bright Banner,* one of those "lost" Italian American novels of the 1940s.

Once I received a letter from a middle-aged Italian American housewife who was a college senior preparing a paper on Italian

American women writers. She wrote me that she wasn't able to draw a conclusion, and that her paper reflected her ambivalence toward her subject. She had read both my Introduction to *The Dream Book: An Anthology of Writings by Italian American Women* and Rose Basile Green's earlier study *The Italian American Novel.* She thought she was in agreement with this statement of Green's: "Italian Americans no longer consider themselves a separate group whose inner-directedness needs emphasis in literary efforts having strictly ethnic themes. . . ." Yet she found comfort in works in *The Dream Book* which were obviously inner-directed statements of ethnic themes. She wavered over Green's dictum that "themes must relate to the general structure of American culture in order to be a valid part of its literary record."

"I am at war with myself," she wrote me, "to be or not to be ethnic."

In answer to her quandary, I replied, "I have never believed that an author who is a Black, a Jew, a Native American, a Wasp, or what-have-you, can successfully speak to the human condition through his or her ethnic fictional characters but that an Italian American cannot."

I understood her confusion. Teachers and critics like Green or Ciardi, not to mention our own perception of those who are successful writers in this country, have presented her with a false conundrum. They have made it seem that "American" does not include variations from the long-dominant insider cast of our literature, or, in the broader realm of Western literature, the dominance of the white male giant. But the post–World War II Jewish novel triumphantly broke the Anglo-American hold, and then the Black writers redefined what's literature, and now there are scholar-critics who are broadening the canon beyond its previous parochialism.

Professor Frank Lentricchia, who was portrayed on the cover of the *New York Times Magazine* for the lead article, "The Battle of the Books," is one of these new critics. He says, "for the old time critics like Lionel Trilling, Philip Rahv, Harry Levin, literature was an escape from ethnic identity, not an affirmation of it." And that is not Lentricchia's style: he is an intellectual from a working-class Italian American background in Utica, New York, who is not trying to forget where he came from.

Lentricchia and others like Leslie Fiedler teach works that democratically reflect our total experience in a more representative literature. Intellectual snobbery is out. Even so, I'm not for the old

Pollyanna-type ethnic novel in which the gloss was that once in America everything turned out all right. The truth is harder than that.

It is not true that the so-called inner-directedness of Italian American writers no longer needs expression. The ongoing production of many writers (including Eugene Mirabelli, Tony Ardizzone, Jeanne Schinto, Anthony Valerio) belies that. Dramatist Albert Innaurato's themes are intensely ethnic. Carole Maso, who made a stunning debut with the novel *Ghost Dance,* beautifully portrayed Italian grandparents who lend not only flavor but also complexity to the theme of achieving autonomy.

My correspondent, the student-housewife, seems to have sensed she was being sold a false bill of goods, but because it was offered by teachers and scholars, she is "at war with herself." She is asked to believe that Italian American themes are different from "the general structure of American culture." She is being told that only writing that hews to the mainstream can "be a valid part of the American literary record." This is assimilationist thinking with a vengeance. It is telling ethnic writers to drop their own material, their own identities and deepest feelings in order to homogenize.

This begets self-censorship as writers deny their special material. It also leaves the field open to non–Italian American writers who then use Italian American characters for "color" in a stereotypical way.

But the new critics and teachers know that assimilation is a betrayal and that the whole idea of "Americanism" itself is in question. Professor Katherine Newman, founder of the Society for the Study of the Multi-Ethnic Literature of the United States, calls for forging alternative critical views in order to discard the old theories that "were fitted to a specific body of literature, that of the Anglo-American seaboard culture" and for taking a wider, more encompassing view of what literature is.

Any life is a personal odyssey, lived within specific cultural and historical bounds. *Umbertina* set the odyssey within an Italian American specificity and idiom. But that the women's quests in the novel spring from that experience does not obliterate the overriding human frame of the quest theme.

I know that when I have been most passionately personal I have most engaged the recognition and reception of readers who relate to something basic–i.e., universal–in the material and can make it their own. That is what Ezra Pound was driving at when he suggested that strength in writing lies in combining strong local flavor with unconscious universality. When a locality or person is fully re-alized, then it becomes universal.

What is American literature if not the reflection of our diversity?

And what is universality? We see about us variations in human beings–not only in how they look, but in how they behave, and in what they believe. And yet within this sea of variety the overlying unity is humanness. No matter what the particular differences, each individual is recognizable as a human being. Humanness is the en-compassing category. Universally, there is a human form, human actions, and, more abstractly, a human nature.

Behaviors may differ from culture to culture, but human emotions have a shared commonality even though their expression varies. Philip Roth's or Grace Paley's characters are very involved in their very particular Jewishness, and yet we are able to relate to them in the more general terms of the existentialist search. Allen Ginsberg's poem "Kaddish," about death and mourning, deals with a universal verity through the particular framework of his own Jewish culture. Alice Walker's Black women triumph for all of us.

When the American mainstream narrows itself and becomes ex-clusionary, to that extent it no longer represents the whole of Amer-ican culture but has become specialized and parochial.

Katherine Newman's linking of eccentricity to ethnic writers is very apt. In a sense ethnic authors write against the current as much as experimentalists do, if one can say that the acceptable writing of today *is* the current; it often seems more a becalmment.

The ethnic author's realism and strong narrative line become al-most daring in comparison, say, to the minimalism in much of main-stream writing. The offbeat characters, the complexity of person-ages usually rendered only in stick-figure outline, not in the round, and the adherence to story, all this makes ethnic writing not the usual canon fodder.

My other insight is that I am not the writer my late husband, the Italian author Antonio Barolini, was. Not just because he was ac-complished, prolific, humorous, and swift. He may have been all of that, but comparisons are odious and in this case not to the point. Mainly he was confident; he was acceptable, both in his own Ital-ian culture, and, when we lived here, in this American one where his stories (in my English translation) appeared some years ago in the *New Yorker*. I as an Italian American am more an outsider in my country than my European husband was. The reason why this is so lies partly in the history and social background of the major part of Italian immigrants to this country, partly in the literary mold of the country itself.

When we married, he said we were now equals–both writers. We would ply our art together, enriching ourselves with the addition of each other's language and cultural background.

Except that we were never equal. I wrote not in the confidence of acceptance, as he did, but in the anxiety of being marginalized. I write from what has been called a position of deterritorialization. That my work is called ethnic is not a literary description, but an attempt to turn me over to the sociology department. I have even been told that my American novel *Umbertina* belongs more to the Italian department than to the English. Yet I know from the letters I have received, from the students who have used my work in their papers, and from personal exchange that I have had the possibility to affect lives and mental attitudes. What affects us in what we read becomes equipment for living. That is what literature does.

I could not, in the few generations my family has been in America, gain the same foothold of certainty and confidence that centuries of permanence had done for Antonio Barolini. I could not write, as he did, from a sense of himself, since I did not know for sure who I was. But I could and did write of that sense of ambivalence and conflict, asking, as an outsider, How do I become who I am?

It is this existentialist search, said the poet Czeslaw Milosz, an émigré to America since the 1950s, that strikes *the* predominant theme of our literature: "the very core of American literature," he said, "has always been the question, Who am I? . . . My integration into America is made easier because its inhabitants have always suffered from homelessness and uprootedness, later called alienation."

This American theme happens to be the preeminent Italian American theme. So that cancels Rose Basile Green's advice that Italian American writers should opt, in her words, for the "general structure of American culture," or accept that an ethnic theme is not a universal one. We can't be more American than we are!

If I go back through the years to try to locate what was at the root of my wanting to write, it was my wanting to explain to myself what troubled me; I had to make sense of the conflicting signals that the school, society at large, and family at home were giving me. Books did not tell me who I was. Nor did anyone care because the anxiety of the ethnic outsider had little place in mainstream literature at that time.

I had nothing strong to sustain me in my difference, as Jews with their strong sense of identity, religious or secular, do; or, as I know now, Black writers with their cohesive oral tradition and long familiarity with the English language have.

I was odd not so much because I wanted to write, but because I was an Italian American female and wanted to be a writer. There simply were no models for such an outlandish idea.

Even feminist publishing, which has done such an outstanding job of bringing to light neglected women authors, still has not found the missing Italian American women. We are still in uncertain territory: not yet welcomed into the national literature, not a recognized minority group with special publishing venues. As a group, we might have been better off if we had been worse off. In recent years there have been enormous incentives and recognition for minority publishing—witness the blooming of Black, Asian American, Chicano, and Native American literature.

German novelist Peter Schneider in an essay in the *New York Times Book Review* wrote that fictional narrative deals more with the emotional life of people than with technology or society—therefore, the material at its disposal is limited to variations on a handful of literary archetypes.

The human soul is universal and deals in universal archetypes. How else can we read and relate to the literature of other cultures? "Poetry is finer, and more philosophical than history; for poetry expresses the universal, and history only the particular." Aristotle said that in his *Poetics*. And in the Crocean sense, *all* fine writing is poetry.

Stories are renewed by freshness of material and contemporary interpretations: the old story is retold with new characters, new images, new language. Which is why I could so assuredly answer an interviewer when she asked, apropos of *The Dream Book,* what have Italian American women to say that Blacks, and other women, haven't. The answer, I said, is that each group restates the basic existential problem of emergence, development, autonomous identity. All literature is this restating in new terms. The fundamental story is retold with new casts of characters, new images of details, fresh language. Besides which, I saw the Italian American woman as hyperbole of *all* women.

For Schneider, this is the literary paradox: Just as literature is bound, in its selection of material, to a handful of archetypes, so it is committed, in its representations, to a permanent revolution. This is the place of language and style: how one tells the story here and now.

When Schneider writes, "The larger historical canvas is only of interest if it can be conveyed in terms of the fate of an individual or a particular group," I think of Nobel Prize winner Grazia Deledda, who set out to write the literature of Sardinia because there wasn't any. In doing so she created an opus of universal stature. Italian Americans have, perhaps, a similar task—to chronicle Italian America, the story of the great journey of the Italian people to this country and their transformation here.

We are, in the Latin phrase, *in fieri,* "becoming." We must get beyond self-censoring our own material and experience. We must know that our themes *are* also the quintessentially American—no, universal—ones of a complex people burdened with the conflict of choice, experiencing not only material success but shifting losses and gains in the process of forging a new identity.

My words are not new. Here they are in an earlier version from that great ethnic woman writer Gertrude Stein, who wrote in *The Making of Americans:* "It has always seemed to me a rare privilege, this, of being an American, a real American, one whose tradition it has taken scarcely sixty years to create. We need only realize our parents, remember our grandparents and know ourselves and our history is complete.

"The old people in a new world, the new people made out of the old, that is the story that I mean to tell, for that is what really is and what I really know."

The Case of the Missing
Italian American Writers

It was a bizarre moment during a New York University conference on the Italian presence in America: at a four-person panel whose topic was Italian American literature, three reported on what had been written and what was being written. The fourth panelist, Gay Talese, got up to say there was no Italian American writing worth talking about because there were no Italian American novelists. Modestly he gave himself as a case in point: as a nonfiction writer, successful, yes; famous, yes; honored, courted, and interviewed, yes; rich, quite; but oh, so unhappy with his Italian American background which, he said, was precisely what kept him from being a novelist.

Gay Talese turned to journalism to barricade himself in facts and to distance himself from expressing his feelings in fiction. He attributes his being a reporter of other lives rather than a novelist refracting his own experience to the dread inspired by his family should he reveal in autobiographical fiction any of their secrets. And all the time he envied those American writers who could freely let all their emotions, passions, resentments, and family wars into their fiction. Talese started a novel on his father and then put it away, unfinished, into a drawer. It was eventually transformed into *Unto the Sons,* a huge, unrelenting documentation of his father's Calabrian background and a rehash of Italian immigration history. It does not, as fiction might have done, transform facts and characters into art.

Talese's dilemma weighs on him. He stated it again on the front page of the *New York Times Book Review* on March 14, 1993. That he may be blocked by family is one thing, but for him then to project his fear of censure onto the group he calls "Italian American novelists," and to say that they're all blocked by the same dread, is an astounding fabrication. It goes against all the evidence of how novelists who are Italian American have, in fact, used family as prime material in their work.

It happens that Gay Talese and I are descendants of immigrants from the same Calabrian hills that he describes as drenched in superstition and warped by misrule into a region of cowering people united only "in the fear of being found out." Supposedly as Americans of Italian descent we still cower. However, not only do I not find my two sets of Italian grandparents in Talese's description of a benighted people, but I have not been blocked from relating their story. On the contrary, I found my family's Calabrian background a rich mine that I used fully in my first novel *Umbertina* without a quiver of anxiety about "that Mediterranean region's ancient exhortations regarding prudence, family honor, and the safeguarding of secrets. . . ."

Indeed, putting my forebears back into history and telling their story seemed a right and worthy thing to do. And so it has seemed to a century of Italian American novelists who belie Talese's defensive and nonsensical argument that we're all rendered mute by family code. Liberated by the very act of writing, many of us have translated our family-based dilemmas into fiction.

There have always been taboos against writing about one's tribe; we have only to remember the fracas that ensued after Philip Roth put Mrs. Portnoy on the map as *the* Jewish mother. He was denounced as calumniating his people and making public matters about Jewish families that were not for wider knowledge. And have the Dubliners ever really forgiven James Joyce his portraits of them? Joyce set out to disclose and defy them in the voice of Stephen Dedalus: "When the soul of a man is born in this country, there are nets flung at it to hold it back from flight . . . nationality, language, religion. I shall try to fly by those nets."

Talese, on the other hand, has fear of flying.

Consider what Virginia Woolf had to say of her parents: "I was obsessed by them both, unhealthily, and writing of them was a necessary act." And consider the long, established tradition of culture from which she came: "The atmosphere of her home is saturated with all that is finest and mellowest in English culture and letters," E. M. Forster reported.

The terms to oppose one to the other are, perhaps, mellow versus raw, rather than the "recognized" versus "unrecognized" of Talese's lexicon which tilts the advantage to those with a long history of literacy. Those of us who are not the daughters and sons of Sir Leslie Stephen, but come from anonymous, non-English-speaking immigrants, have had painfully to acquire not only the language but the confidence of being literate.

It is, then, the rawness of the new writer's experience that equates with what the seasoned writer has been bequeathed in mellowness. Both raw and mellow have positive angles, one is not "better" than the other, or more "major" than the other. It is a question of *difference*.

Writing does risk everything. Being an artist, a writer of novels, means wrestling family or national loyalty to the ground to overcome restraints to the truth. If not, writers would be studio photographers airbrushing away the flaws and blemishes, unheedful of Oliver Cromwell's injunction *not* to misrepresent with flattery but to show him warts and all. It's truth writers must go for, not safety, and, yes, it takes gumption.

That Talese suffers writer's block over private revelation is his own business, but his extending that failure falsely to all Italian American writers makes it ours.

Was Talese's confessional outburst timed to coincide with the publication of *Unto the Sons?* Was he actually saying, there is no one else who has written this story, so read me? Suddenly he was going on like a broken record at appearances and in the *New York Times* saying his book might have been a novel but Italian American guilt kept him emotionally blocked from transforming the raw material literarily and writing deeply of his feelings in fiction.

To hear this repeated despite evidence to the contrary in the novels of other Italian American writers became tiresome. Was his motive to garner book sales by stirring up controversy and making everyone aware of him? Had he learned a trick from Camille Paglia who reported that *Sexual Personae* only took off after she appeared on the Op-Ed page of the *New York Times* with a provocative piece headlined "Madonna–Finally, a Real Feminist." By being controversial about Italian Americans in the hospitable pages of the *New York Times,* which seems to privilege that kind of story, both Paglia and Talese called attention to themselves.

With Talese, however, it's both showmanship and disregarding the record. Rather than question why, as he puts it, "there is no widely recognized body of work in American literature" that deals with the Italian American experience, he seems to have internalized the bias he's absorbed from media and publishing circles in regard to Italian American writers. His pride is hurt by being associated with a group that has produced, he says, few writers of eminence–Pietro Di Donato he considers to have written only one book, Don DeLillo doesn't touch Italian American material, and in his view there are no women novelists; there is only Mario Puzo.

A proven investigative reporter and patient researcher for his own past books on the *New York Times,* on adultery, or on a Mafia don, Talese nowhere questions the negative stereotyping of Italian Americans which he quotes from editors and publishers; he merely accepts and repeats it.

Out of his psyche endlessly roiling come the charges: Italian Americans are so dependently wrapped up in a presumed family code of *omertà* (which is actually the conspiracy of silence that obtains in the underworld) that they cannot write fiction; Italian Americans don't read, aren't interested in education, don't buy books; Italian Americans really can't be writers because they're still Old World villagers, unprepared to endure the solitude which writing requires.

It is a burning issue with Gay Talese that Italian Americans are not, in his estimate, better than they are; do not produce best-sellers; are not, as he, invited celebrities on television talk shows. Taking on the persona of his own feared father (the very thought of whose displeasure kept him from being a novelist), Gay Talese himself becomes the terrible chastising parent whom we, his *paisani,* far from enhancing, have tainted by our obscurity.

Whereas Gay Talese describes himself with a sense of loss as a "hybrid" or "fractional" American, others of us have been enriched by the possession of dual cultures in our lives and in our work. Not only Italian Americans, but all groups–the Jewish antiheroes and Ellison's Invisible Man and hosts of others–grapple with a central theme of our literature: the quest to discover the connection between a specific identity and being American.

The very feeling of being outsiders, the estrangement from both old traditions and new ways, the clash of generations as the children of immigrants remade themselves outside the traditions–all this has been the very stuff of literature for Americans, Italian and otherwise.

This was made visibly clear to me when I was a resident writer at the Rockefeller Foundation's Bellagio Center on Lake Como in Italy. Each morning as I left the villa for my workplace, I was stopped by the view: spread below me and cradled by the Alps, Lake Como branches into two arms, Lake Lecco to the east and the continuation of Como to the west.

It was emblematic: a pattern of life and work was made strikingly clear as I saw in the lakes both the main body of who I am, American, and the Italian tributary. From these two confluences am I and my writing formed. My straddling position could be none other than that of the Italian American.

If I could compare that tiny happening of mine with a renowned one, it would be the moment of insight Freud recorded on first viewing the Acropolis. He called his experience "a disturbance of memory"—disturbance because he attached to it a guilt feeling toward his father for having gone so much further than he both in the trip to Greece and in his life's work.

I, too, had the feeling of having gone farther than my parents, but my vision of Lake Como was tinged with no guilt; to be able to encompass dual views as an Italian American seemed simply a gift. I can have an Italian heritage as a part of my life without the shame and denial that marked my own parents' view of the country from which their parents had come. If there were any Freudian aftereffect for me, it was the realization that by going from illiteracy to literate beings, we Italian American writers have taken on the burden of recalling our forebears in story to discharge what we owe them.

It is not that Italian Americans have not used their most intimate material: the novels and stories of John Fante, the plays of Albert Innaurato, the poetry of Diane diPrima all deal with family and transformation, with the push and pull of dual cultures.

The evidence shows that we have been peculiarly tied in our material to the fathers, to family—that we have not ranged far from home; the very tensions of ambivalence and inner qualms we have experienced in our struggle to emerge from Fortress Family on the way to selfhood have become our most cogent literary material.

Gay Talese's neglect of this point, as well as his chagrin at the lack of notable enough names among Italian American novelists, is only a symptom of the larger problem, which is our exclusion from the record. If we're not reviewed, how can we be known? Talese himself can take some responsibility for this; he has reviewed Puzo for the *New York Times,* but what other Italian American authors?

Then there is the question of audience. Do we, as he seems to think, echoing his editor-wife, write only for others like us? Nan Talese has been heard to say that Italian Americans aren't published because they don't form a large enough reading group. What a red herring that is!

Italian Americans are not writing to be read only by Italian Americans any more than African Americans write only for African Americans, or the West Indian Nobel laureate Derek Walcott is writing only for West Indian Americans. We all write as Americans for everyone who will read us, including Gay Talese who is invited to become acquainted with those he's avoided.

Italian American writers will always bear the ethnic identification and particular shadings that our names signal; but these particularities are transcended in writing of the human condition. I know that I write from an Italian American sensibility on a hundred-percent American theme: the transformation from one worldview to another from one generation to another.

Unsettling, then, it was when an acquaintance in Westchester, where I live, asked me why I always wrote about Italians.

I don't, I said, I write about Americans.

To her Americans were the people John Cheever, another Westchester resident, wrote about. She did not consider that suburban white Anglo-Saxon Protestants constitute just as much an ethnic enclave as a Bronx neighborhood of Irish, say, or the Harlem of African Americans or, conversely, that Italian American characters are as American as Wasps, Blacks, Jews, or whatever.

This is a mind-set that a reporter like Talese would do well to explore rather than repeat entrenched prejudices based on stereotyping.

Ironically, just a few months before Talese's piece on the "missing" Italian American novelists appeared, I was invited to participate in a conference entitled "Interculturalism and the Writing of Difference" at the University of Bordeaux. Included in its sessions were discussions of those very Italian American authors, alive and well in France, whom Talese declared missing.

I liked the French way of terming them writers of difference rather than "ethnic" or "minor" writers–for that opened a range of interest quite overlooked in American criticism where difference is interpreted as simply making writers marginal. *Vive la différence,* I say; it is the yeast and ferment of literature.

Meanwhile at home, Talese was contending that even if publishers find worthy Italian American novelists, they rarely publish them because there is no market for their books. Has he ever questioned the ongoing demand for mob books and the publication of takeoffs on Italian Americans in such works as Richard Condon's Prizzi books, Francine Prose's *Household Saints,* or exploitive ghosted nonbooks such as *Mafia Princess?* Talese himself and his cousin Nicholas Pileggi have used the Mafia genre with their best-selling mob books.

Gay Talese's measure of a writer's worth seems to be tied to newspaper best-seller lists; he mistakes current prominence for permanence and gives himself over to what critic Bernard De Voto long ago called the Literary Fallacy—i.e., believing that a list of ad hoc winners is actually the measure of a culture. De Voto was criticizing the Eastern establishment for overlooking the literature of the West, but his fallacy argument holds true for overlooked women or overlooked minorities, as well. Often the result of the effort to define who are the significant writers of contemporary literature is at best a list of temporary literature.

Talese's operative words for a writer are "widely recognized." The questions Talese leaves unasked are what are the preconceptions within the national literature that marginalize the experience of a people? Who makes the rules about who will be "widely recognized" and who will not, and how is this translated into which authors are reviewed, interviewed on television, perpetuated in anthologies? Why has the existing body of work which *does* reflect the Italian American experience received so little attention, and why are those books by Italian American authors buried by not being reviewed?

Italian Americans make pizzas not Pulitzers, says Talese smartly. Besides overlooking awardees Bernard De Voto and his former colleague at the *Times,* Anna Quindlen, his remark is appallingly denigratory.

Gay Talese does not investigate, does not ask questions. He takes as truth that Italian Americans do not support education, the proof being, he says, that no academic chairs are underwritten by rich Italian Americans. But I can counter by naming the palatial Casa

Italiana in New York City, which was built with donations from the Italian American community and given to Columbia University; I think of being invited to the Humanities Institute at Brooklyn College to give the Sal Cannavo Lecture in Italian Studies, an endowed series; I think of the Cesare Barbieri Center at Trinity College, long distinguished by the eminent Italian artists and writers it brings to the campus. Those endowments come immediately to mind; I could find others. Why can't Gay Talese?

There are, a friend reminds me, those pusillanimous beings who accommodate the damaging stereotypes of their ethnic group in "profoundly bad faith," sure that they are the exception, and in order to be in step with prevailing attitudes and to be able to reap the rewards of celebritydom by feeding the mass audience's appetite for those views.

Just as curious as Gay Talese's harangue is the question of why the *New York Times* would publish his essay and give prominence to his misconceptions when other serious writers who know something about Italian American novelists have been denied space in their pages. There appears to be a perfect collusion between Talese's views of Italian Americans and those of the *Times*.

The novelist Ishmael Reed, who has taught *Umbertina,* my novel of four generations of an Italian American family, sent me a wondering note once saying, "I saw Gay Talese on the Larry King show, he said that there was no tradition of Italian American literature because people were afraid to write about their families." Reed, an African American, knew more of what was going on with Italian American writers than Talese has ever wanted to know.

American literature is an ocean, Reed has said, and it's large enough for all the currents that run through it, a body of literature reflecting all facets of what America is–a many-cultured society.

In the meantime, Gay Talese's words notwithstanding, we novelists of the Italian American experience are here present, like Pirandello's characters, authors in search of our audience.

Gay Talese, novelist manqué, would like to extend his personal misery to include all Italian Americans by asserting, "we reluctant Italian American writers are extending the reticence of our forebears, evading scrutiny as they had for centuries . . . laying low."

But it's just not so.

Turtle out of Calabria

On Cape Cod I have a house which looks west to the bay into the setting sun and its afterglow. The house is on a rutted dirt road called Sunset Drive, the same name as the well-paved suburban street where, years earlier, I had my first house, a husband, children, but no sunsets.

Today, as I sweep the side patio, the day is heavy and hot for the Cape. The sky is a gray glaze over gray water. There is no breeze off the bay. Drops seem about to ooze out of the heavy-hanging air.

I sweep a patio that never was—an idea for one that lives only in my head. What actually lies beneath my feet is a rectangular cement pavement into which, before it set, I put a dozen tiles salvaged from the flooring of a previous home, a farmhouse in the Marche region of central Italy. The tiles form a hexagon in the center of the cement. Singles are embedded at each corner where poles support intersticed strips of wood meant to be covered with flowering vines or grapes.

I sweep, tidying, still hoping, anticipating the bright orange blare of the trumpet vine planted summers ago but still only green and leggy as it leans toward its support, far, far from the thick, flowering canopy I envision. I keep glancing at the vine, willing it to grow, to climb, to luxuriate. It does look a little fuller this year. I note tentacle shoots that hold in themselves the promise of growth shooting toward stupendous bloom, the promise that a shady bower is perhaps not impossible.

I sweep because the space has an unkept look which offends me; a past tenant has left old beer cans and his young daughter's plastic playthings all about; the nearby log pile is every which way, spilling over and messy; the builder who worked on the house siding has left his own debris. Last fall's dead leaves are still heaped, and the torn lid of my once new, bright blue trash can just lies there.

What strikes me as I sweep is the greenish patina of weathering on the tiles whose rust color is called *sangue di bue* in Italian, oxblood. I suppose they should never have been put outdoors but I like having as part of my present life the salvage of a past life. It connects me.

In order to site the patio at the southwest side of the house I had the builder remove the bulkhead entrance to the basement and wall up the opening. That proved to be a terrible blunder, a colossal jettisoning of good sense and practicality done only for aesthetic reasons. I have always been subject to pernicious nostalgia and to acting on impulse. But this time the lapse in judgment is really bad: it means that the only access I have to my basement is from the narrow inside staircase off the kitchen. It means that when the washing machine in the basement goes, I can't get rid of it. If the oil tank becomes contaminated with water and is useless, it cannot be removed. And finally when the furnace goes, the problem will be how to get it out and a new one down those impossibly narrow stairs. To undo my mistake I asked the builder if the passage to the basement under the cement can be reopened. A frugal and practical Cape Codder, he snorted at such foolishness.

My patio was to have been a sitting area on the side of the house looking toward the bay where I, and my guests, could sit in the evening under an interweaving canopy of vines and trumpet flowers and sip a glass of wine, or reach up for clusters of grapes, as we watched the sun set and the dusk come on. We'd glide gently on a porch swing; an old trunk (which I bought years ago at a yard sale, intending to restore it), would serve as a table. It would be a simple, natural setting, the kind I loved in Italy and thought I could easily command on the Cape.

But my outdoor space has not become a patio; it is only dull gray cement under raw wood supports bare of foliage. And now it is littered and I am sweeping.

I think of my other homes. Unlike the turtle (snapping, box, mock, sea, or soup) who carries her home constantly with her and will live and die in it, I have only carried forward bits and parts of my different homes. Each one a dream house, definitive; and each one relinquished until finally the message is clear: there is no permanent home. That's like a stab in the heart to me for I was born homesick.

Like the turtle, in my slow, determined way I made doggedness (not farsightedness) my virtue. It's dogged as does it, Darwin said, and he knew his stuff, so I'm not terribly perturbed. I begin to understand that I am of a people, Calabrians, who endured millennia of obstacles, and that *pazienza,* patience, had to be their motto. Patience in the endless drought, patience in the heat, patience in tempests and plagues, patience in fields that grew stones not crops, patience with nature with bad government with fate. I carry the mark of the turtle: stubborn, dogged, patiently carrying on, making do.

From the stoicism of Calabria to the exuberant, intoxicating Excelsior! motto of New York State was the path of one set of my grandparents. Each a *testadura,* hardhead, noted also for an elephantine ability to hold onto an old grudge. "You Can't Go Home Again" was never a slogan coined for them or their ancestors; they were the preeminent people of home, family, *lares et penates.* But now I realize: they had no choice nor any notion of other verities. Being stuck in something is not the same as choosing it.

In this promised land where grace and patience count not much, they learned haste, detachment, separation from family, rugged individualism, competitiveness, greed, the right to personal fulfillment. Those words seem harsher than the stones of the old country, harsher than the old *miseria;* they signify hardship not to the body but to the soul.

In my home on the Cape, the one built on the shining sands of hope and blunder, I see the remnants of my other homes: dishes and linens from my first house in Croton; the flowers plucked in Italy and pressed, then framed and labeled "Spring flowers from Horace's Sabine Farm . . ." I see the old Portuguese basket bought in a Lisbon junk store to the scorn of a friend with whom I spent the summer following my husband's death and her divorce; things from the Marche farmhouse where I filled the feeding troughs of the downstairs stable with plants and installed Antonio's family furniture to make it the living room. Did I think I could transplant the bourgeois furnishings of his Veneto family into an out-of-the way farmhouse and expect everyone to come visit me there? I soon realized I had to leave Italy to make a living in my own land and to raise my children where Always Upward is motto and goal.

I sold the farmhouse with most of its furnishings to a woman who lived over the hills in the town of Fermo. But the old credenza and the table with the impress of an iron on it that were used two hundred years ago in a Veneto kitchen were trucked over the Apennines and put into crates to follow me back to America. The new owner wanted the place as a country retreat. Years later I heard that a band the locals identified as "Turks" descended on the farmhouse during her absence and ransacked it, as in the days of old seafaring marauders. They made off with *zia* Giulia's dormeuse, with the leather settee and chairs from *zio* Giuseppe's law studio, with everything I had not been able to take with me. Should I ever get to Istanbul, will I come across those pieces from Antonio's family and my married life in some great outdoor bazaar?

Finished with the patio sweeping, I bike down Bridge Road toward Eastham center, passing the old Burying Ground which is actually the new one of 1754 replacing that of 1660. The cemetery is a venerable and simple place. I like the Christian names—Thankful, Mercy, Albion—and the surnames, Dyer, Snow, Nicholson on the gravestones. A sign warns against tombstone rubbing; the stones are fragile, weathered, worn, some reinforced by a polyurethane backing. They stand, or tilt, in a grassy meadow; in dead center stands one carved with a death's head at its top. It reads: "In Memory of Deacon Samuel Doane who died March 14, 1795 in the 73rd year of his age." Below that are these lines:

> Death is a debt to nature due,
> As I have paid it, so must you.

It comes to me, considering the gravestones, that the Yankee creed of fiscal responsibility extended unto death as well as in life. The old Cape Codders used "debt, due, paid" as a natural vocabulary to the commerce of life and death. It strikes me as completely contrary to the Italians warding off of death with all the *scongiurie,* entreaties, at their command, the imprecations, amulets, novenas, rites of *malocchio,* and prayers to Saint Rocco whom the Calabrians (who else?) installed as saint of the impossible when all else failed.

It is not rectitude and the straight narrow path that interest my paisans, nor solvency, nor liquidity, nor estate planning, nor debts paid up and no liens outstanding. It is the amplitude of life and its contemplation that focuses the Italian imagination. For that I need a hammock not a Puritan graveyard.

In fact my instinct went to a hammock when, returning from Italy, I settled on a street of tall shade trees and Victorian houses in a Hudson Valley river town. There was a small barn behind my

Carpenter Gothic house where according to graffiti on the walls a sleigh-making operation had been carried on in the 1860s. And in the tiny yard between house and barn I craved a hammock despite the fact that only one tree grew there, and that one not placed conveniently to either structure for attaching the hammock between them. I spoke of my yearning to Jesse, an ingenious black man who worked at many trades including home services and had repaired storm windows for me. He simply said, "I respect your wish to have a hammock."

What he did, then, was to sink two posts into cement at the proper distance to support a hammock. The posts were not the same as trees, but Jesse's honoring my wish for a hammock made me go along with it. Still, the swinging was not the same.

Sweeping the patio at the Cape helps me reflect once again how life is made of accommodations and compromises between the wished-for and the real. Here I conclude that a hammock might well swing between the one tree which grows alongside the patio and a supporting post of my dream arbor. Not ideal, but doable. I'll buy another hammock and hoist it diagonally from the locust tree to the post where I hope the triumphant red-orange blast of the trumpet vine will yet ring out.

I do not willingly give up things of my past; it is not with my volition but always a sense of force majeure that I jettison and eliminate in order that a portion, at least, can be carried forward. If I do not sacrifice something, I end up with nothing. This has also been true of my writing life. It has never been a straight shot, right on target, but rather decades of persistence, setbacks, renewal, belief, trust, reward, sometimes betrayal. The same *pazienza* required and learned as that which served the old Calabrians in their fields of stone. Something I have always carried forward: it is my survival. My persistence. My hard head. My turtle shell.

Reintroducing
The Dream Book:
An Anthology of Writings
by Italian American Women

Paths are made by walking. Books are made by questioning.

My questions–long dormant–surfaced in the early 1980s when I was invited to address a conference for Italian American women. I was asked to speak about the women of their background who were, and are, writers.

Who are they? I wondered then. To be able to call up the few names I knew was not sufficient to wipe out the prevailing notion that there are no Italian American women writers as there are, so notably, Black women writers, Jewish, Asian, Hispanic. In histories, sociological tracts, bibliographies, and learned conferences the names mentioned as Italian American writers were exclusively those of male authors; it was a totality of male presence that effectively undercut the importance and witness of women in the Italian American experience. And as I wondered about the unnamed women, there echoed in my mind what a reader of my novel *Umbertina,* had written me: "When I first saw your book I was drawn to your name, a novel by a woman with an Italian surname is rare."

I knew she was right, but why? Who were the others? Why had I never heard of their work? Why was it that though we Italian American women existed as writers, we were not perceived? Before I had many answers, I addressed the conference with a talk called "Breaking the Silence," more a statement of hope than of fact. But

I had started on a path. The rest came to fruition with the searching that led to *The Dream Book: An Anthology of Writings by Italian American Women*.

When the Before Columbus Foundation gave my collection an American Book Award in 1986 it was cited as a groundbreaking work, for my Introduction had placed Italian American women authors for the first time in a historical-social context and presented their work in various literary genres as a cohesive voice.

The Dream Book was intended not as an act of separatism, setting a specific ethnic group apart from the main body of American literature, or, indeed, setting Italian American women writers apart from their male counterparts, but rather as an act of inclusion and completion, restoring to the body of the national literature the names of women authors who had been overlooked even as men were being documented as the only examples of Italian American writing.

For when the record is not recognized, it is in effect denied. This was the case for Italian American women writers.

The question had always been, why were Italian American women silent? It might well have been, instead, why were they not heard?

Where was their written work, the testimony to their lives and experience? They had been dismissively referred to as "Women of the Shadows" from the title of Ann Cornelisen's book about a non-applicable group, the poor village women of southern Italy, thus casting the writers by association into deeper stereotypical gloom. In Alice Walker's words on the *Dream Book* jacket, "For years I have wanted to hear the voice(s) of the Italian American woman. Who is she? I have wondered. What is her view of life? Does she still exist?"

Yes, the Italian American woman writer exists, and her experience is registered in an honorable literary record; if her voice remained silent to the larger culture, it was because no established critic or reviewer amplified it. If the writers seemed women of the shadows, it was because the spotlight of attention never reached them.

Although *The Dream Book* brought the women to light, there is still the lingering and misinformed notion (notoriously fostered by Gay Talese on the front page of the *New York Times Book Review* of March 14, 1993, in a misperception entitled "Where are the Italian American Novelists?") that there are no Italian American women writers as there are, so notably, women writers of other ethnicities. But that view simply begs the questions that have never been asked: what are the factors and circumstances in Italian American history that have combined to keep valid writers from being known? Why has the majority literature, exhibiting cultural parochialism, ignored them?

Women, particularly, were long overlooked not only by the established majority, but also by feminist critics engaged in the recovery of women writers, and certainly by an inimical publishing world. That does not, however, excise Italian American women writers from existence, precarious as that existence may be. They are the true "lost women writers," still to be recovered as their Black sisters so notably have been.

Although in the course of preparing *The Dream Book* I met many Italian American women writers–in person, in correspondence, in their work–others remained unknown to me, deceased, or "lost" or still unpublished. Exceptionally (an exception that proves the rule), it was in Andrew Rolle's *The Immigrant Upraised* that notice was given of Antonia Pola, an author who was silenced before she was formed. Her work, as far as is known, remains one book only, the 1957 novel *Who Can Buy the Stars?*–so tentative, unpolished, and yet so forceful in a woman's voice crying out for notice long before the women's movement opened a way. There are women even more lost than Pola, for she left a book while others remained unpublished, unknown.

I wanted to "name the names" as much as I was able and to put on record a part of our national literature which had been overlooked or thought unworthy of attention. The collection, which dramatist Karen Malpede wrote me "feels like coming home," never claimed to be exhaustive. It was a start.

I got a great deal of personal enrichment from my contact with many of the contributors. They enlarged my thinking, moved me by their stories, and broke, by their presence, the confinement of isolation and oddness in which we singly struggled. They brought the warmth and sharing of personal revelation to my work, the joy of their enthusiasm, and the answer to the question, Where are the women?

Several writers were very generous in bringing to my attention others of whom I was unaware. Novelist Dorothy Bryant told me of Alma Rattini Vanek, former student of Bryant's creative writing course, then seventy-eight years old. I went to see Alma on the heights of Berkeley where she and her husband lived with orange trees in the front yard and rear window views out to the Bay. Alma's Italianness was reawakened by my search, and it came in an outpouring of memories which she shared with me.

She told of being born in a mining camp at Telluride, Colorado, where her parents had immigrated from the Trentino-Alto Adige region of Italy, on the border with Austria, at the beginning of this century. And then she put into my hands an old, yellowed, oilcloth-covered manual she called the dream book. I opened the ragged-edge, loose-paged book. On a front page, in awkward, uphill handwriting was the notation in Italian of one Angela Zecchini who, with many misspellings and an incorrect date for the inception of World War I, recorded this terse account of her life: "I was born in 1884 in the commune of Folgaria, district of Rovereto. Departed the old places the day of May 7th. Arrived in Telluride June 12 and on July 20 [*sic*], in Europe, there erupted a powerful war of the European powers. Written October 7, 1914."

That handwriting was the first I had ever seen of an immigrant Italian woman; and the book itself was the first piece of immigrant "literature" I had ever encountered. It was, Alma told me, a book the Italian women of Telluride used constantly, the Baedeker of their dreams. Through it any dream could be interpreted by consulting meanings in the alphabetized subject entries; looking up dreams gave them explication for the strangeness around them and a clue to their *destino*.

I tried it, too, for that very morning my daughter Linda had told me her dream of my holding a baby in my arms. I myself had dreamt of stacks and stacks of white paper. In the Italian language dream book I looked under *"bambino"* and *"carta."* The reading was of an auspicious beginning for a creative venture. I took it for the sign of the anthology I was beginning, and from that original dream book came the title and meaning for mine.

The old, tattered, and much-fingered Italian dream book had been the companion of those displaced women in Colorado, giving them hope or warning, speaking to them of their hidden longings, fears; it had been their counsel and guide, as, in another immigrant society, the Bible was for the English Pilgrims.

Alma related how those isolated women in Colorado shared any popular Italian novel which might find its way to them. Her mother and the others craved those stories which embodied their other lives in the language of their birth. A *romanzo* would circulate among all of them until it fell apart from sheer reading and rereading, satisfying in part their need to transcend their lives. But having a novel to read was the rare occasion.

For everyday, they had their dream book. Their men, the rough miners, might ridicule and scorn them, but the women knew the power of dreams. They charted their ways through the unknown with the help of divinations from the little book. It had to serve until the day came when their daughters and granddaughters would be mistresses of the new language, able to lay out lives and signs in their own words in order to make sense of them, and understand the past.

The neglected literary record of Italian American women's experience *as narrated by themselves* is a great lacuna in the national literature. To present a people from only one viewpoint—the male—is to falsify their total creativity.

Thus, being Italian American, being female, and being a writer was being thrice an outsider, and why this was so is partly in the history and social background of the immigrant women who came to this country, partly in the literary mold of the country itself.

The loneliness of seeming marginal is something well understood by an Italian American woman with literary aspirations who seems to stand alone, unconnected to any body of literature or group of writers—an anomaly, a freak occurrence, a frequent nonrepeater, ephemeral.

More difficult than the question of why Italian American women writers were isolated and few was the question, If grouped, do they form a cohesive identity and have a specific resonance to their writing? I believe it to be so. The superabundant tradition from which we derive has given us a powerful identity; has bequeathed specific strengths and weaknesses; has presented common problems as well as passions. The writing reveals the commonality. For no matter how oblique the themes or broad the views, overtones of who we are and how we feel, as formed by our values and history, show up in the work.

A common base for Italian American women writers was the prior realization, as readers, that it was all but impossible to find writing in which to recognize the transcultural and transgenerational complexities of who we are, where we've come from, and what the journey has been.

Sandra M. Gilbert (née Mortola), who is well known under her nonidentifying married name as a literary theorist, feminist critic, and editor, but perhaps less known as a poet of passionate Italian American identity, stated the problem in a letter to me very precisely: "I am always struck by how few people have written about what it meant to be *us!*"

At the same time that there is a longing to validate one's identity, there are qualms about being too narrowly defined. Barbara Grizzuti Harrison remarked in a panel discussion that she did not think of herself as an Italian American woman writer, but as an author who is all of that and more. That's agreed. It is not the qualifiers that are important, it is the writing. But it would be disingenuous to deny the influence of the ethnic factor, and the outsider position it's put us in. It was the aim of *The Dream Book* not only to create a record of literary achievement, but also to help Italian American women find strength in solidarity, and a means to greater visibility and voice. From the outpouring of commendatory reviews, readers' letters of self-discovery, teachers' use of the book in courses, and continual citations in scholarly works, that goal seems to have been attained.

Still, in the end, each writer must transcend ethnic-gender qualifiers through the work itself. There is a great range among the Italian American women writers—of age, education, geographical provenance, occupation, as well as in their work and experience as writers and in their literary reputation. Some have a remote Italian connection, others were born in Italy. The degree of generational distance from Italy, or even the part of Italy one's people came from, can influence a writer. There are perceptible differences in style—from the older, wry, humorously cast family stories of Marie Chay or Rose Grieco to the more hidden allusions in the younger generation of writers like Agnes Rossi or Mary Caponegro. From the vivid realism of novelists Julia Savarese or Marion Benasutti to the intense, linguistic control or esoteric surrealism of poets Ree Dragonette and Leslie Scalapino is a great distance. It indicates angles and complexity denied to the popular image of the Italian American woman.

There is an emerging Italian American woman the newness of whose education and economic independence has, in the best American tradition, advanced her from working to middle class; but the transition, tricky even for a Babbitt or Gatsby, is even more vexed for someone who wants mobility upward together with the freedom to grow and change, but also values the firmness of that early home base where the rituals and food and cultural traditions of her family and childhood reside. Many women are the first of their family to attend college, and quite a few like Grace Lamacchia, a professor at Pace University, have Ph.D.'s. Lamacchia is the author of *Collision,* a story collection which includes "A Doctor of Stories," the wry and touching account of her moving beyond her Bronx working-class neighborhood as she achieves her degree in literature and tries to explain to her bewildered father, a retired plasterer, that after all those years of study she is not going to be a doctor in a hospital but one who dissects stories.

The grandparent is a rich mine of the Italian American imagination–mythical, real, imagined, idealized, venerated, or feared. The grandparent embodies the tribe, the whole heritage, for that, in overwhelmingly the most cases, is as far as a present-day Italian American can trace his or her descent. Often, uncannily often, what the women write of, where they start, is with a grandmother, with those old women, sometimes illiterate or very little schooled, who had only their dreams, premonitions, and feelings to read for guidance. Going back beyond the Americanized generation of their parents, the writers feel an intense connection with older generations and revere their iconoclasm, peculiarity, unconventionality, and strength. Some of this wild oddness of the elders (before homogenization into standard American) was recalled by Beverly Donofrio in her piece "My Grandma Irene," which appeared in the *Village Voice.*

After the immigrant grandparent, or, at most, great-grandparent, there are only faceless hordes stretching back into the past–unknown, unvisualized, unnamed. Most Italian Americans embody the paradox of coming from very ancient roots of an ancient civilization but knowing their past only as far back as a grandparent. Most often there are no written records beyond the grandparent to tell us more of our ancestry; there are no Victorian photo albums in velvet covers. In our grandparents is incorporated all of the past, all of tradition and custom, and, we imagine, some archetypal wisdom and native intelligence. We start from the people who came here.

Rosemarie Caruso's vision of her grandmother walking down to her from the moon came in a dream–a benevolent vision where the harsh reality never enters–which inspired Caruso's interesting exploration of tradition between mothers and daughters in a play called *Shadows of the Morning Moon.*

How often the grandmother figure turns up in dreams! From *The Dream Book,* Sandra Gilbert's poem "The Grandmother Dream" evokes the "Sicilian grandmother, whom I've never met / . . . sitting on the edge of my bed. . . ." Diane diPrima's moving rededication of herself to the ideals of her grandfather is given stirring voice in her poem "April Fool Birthday Poem for Grandpa."

Carole Maso's stunning first novel, *Ghost Dance,* included unforgettable images of two Italian grandparents, one turned to the old ways of the past, the other future-looking. Tina DeRosa explored strong ties with grandparents in her novel *Paper Fish.* My own novel *Umbertina* developed from the imagined strong grandmother who inspires her descendants.

The veneration, the awe, the wish for the strength of the ancestor is an enduring topos, ineluctable and omnipresent, a reference for almost every Italian American writer even when not specifically a grandparent but some older relative as in Mary Gordon's essay on her great-aunt, "Zi' Marietta." Mary Gordon an Italian American? it might be asked. It was Gordon herself, at the beginning of her writing career, who presented herself as Italian American when she entered the UNICO national literary contest for young Italian American writers. To be noted is that while the 1976 winner of the UNICO contest was a young man who has not been heard of since, the three young women who got honorable mention were Camille Paglia, Teodolinda Barolini, and Mary Gordon, all of whom went on to publish notable work.

Gordon's maternal grandfather was Italian; he married an Irish woman who put the Irish Catholic stamp on their nine offspring so thoroughly that, in Gordon's own words, "the Irish drowned out, without a whimper, the Italians—a conquering nation meeting up with a docile colony it need only step over to rule." But it was not merely opportunism that led Gordon to identify herself as Italian for the sake of entering the UNICO literary contest. I think of the Italian connection for Gordon as an intense internal one, called upon subliminally, to correct the rigors of Irish Catholic puritanism which she so often decries in her work.

In "Zi' Marietta" Gordon recalls the old woman's silver-backed brush and comb and her admonition: "Brush your hair five hundred strokes a day and put olive oil on your hair after you wash it. American girls kill their hair. Your hair is alive; it is your glory as a woman." The articles were left to her at her great-aunt's death, Gordon writes, and "Now I have begun to use them, not often, but at those times when I most need to feel like a beautiful woman who has come from a line of beautiful women. When I most need that weight, Zi' Marietta's heavy silver comb and brush are there for me. . . . The silver comb and brush lie on the top of my dresser, heavy, archaic, ornate as history, singular as heritage."

And, it may be added, symbolic of Italian stylishness and the aesthetic and sensual sense of self that are part of Gordon's heritage. To all Italian American writers, it seems, the archetypal presence of an ancestor ("ornate as history, singular as heritage") is present.

In their writing Italian American women expose the signs and symbols, the auguries and directions of lives which were—and are—subject to great ambivalence, to dual pulls from opposing cultural influences, to dual vision. They assign meanings through their poetry, novels, stories, essays, and plays. In the written word—*their* written word, finally—interpretation and direction for lives and futures can be found. Their writings interpret the experiences of a collective past and bring into view what has been inexplicable, painful, dubious, conflicting. By writing their stories and reading each other, Italian American women have come to know themselves.

The Historical and Social Context of Silence

A question to ask, rather than why Italian American women were silent so long, is what were the conditions that impeded the act of writing? What were their lives as they were transplanted from one culture to another?

The words of a cultural representative from Italy to New York in the early 1980s seem emblematic of a long engrained attitude toward Italian Americans. A reference to Italian American women writers had been met with words of impatience and even a certain derision: "Who *are* they? Why aren't they stronger? More important? Who has heard of them or ever seen their books on racks at an airline terminal? How many people would any of them draw to a lecture?"

Significantly, at the same time, in 1980, the Agnelli Foundation issued a monograph, *The Italian Americans,* stating it was time for the mother country "to revivify relations with the descendants of emigrants from our shores . . . that there be a rapprochement between the Italian American world and contemporary public opinion in Italy."

In a time of hype when the prevailing standard is whether or not one has been interviewed on television for fifteen minutes of celebritydom, the Italian representative's statement was a dispiriting display of lack of critical judgment and historical understanding, and of a popularity-chart mentality which lingers in the mother culture and asks impatiently of its descendants abroad (the runaways from home), why aren't you better than you are?

The why is in their history.

And it is not negative history, a litany of ineptness or missed opportunities. Quite the contrary: given the adverse factors of extreme deprivation and provenance from areas that provided them with no practical preparation of language, civil or political skills, schooling or even basic literacy, the Southern Italians who made up the bulk of the late-nineteenth-century or early-twentieth-century exodus did, in large part, translate their innate strengths and canniness into successful American terms. They did secure an economic foothold in their new environment and started the educational process that has led their children to the professions, to politics, to managerial positions.

At the same time they also secured a sense of double alienation. The Italian immigration to the United States was preponderantly by people who were not wanted or valued in their land of origin, then found they were not wanted or valued in their new home country when they aspired to more than their exploitation as raw labor. Some of this discrimination still sticks in the Italian American memory, regardless of social advance.

That the literary arts lagged behind pragmatic ones in development is not hard to understand. A people without a written language and a literature (for Italian was as foreign to the great mass of dialect-speaking immigrants as was English) had first to acquire not only the words and concepts of their new world but the very notion of words as vehicles of something beyond practical usage. In contrast, the ease and style of African American writers attest to the centuries of their exposure to and absorption of English. For Italian Americans, a realistic people for whom hard work and modest economic gains took precedence, that literary writing does not immediately—or even usually!—produce financial rewards meant it had to wait.

Italian Americans cannot be conveniently generalized; they are differentiated by a multitude of variables, including class, political activism, occupation, religion, education, the region of Italy from which their ancestors came and where they settled here, and to which generation in the United States they belong.

But, by and large, the women have a commonality.

They are women who, with rare exceptions, had never before been authorized to be authors (of themselves, of the word)—not by their external world, nor by their internal one. A woman like Bella Visono Dodd (1904–69), born in south Italy and brought to this country as a child, managed to have an education and become a college professor, later acquiring a law degree; she was known as a labor activist and public speaker on the rise in the Communist Party. But glory was transitory and at high personal cost, as she relates in her ominously titled but curiously unrevealing autobiography, *School of Darkness* (1954). She defied the old ways for the sake of her successful career and for marriage to Mr. Dodd. She remained childless only to lose her marriage and her closeness to her family of origin and their ways, and then to find herself cast out of the party to which she had given so many years of her life. Her story ends with a desperate sense of loneliness and a return to the religious beliefs of her childhood. It is a stark and foreboding morality tale of the overachieving woman, one that could give little comfort to any mid-century Italian American woman looking for someone to emulate; it remains a testament of how even a supereducated Italian American woman was unable to transcend her background to write deeply of relationships and to evoke in vivid personal terms the depths of her internal turmoil.

The very thought of making one's life available to others through publication was alien to earlier Italian American women, and even Dodd, quite extraordinary at the time in writing an autobiography, was not forthcoming concerning many areas of her life; she seems to have approached her story more as an act of contrition for past sins than as an illumination of the choices she made.

Italian American women did not come from a tradition that considered it valuable for them to narrate their lives as documents of instruction for future generations; they were not given to introspection and the writing of thoughts in diaries; they came from a male-dominant world where their ancillary role was rigidly, immutably restricted to home and family; they came as helpmates to their men, as mothers of their children, as bearers and tenders of the old culture. The creativity went elsewhere—into managing the homes, growing the gardens, making the bread, elegant needlework. Though they brought native strengths—sharp wits, tenaciousness, family loyalty, patience and courage, which are skills for survival—they did not acquire until generations later the nascent writer's tools of education, confidence of language, the leisure to read, and the privacy for reflection.

When you don't read, you don't write. When your frame of reference is a deep distrust of education because it is an attribute of the very classes who have exploited you and your kind for as long as memory carries, then you do not encourage a reverence for books among your children. You teach them the practical arts, not the abstract ones.

Italians attach little value to exact meaning and the literalness of words. *Parole femmine,* they say in Italian: words are feminine, words are for women, frivolous and volatile, a pastime in the marketplace. *Fatti maschi:* deeds are masculine; men engage in action which is concrete, real. Italians are unlike the Jews, people of the Book, for whom the survival of race identity was closely tied to a constant reading and analysis of the Bible; and unlike Fundamentalist Christians, believers in the Word, who implicitly trust words and honor them as revealed truth.

It is useless for disgruntled self-appointed critics to ask why there are no Norman Mailers or Eudora Weltys among Italian American writers, as if our writing could or *should be* homogenized into a Wasp, or a Jewish, or any other framework. What has been written authentically from the unique experience of being of Italian background in America may yet prove to be more valuable in the long run than writing that conforms to prevailing majority notions.

The long history of the Italian people has made them skeptical; it is as if, numbed by the rhetoric which continually whirls about them, inured to the conventional formulae of empty *complimenti,* they tend to lose all notion of words as conveyers of anything "real." What is real is life in the *piazza,* church ceremonies from birth to death, the family at the table.

Words themselves are meant for fanciful approximations, polite artifice; they are relative and circumstantial, illusory and masking, but not for relying on. Even more distrustful of words, then, are those who cannot read or write them, thus the distancing from that most abstract act with words, the writing of imaginative literature. It would take time before the habit of literature was widely rooted among Italian Americans.

The first survey of Italian American literary activities was a bibliography compiled by Olga Peragallo and published in 1949. She listed fifty-nine authors (with an amiable inclusiveness that welcomed Nicola Sacco and Bartolomeo Vanzetti), eleven of whom are women and of those only two whose names are known today: Frances Winwar and Mari Tomasi. In a preface to that work, the late Italian critic, author, and professor emeritus at Columbia University Giuseppe Prezzolini lent his keen and acerbic observations. He noted that at the time of Peragallo's compilation, there were, by census count, 4,574,780 Italian Americans in the United States, of whom 3,766,820 still declared their mother tongue to be Italian. "This leaves," he wrote, "only 827,960 who spoke English at home; that is a very small minority from which one could expect writers to come forth. . . ." He also noted of the fifty-nine writers that "the amount and value of their literary output would certainly be greater if the members of the first generation had come to America endowed with a culture of their own and if they had been able to absorb also the culture of the United States. They found two barriers: the language and the social background. . . . Since these families were driven from Italy by poverty, the ghost of poverty followed them throughout their lives and influenced the education of their children."

Those children, including any hypothetical aspiring authors, were but one or two generations into the use of the English language in any way, let alone as a literary vehicle; they had to acquire the skill of becoming book readers. It was their American schooling which provided the beginnings of relating to literature, a literature not of their own world nor of their own experiences, but of Anglo-American models which would, in turn, feed their sense of alienation.

And though, by the early years of this century, some men of Italian American background had begun to write and publish books, for the women it was to be a much longer, harder, and later development. Again, there are exceptions. Two notable women stand out as beacons rendering even deeper the dark void around them.

Sister Blandina Segale (1850–1941), a teaching nun of the Sisters of Charity, whose letters describing her mission to the Far West from 1872 until 1893 were published in book form as *At the End of the Santa Fe Trail* (1948), is the earliest known author among Italian American women. She was of Northern Italian stock and arrived in this country in 1854 at a time when Italians were so few and far between that there was no developed prejudice against them as would later be the case. She was educated, bilingual, and her letters show a cultivated person who delighted in arranging a Mozart Mass for Christmas in a mining town, who made knowing allusions to Dante's *Commedia,* and who taught a quartermaster's daughter Italian by reading Alessandro Manzoni's novel *I promessi sposi* with her in the Santa Fe outpost where they were stationed. Sister Blandina became a civic influence in the Western territories, and a social activist who was instrumental in ending lynch law.

She wrote, as she says, in scraps of time, on scraps of paper, throwing the pieces into her desk drawer for a moment of leisure when she could enter them into her journal as a faithful record of the mission life and work of the nuns in Santa Fe under the authority of Bishop Lamy. In Sister Blandina's case, there is a tantalizing noncrossing of paths with another recorder of mission life, the author Willa Cather, who was to immortalize Lamy and other French-born Jesuits in her novel *Death Comes for the Archbishop.* Regretfully, Cather omitted not only the work of the Italian Jesuits in the West but certainly the achievements of the female religious in the Western territories.

Willa Cather's oversight is rather symbolic of the displacement and neglect of Italian American women writers. From Sister Blandina on, these writers have been omitted from the record.

Sister Blandina was far more autonomous than other women of her day, and many generations ahead of the later-arriving Southern Italian immigrants among whom she would return to work in Cincinnati for the rest of her long life. Her memoirs leave no doubt of her enterprise, her adaptiveness, her self-reliance, and her deep satisfaction in her work. She is justifiably impatient with those who wonder how she could give up "everything" to be a nun.

Despite Sister Blandina's having all the resourceful and adaptive qualities of the celebrated Anglo-American pioneer women, her story has been omitted from collections celebrating women in the West. Her singular voice is unique among the written records of immigrant Italian women in the form of diaries, memoirs, or letters.

In 1961, a novel by Marie Chay called *Pilgrim's Pride,* pieced together from individual stories based on family lore and first appearing in a number of noteworthy journals including the *Saturday Review,* documented the experience of her Northern Italian immigrant grandparents in the same mining territory that Sister Blandina had worked in. Chay's novel is humorously written; it had to be to be publishable, for a skewed and stereotypical vision of Italian Americans made them acceptable on the margins of the national literature as easy-to-take, humorous ethnic types rather than as substantial individuals fraught with the full range of human problems and emotions. Chay's dedication page carries an interesting disclaimer which indicates that there was more depth and darkness to her characters than was allowed into the book: "Thanks to the imagination and memory, the people are no longer what they once were, and the harsh, sad and tragic events they often went through are now something that even they might laugh about."

Sharing the stereotype of Italians as sunny, easygoing types is Camille Paglia, who flaunts as her trademark "That's Italian!" whenever an explanation for some of her extravagant notions is required. She routinely overstates, as in this passage from her *UNICO* essay, "Reflections on Being Italian in America": "The vivacity of our responses to the realm of the five senses makes it nearly impossible for us to suffer from that alienation which is the modern dilemma; the sense of absurdity and meaninglessness is a northern-European invention. Gothic gloom has never made much of an impact upon the sunniness of the Mediterranean temperament." Already a Ph.D. from Yale and in her fourth year of teaching literature at Bennington when she wrote that, Paglia seems not to have heard of Pirandello, who invented the theater of the absurd, nor does she seem to know the despairing and powerful novels of Verga, the sombre poetry of Montale, or to know anything of the unsunniness of actual Italian American life. She has certainly no inkling of Andrew Rolle's psychohistory, *The Italian Americans: Troubled Roots* (1980).

Preceding Paglia, Rose Basile Green, in her comprehensive study *The Italian American Novel* (1974), offered a similar notion of sunniness in the thesis that the basic optimism of Italian American writing will eventually win it success and a place in the American showcase of literature. Yet beneath the clichés of optimism and sunny temperament, there are other, shadowy, complicated layers in the Italian American character manifest in the literature. A way to dismiss a people is to see them in simple terms, as the critics have, and not give recognition to the reality of their yearning, defensiveness, humiliation, and anguish as reflected in their plays, novels, poetry.

The second notable exception, after Sister Blandina, to the late appearance of Italian American women in writing is Frances Winwar, born Francesca Vinciguerra in Taormina, Sicily, in 1908. She came to this country at a young age and was fortunate in having educated parents and a father who gave a great deal of attention and encouragement to her. Going through American schools and acquiring English with precocious ease, she started writing poetry, and her first publications were poems in Max Eastman's *The Masses* when she was only eighteen. As was the case with later writer Mari Tomasi, Winwar had the inestimable good fortune to find a mentor in the then Wasp publishing world: Lawrence Stallings, the literary editor of the *New York World,* hired Winwar as a book reviewer. She went on to become a successful, prolific writer, not unhelped by the anglicization of her name which, she has related, was a condition of the publication of her first book, *The Ardent Flame* (1927). Astutely, it now seems, she destroyed her first MS, an autobiographical novel, and thereafter was able to turn away from herself in order to concentrate on historical novels or the biographies of literary figures. This distancing from herself and her origins must be taken into account as part of the price paid for getting on in a publishing world not interested in Italian American material, regardless of the quality of writing. In Winwar's case the writing was distinguished enough to win her the esteemed and lucrative first *Atlantic Monthly* nonfiction award in 1933.

Winwar's nonidentification as an Italian American (paralleled these days by the very successful Evan Hunter-Ed McBain who was born Salvatore Lombino, or by women whose married names camouflage their origin) was reflected in the remarks of a curator of a large collection of books and manuscripts by American women. Asked if any Italian American women were represented, she said, "No, this collection represents *la crème de la crème.* For instance, if Christina Rossetti were American, not English, she'd be here." Then, asked about Frances Winwar, she said, "Oh, yes, of course she's included, but I never thought of her as Italian."

The historical and social context of literary silence, and the clues to the missing women writers, can also be found in Italian family mores.

It is a story of conflicting cultures, alienation, unschooled parents' fear of the American school which they sensed, rightly, was taking their children from their authority, the growing resentment of American children toward their Italian parents, the resulting split in loyalties and personalities, the passing of the old ways, and the painful rites of passage into the new.

Italian women who came to this country did so as part of a family–as daughter, wife, sister; or "on consignment," chosen, sometimes by picture or sometimes by hearsay from an immigrant's hometown to be his wife. But always in the context of a family situation. There was no pattern of the independent Italian woman emigrating alone to better her lot as there was, for instance, of Irish women who, advantaged by having the language, came over in droves to be hired as maidservants, many then living out their lives unmarried and alone. But an uneducated Italian woman could not exist, economically or socially, outside the family institution which defined her life and gave it its whole meaning. She came bonded to her traditional role. The oral history of Rosa Cassettari, published in 1970 as *Rosa: The Life of an Italian Immigrant,* is that of a young girl given by her guardian to an immigrant in Arkansas. Rosa's story was recorded by Marie Ets Hall, a social worker at Hull House in Chicago, and reflects the lives of many other immigrant women who never had the chance to tell their stories.

The Italian woman had little choice but to put herself under the protection of a man. Women outside the family structure were scorned as deviants from the established order; they were either wicked or pitiful, but always beyond the norm. Unmarried or widowed women, who were thought, in their singleness, to be consumed with envy and full of spite toward women partnered with men, were thus commonly held to be the chief casters of the evil eye. In Grazia Deledda's novel *The Mother,* filled with the intensity and superstitions of the harsh Sardinian world of a century past, a mother watches her son, a priest, fall under the spell of a woman who, being "rich, independent, alone, too much alone," was outside normality and thus a threat to all around her. In a patriarchal society, any female (save nuns) whose life was not defined by a man's would be suspect.

Rosemary Clement (a name truncated from Clemente during immigration processing) has Lena, a character in her play *Her Mother's Daughter,* boast: "I'm a thinker–I thought myself right out of getting married." But eventually Lena's place in society is legitimized when she becomes a mother to her young orphaned niece and nephew, thus redeeming her womanhood and removing suspicion of ego-centricity from her life. In Clement's *October Bloom,* the psychological warfare between the old family and the new woman is still being fought as a young girl's desire to go away to college is opposed by her mother. Beverly Donofrio's vivid memoir, *Riding in Cars with Boys: Confessions of a Bad Girl who Makes Good* (1990), also recounts how her own desire for education was thwarted and how her reaction was played out in a wildness that could have left her life a permanent ruin.

As with Caruso and Clement, the Italian American playwrights Donna De Matteo and Michele Linfante have written works with deep connections to the mother-daughter bond—a connection heightened in a culture that still worships the ancient goddess as Madonna—and to the wider world of women. A model of the Old World Italian woman who was resourceful, strong, and able to live by her wits and hard labor when it was demanded of her (as it often was when her husband preceded her to America and often was gone for years at a time without any word) appears in Lucinda LaBella Mays's 1979 novel *The Other Shore.* In Mays's book, the mother must pit herself against the elements, poverty, outside hostility in order to survive. She keeps herself and her child alive by her unremitting sacrifice and strength until the long-awaited ticket to America arrives. The child, Gabriella, will find for herself that the long-dreamt-of street of gold is actually the American public school. She will separate her life from her mother's through education and self-direction, thereby providing an elevating but historically uncommon ending.

For this much is certainly true of Italian women: they have resources of strength which are denied in the stereotype of them as submissive and servile to their men. At the beginning of the twentieth century, Jacob Riis, who photographed and wrote of the immigrants in their tenement life on the Lower East Side of New York, noted, "There is that about the Italian woman which suggests the capacity for better things." Did he mean her tenaciousness, her endurance, her grace under pressure, her faith? Those are the qualities her granddaughters, in particular, cherish and have reintegrated into their lives, adjusted for new uses.

There are certain mind-sets, however, brought over with the immigrants, which take longer to reshape. Self-denial was the psychological preparation among peasants for survival in regions where *la miseria* was the norm of life and there was no chance of a better one: denial of aspirations; denial of any possibility of change; denial of education to children as being futile; denial of interest in anything beyond one's home walls; denial of goals as being unreachable and therefore an emotional drain and psychological impairment. Strength, psychic and physical, was conserved just for sheer life support. If they could not better themselves in the old country, what they could do, and did, was to leave. It was an act of enormous courage and faith, but inevitably there clung to them remnants of the old *miseria* mentality, for survival had once more to be secured, and this time in an alien land.

The ingrained suspicion of education used to be expressed in the saying *Fesso è chi fa il figlio meglio di lui*–it's a stupid man who makes his son better than he is. In America schools were not always regarded as the road to a better future; often they were seen as a threat to the family because they stressed assimilation into American ways and gave children a language their parents did not have. Reading was ridiculed as too private, too unproductive, too exclusive an enjoyment–free time should be spent with the family group, not on one's own. What the family wanted was cohesion and no threat of change; learning gave children ideas, made them different; and writing produced nothing. These were the criteria of a people involved completely in economic survival. And for their time and place, they were right. Reading and writing are the rewards of a well-established class.

Here, as in Italy (and, indeed, in all rural societies) the family was the chief fortress against the unknown. This commitment to family was placed solidly upon the shoulders of women, and because of their service to it, it was they who were most denied educational opportunities. Though the number of Italian Americans in college has doubled since mid-century, Italian American women still lag behind both their men and women of other groups when it comes to higher education, and this despite the models of educated, achieving women like Ella Grasso, governor of Connecticut; Geraldine Ferraro, candidate for the vice-presidency of the United States; Eleanor Cutri Smeal, past president of the National Organization for Women, and Dr. Aileen Riotto Sirey, a successful psychotherapist in New York and founder of the National Organization of Italian American Women, a remarkably successful union of accomplished professional women who sponsor mentoring and other programs.

Studies show that Italian American students in the main still demonstrate a predilection for pragmatic and vocational studies over the liberal arts, and are relatively uninterested in cultural activities, do not get involved in extracurricular activities, and in general feel alienated from faculty and other students at their colleges. A 1986/87 study of Italian American college students at the City University of New York yielded the disquieting finding that "Italian American young people still have difficulty in establishing personal independence from their close, and in many cases, 'enmeshed' families." The profile of the female student of Italian American background is of someone extremely anxious and suffering from low self-esteem, often depressed, and with an "irrational anxiety about appearance and other issues of self-worth."

At best women are getting a mixed message: Yes, better yourself through education, but don't get beyond your family; learn the wherewithal to gain economically, but not how to develop an independent mind and spirit which might take you away from us. Still present is the concept of education as a practical tool to help one earn more money, not as the door to autonomy and lifelong self-development.

A film of 1970, *Lovers and Other Strangers,* reiterated the theme of not growing beyond the old style of doing things; the father in an Italian American family confronts a son who is contemplating divorce: "What do you mean you're not compatible? What do you mean divorce? What are you—better than me? Look at me, do I have to be happy to be married! What makes you think you got to be happy? Why do you think we keep families together? For happiness? Nah! It's for *family!*"

Thus is the dialectic set up—there is resistance to change, but change is inevitable. In the very title of Louise DeSalvo's incisive essay "A Portrait of the *Puttana* as a Middle-Aged Woolf Scholar," is the recognition that an educated woman was (is) looked upon with deep suspicion: an emancipated mind puts her outside familial control, beyond male authority, and that has to mean intolerable anarchy. The psychological warfare of former generations is perhaps only now abating.

Italian American writing is full of the dilemma of the individual on the road to selfhood who is caught in the anguish of what seems betrayal to family. Yet breaking out of the family, or the neighborhood, is a step in the search for one's autonomy.

The very solidity which is the success of the Italian American family makes it hard to break away from; and to be a writer means breaking away and distancing oneself from where one came in order to see it better, more truly. This puts the Italian American woman writer in a precarious position: that is, do you keep close to family, enjoying its emotional warmth and protectiveness, and lose your individualism; or do you opt for personal independence? Do you go against the grain of your culture to embrace the American concept of rugged individualism? Do you choose loneliness over denial of self for the family good?

The working out of independence/dependence factors is critical in the development of both men and women and for people of all backgrounds. But some cultures, in effect, demand too enormous a ransom to release the individual from benevolent captivity.

Strangely, the ways of the past have hung on with Italian Americans even as Italy has radically changed from what it was just fifty years ago. An industrialized and transformed Italian society makes an Italian American community like Marianna De Marco Torgovnick's Bensonhurst in Brooklyn, which tenaciously holds onto the old isolation, seem a remote backwater by comparison. Now a scholar, author, and professor of English at Duke University, she wrote of her early background in *Crossing Ocean Parkway*, noting the sea change she underwent.

There is an irony here, for the Italian thrust and talent as a people was always toward individualism. The Renaissance was created of giant personalities. But none of that high culture touched the masses of people who would form the major immigrant population and who, in arriving in America, would find their rebirth here.

Sounding like an analyst pointing the way to group maturity, Jacob Burckhardt wrote of the Italian people in *The Civilization of the Renaissance in Italy:* "this it is which separates them from the other western people. . . . This keen eye for individuality belongs only to those who have emerged from the half-conscious life of the race and become themselves individuals."

The immigrants who left Italy took the first step toward lifting themselves from that "half-conscious life of the race" in the very act of taking passage to America. That act linked them and their descendants to the American ideal of the self-made person. And the paradox is that by becoming self-made in America, Italian Americans may finally be more authentically Italian than they ever could have been by remaining submerged in the old way in Italy.

In a sense Italians transplanted to America were asked to mature immediately from a state of childlike dependence (on family or church or landlord), to a state of self-reliance in order to be what America said they should be. It went against the grain of their very being and most deeply held convictions about life.

Mario Puzo, touching in *The Godfather Papers* on the enormous exodus of the poor from the south of Italy, says: "they fled from sunny Italy, these peasants, as children in fairy tales flee into the dark forest from cruel stepparents." Interesting that he casts it that way. It seems a very apt simile—if they came as children, they either had to grow very quickly or remain as vulnerable as children, dependent on family and familiar surroundings, their impetus halted.

The Italian American woman comes out of a family-oriented, patriarchal view of the world in which women stayed at home or, at most, worked alongside her immediate male kin, but was always dependent upon a male—her father, brother, husband, and, eventually, if widowed, her sons. Family was the focal point of the Italian woman's duty and concern, and, by the same token, the source of her strength and power, the means by which she measured her worth and was in turn measured, the reason for her being. Historically, the woman's role as the center of family life was crucial because of the importance of the family over any other institution; the only unit that protected its members from the abuses of others and helped them recover from natural disasters.

Within Italian culture, the woman's role and definition in the family were reinforced by the strong Italian cult of the Madonna—the Holy Mother who prefigured all other mothers and symbolized them, the quintessential *mamma mia*. But as Andrew Rolle, who has made a unique contribution to the psychological understanding of Italian Americans, has observed, "The Madonna had been a mother but scarcely a wife." And so, too the Italian woman reduced her sexual role as her husband's lover to take on that of *mater dolorosa*.

This acute observation helps explain the often vexed sexuality of the Italian American woman and why she was in the past so little a companion and friend to her husband. What she was mainly was Mother, the continuum of life to whom her children will be bound forever by the stringent strings of respect, weekly visits, confidences, obedience. Such restrictiveness may explain the performer Madonna's obsession with publicly acting out sex when she sang "Papa, don't preach": she was vehemently cutting loose from the childhood bonds of Catholic education and strict patriarchal family mores.

Becoming ourselves is why some of us write, the being is part of the writing. Pietro Di Donato, who died in 1992, described *The Gospels,* his work in progress, as his revenge, his answer to all the past constraints: "I am writing [*The Gospels*] because I was . . . a true believer, and I outgrew that and have to replace it with Gods of my own creation. . . ." Or, as Marguerite in *Umbertina* puts it, "What world is there that's not beached first in ourselves?"

The caustic of the American experience changed the old role to a new one at the cost of an enduring psychological split and a tension which have, in Italian American women writers, become the material of much of their work.

The women who are second- and third-generation Italian Americans know and honor their special background, but they also question it and are aware of deeply ambivalent feelings about family and about those bonds, both healing and constricting, which are suffered as the heavy cost of preserving tradition. Barbara Grizzuti Harrison in her essay "Godfather II: of Families and families" has stated the dilemma: "I think of the strength of Italian women, of strength perverted and strength preserved. And I am painfully confused. I want all of these people to love me, to comprehend me; I want none of them to constrain or confine me. And I know that what I want is impossible."

In a harsh environment, woman was recognized as the central pivot of the family, just as the Navajo's traditional hogan is built on four poles named after female deities, so that the support of the home literally rests upon the female principle.

Richard Gambino's *Blood of My Blood* (1974, 1995) examined the background of the Italian American experience and its past dynamics. It described well the positive qualities expected of the female who was to become wife and mother; she was socialized at an early age to be serious, active, sharp, and practical. In the chapter Gambino devotes to women, "*La Serietà*–The Ideal of Womanliness," however, he espouses too idealized a male vision of woman's place. True, she was the center of life of the whole ethnic group; true, it was she who expressed the emotions of the men; true, she had to be useful to her family, for her value was based on practical usefulness; but women view it as less acceptable than do men like Gambino that this ideal of *serietà* should be the end-all and be-all of a woman's life. Gambino finds women's traditional role pleasingly full of the dignity and gravity that would honor an ancient Roman matron. Contemporary women stuck with the role are less gratified with it than Gambino has ventured to imagine.

"I have it like heaven now," says the widowed Rosa Cassettari towards the end of her life; "no man to scold me and make me do this and stop me to do that . . . I have it like Heaven–I'm my own boss. The peace I've got now it pays me for all the trouble I had in my life." Even unlearned and unlettered women like Rosa, once they got to America, gained a sense of there being potentially something more to their lives than family service.

Why, if the *donna seria* is such a paragon of sturdy virtues, has the Italian American male (including Richard Gambino), as he evolves educationally, professionally, and socially, fled her company so completely? As one member of Dr. Aileen Riotto Sirey's ethnotherapy group admitted, "I never wanted to marry an Italian girl, I wanted to marry a Wasp, someone who was educated and could help me to get ahead."

It is a verifiable phenomenon that educated Italian American males marry outside their ethnic group. Fleeing the traditional woman and her feudal role, Italian American men find social mobility and better company in educated Jewish or Irish wives. Still, they want their mothers and sisters to keep the traditional ways to which they return on festive occasions, filled with nostalgia and sentiment for old ways that can safely be left behind when it's time to go.

That flight was given recognition in a popular film of some years ago, *Saturday Night Fever,* in which the woman protagonist, named Stephanie MacDonald, becomes the symbol for the Italian American hero, Tony Manero, of what is better, achieving, upward in life. Tony, played by John Travolta, leaves his Italian American Brooklyn neighborhood (and the Italian girl who pines for him) to follow

Ms. MacDonald by crossing the bridge into her realm, Manhattan, thus signifying his willingness to grow beyond his ethnic group.

The one thing, according to the men, that an Italian American woman must not do is change. Since everyone leans on her for support, she must be permanently accessible and permanently unchanging, a lynchpin of traditional values. She can not exist as an individual with her own needs and wishes for that would topple the whole patriarchal order and undermine the common good of the family. That is a heavy price to pay for the pedestal and a Holy Mother image.

A very contemporary use of the self-nullifying theme in the Italian woman's life is in Rosemarie Caruso's play, *The Suffering Heart Salon,* where the ritualization of women's sacrificial lives is played out in a New Jersey beauty salon and embodied in the line "You don't like it?–do it anyway!" Caruso compares women to the sanctified host of the sacrificial Mass, which exists to be consumed by the officiating priesthood of men. In their sacrifice is their blessedness, and specialness. Thus they are revered by those who consume them, and made to feel consecrated by their role. In contrast, their daughters assert a need for self-identity and want to free themselves from the past patterns; in their self-actualization they *must* react against their mothers; but in denying the value of the mother's role, they lay upon themselves a terrible dilemma.

As early as the 1943 publication of Michael DeCapite's novel *Maria,* a different kind of Italian woman from the submissive types portrayed in Di Donato's *Three Circles of Light* or the Mafia women popularized in *The Godfather* and elsewhere was presented–one far beyond the stereotypes they had already become in the larger culture. *Maria* is a penetrating study of a woman in conflict with the role she is expected to fulfill, a woman who yearns for something else.

First depicted as a young girl, Maria submits to the marriage her father arranges with a harsh, silent, and ultimately stupid man. She experiences divorce and abortion when both were not only unusual in American life, but matters of extreme gravity in an Italian enclave. She befriends a Jewish woman; she expresses sexual interest in a man not her husband; she finds intense satisfaction in her comradeship with women at work. She knows the reality of life and achieves a sense of belonging in her city environment and at work. Only her final action, when she rejects her second husband through feelings of guilt toward her eldest son, seems contrived. It's as if Maria, by accepting the maternal role as more important, is acting as the male author thinks she should. Still, it is a choice, not something forced upon an unformed person, as her first marriage was; in the difficulty of the choice lies the seeming nobility of her self-sacrifice. Despite the novel's ending on the traditional note of a mother's sacrifice, one feels the truth and depth of feeling of the character; Maria is beautifully realized and is resonant with an inner turmoil not normally accorded Italian American women who seem to act only as automatons of their tradition.

But such female characters have not fared well with critics, who are more comfortable with predictable stock figures, having certain assumptions about Italian Americans that they find hard to relinquish. Thus, Julia Savarese's novel *The Weak and the Strong* (1952) got a very harsh reception. Critics called her strong descriptions of poverty and the Depression era "bleak," "tough," "unrelenting," and—the ultimate pejorative!—"humorless." Of course, for an established male writer like Di Donato, or women writers like Jean Rhys or Flannery O'Connor, that kind of unsentimentality would be *verismo* of the highest order.

In Antonia Pola's *Who Can Buy the Stars?* Marietta, impatient with a weak husband, has the stamina to become a bootlegger as she tries in vain to buy happiness for her family and herself. Mari Tomasi also created women who acted independently of the notions of how they should act and suffered reviewers who misread her work as "Quaint . . . unpretentious . . . pastoral".

The women's voices, whether in literature or in the recorded interviews of Professor Valentine Rossilli Winsey, in their poignant resignation or in anger, strongly contradict the image of Gambino's ideal stoic matron, *la donna seria*. A chorus of female voices speak of unhappy marriages, no choices for their lives, and a kind of bewildered regret for what life has been. All that sustains them is that they did what was expected of them.

The Italian immigrant woman met her duties and responsibilities and showed again and again her strength, her resilience, and her timeworn patience. Indeed, her success in keeping the family together has earned her recognition and tributes from sociologists and other scholars.

But no barricade around the family unit is large enough or strong enough to keep out the winds of freedom wafted on the new world air. The minute their children set foot in the American school and imbibe the notions that in this land all is possible and each person has the right to be self-fulfilled and seek a personal happiness, something happens to the old bonds. They do not disappear, but they loosen. They allow for new thoughts, new arrangements.

It became apparent that in Anglo-American life (for that was the dominant ethnic pattern and became the standard by which American society judged all other ethnicities), the family had less importance than political or economic institutions, or even the school system. It was soon perceived that "Americans" rated self-sufficiency over family ties. Individual success and achievement were what counted, not sacrificing oneself for the family. As a result, the value of the Italian woman was diminished in the new land—she became old-fashioned, backward; she became the focus of well-meaning social workers who wanted to "save her" from what they viewed as an undemocratic patriarchal system without recognizing that in that very system she had found validation and had nothing, immediately, with which to replace it.

The psychological battering endured by the Italian American woman has been considerable. Professor Winsey quotes the poignant remark of a solitary old immigrant woman reflecting on her experience of life in America, which keeps her children and grandchildren so busy running they have no time for her. "Bread rises," she said, "only when it's allowed to stand awhile. The soul, too, has its own yeast, but it cannot rise while it's running. It's certain that I got things here which in Italy I never could have gotten. But I had things in Italy which in America I still cannot find—yeast, yeast for the soul!"

The Italian woman's soul was in her consecration as core of the family, upholder of its traditions and the transmitter of its values. In that role her hardships and sacrifices were repaid, her value was inviolate, and this gave her a positive sense of her self and of her power—a power that was, however, often manipulative and always relative, confined as it was to the home environment and not used in the world at large. In America she was quickly dethroned from venerable matriarch to old woman in the kitchen stirring the sauce, heartwarming, maybe, but actually a figure of ridicule, a caricature. She and the stern values she stood for were no competition for the seduction of America which beckoned her children away from stern duty, away from tacky self-sacrifice, away from the old way.

Not able to Americanize on the spot, the Italian immigrant woman suffered instant obsolescence (an American invention), and became an anachronism, a displaced person, a relic of a remote rural village culture.

There is no doubt that family structure was an essential aid to the successful transplantation of Italians in America; it continues to provide stability and important verities and a specific Italian American identity. But now it is its tensions or the strains of intercultural marriage that have been explored by such works as Barbara Grizzuti Harrison's autobiographical *Visions of Glory* (1978) and the novels *Miss Giardino* (1978) by Dorothy Bryant, *Tender Warriors* (1986) by Rachel Guido deVries, *The Right Thing to Do* (1988) by Josephine Gattuso Hendin, and Rita Ciresi's *Blue Italian* (1996).

Contrary to folklore, humorous stereotypes, and appealing portraits of the traditional Italian woman as pillar of her family, Italian American literature abounds with portraits of women who are harsh, frequently cruel, crushing, unfeeling. They are embittered and malevolent; and, given the strictures of their own lives, there is plenty of reason why.

Some mothers, as in Jennifer Lagier's poem "Second Class Citizen," in Marion Benasutti's fictionalized memoir *No Steadyjob for Papa* (1966), or in Rosemarie Caruso's plays, are portrayed with a humor that nonetheless still reveals layers of apprehension or bleak disappointment in their lives, an edge of rancor toward their lot. Or there is the figure of the angry mother in Jacquelyn Bonomo's poem "The Walk-in Closet," and the troubled mother in Linda Monacelli-Johnson's "Home Movies":

> When a bourbon bottle
> became the lens, I discovered
> I was born of you to be your
> mother.

In the haunting words of Janine Veto's poem "Naturally, Mother":

> Freud aside, all our fathers
> do not matter
> A woman bleeds through her mother

But family in all its facets—not only the dark side—is what gripped the imaginative powers of the first Italian American writers and, most forcibly, women, because their roles were so enmeshed in that powerful mark of their culture. Thus, the family's benevolent warmth and support are portrayed in Rose Grieco's stories and in Dorothy Gentile Fields play *1932* about an Italian American family in the Depression years; compulsive nostalgia and life ritual are the subject of Diane diPrima's *Dinners and Nightmares,* about shopping for eels for an Italian Christmas Eve; and Maryfrances Cusumano Wagner's poem "Preparations for an Italian Wedding" predicts, "You will be glad you followed tradition; / you will at last understand your mother."

More than for men, the displacement from one culture to another has represented a real crisis of identity for the woman of the Italian family, and she has left a heritage of conflict to her children. They, unwilling to give themselves completely to the old ways she transmitted, may end up with burdens of shame and ambivalence or a sour self-hate as the pernicious inheritance gets passed on; even third and fourth generations feel the remnants of conflict.

For the modern woman it means that traditional power (based upon selflessness and sacrifice) has been transmuted into a more gratifying autonomy and self-awareness. If not power over her children in the old way, she has instead power of choice in her own life and the possibility of a democratic family style.

And yet there remain valid ties to the past, and feminists of Italian American background look for and find strengths in the old traditions, especially in those parts of the model of *serietà* which Gambino described as assertiveness, commitment to work, activism, and practicality–qualities, it turns out, that are normal expectations for *all male* Americans! Utilizing the Old World values of the ideal of Italian womanliness in the service of the contemporary quest for individuation, the evolving and maturing Italian American woman has learned to shift the focus of those qualities from the exclusive service to others to service to herself as well. That is the balance she explores in her writings. The pull back toward family is powerful; the push forward toward self-enhancement is ineluctable. How to arrive at an equilibrium is something that Louise DeSalvo's essay explores not with the quaint self-deprecating humor of the past, but with pungent and sophisticated insights.

Despite their specific material, Italian American women writers speak for all women: their emergence is that of all women who once lived in the shadows of others.

There was a dark underside to the bright picture of compact Italian American family life so praised by sociologists and onlookers. The professional apologists who extol the Italian American family had better listen to the women and to their literature–to the voices of women writers who are telling it as it is. Home life was never as satisfying and untroubled as the men said it was; it was what it was for historic and social reasons that are now surpassed.

Put Italian American women in the context of their origin, their time and place, and the collective psyche which formed and held them, and it becomes comprehensible why they have taken long to test language and flaunt tradition as writers, long in giving themselves the authority to be authors.

Gay Talese's misperception, however, is that *his* failure of nerve has kept *all* Italian American novelists from writing about family (or whatever), whereas, in fact, the contrary is true: the family has proved their most cogent material. Through wilfullness or ignorance, Talese simply discounted past decades of Italian American writing. Nor is he presently aware that the old culture of shame, of not giving up secrets, has been replaced, one by one, by a new Italian American woman writer.

Singlehandedly, Cris Mazza revokes shame by the deliberate shamelessness of images in her collection of stories, *Animal Acts*. There is nothing that she and her sister writers (Mary Caponegro, Anna Quindlen, Jeanne Schinto, Carole Maso) flinch from writing. For them there are no more shadows.

Seeds of Doubt: The Internal Blocks

In America, the newly arrived faced the cultural imperative of the dominant society: to "pass" you had to lose your distinguishing identity and somehow become a stranger in your own life.

This part of Maria Mazziotti Gillan's poem "Public School No. 18: Paterson, New Jersey" perfectly catches the dilemma:

> Miss Wilson's eyes, opaque
> as blue glass, fix on me:
> "We must speak English.
> We're in America now."
> I want to say, "I am American,"
> but the evidence is stacked against me.

Evan Hunter (who, born Salvatore Lombino, made a nomenclatural leap into America's mainstream) explored in his novel *Streets
of Gold* the transmutation of Ignazio di Palermo into Dwight Jamison and his attempt, in an anglicized persona, to attach himself to
the American dream. The realization of the futility of it all comes
because, in his self-made Waspness, Dwight Jamison finds he does
not exist, he is a figment of the American imagination.

It was the myth that failed. The myth that told us we could and
should be equally American in the Anglo mold, but forgot to mention that to force people to become what they are not produces not
equality but enmity—enmity with one's self. Gillan, winner of the
prestigious May Sarton Award for her writing, states it again:

> Without words, they tell me
> to be ashamed.
> I am.
> I deny that booted country
> even from myself,
> want to be still
> and untouchable
> as those women
> who teach me to hate myself.

By an early age I, too, had a good start on what is a major motif
in Italian American writing—the sense of being out of line with
one's surroundings, neither of one's family nor of the world beyond
the family: an outsider in every sense.

What, long ago, really crystallized my desire to write was a slim
little book of poems, *Seeds of Doubt,* by Syracusan Alma Aquilino. It
was an extraordinary revelation. All I recall of that long-lost book
is the feeling of melancholy the poems conveyed—a delicious sensation in adolescence. The poems themselves were not as memo-
rable as the fact of their existence, but it was the title that made the
impact: it reflected my own uneasiness, my own sense of doubt
about my identity. I think of Alma Aquilino's book as my koan of
insight. But even more powerful was the fact—unheard of!—that a
woman with an Italian name had written a book. The little book
was a message that I was not alone in my aspirations. The most important fact of the book was the Italian name on the cover.

My schooling had provided no texts by authors with Italian
names, no hint that people of Italian background had a rich litera-

ture. Rather, the illiteracy of the Italian immigrants was stressed without the countering view that illiterate people do have an operative social system and a culture outside of books. James C. Raymond's *Literacy as a Human Problem* stated that neither wealth nor literacy guarantees superior sensibility; either can engender a warped set of values, fashionable vulgarity, and callousness toward the disadvantaged. People who are highly literate, are tempted to regard literacy as the measure of human worth, in the same way people who are very rich regard money as worth.

No Italian achievement in social or humanistic arts was ever mentioned to dispel the message that Italian Americans were somehow less than the Tom Sawyers and Becky Thatchers around them. This sense of being alien in America pervades other ethnic groups as well. Feminist writer Vivian Gornick decried what she saw as the squashing of ideals present in earlier generations of Jewish social activists and the overlaying of revolutionary goals with the whitewash of Protestant ethics in order to fabricate stereotypes of middle-class virtues. This is possible, Gornick pointed out, because of the overwhelming prevalence of Wasp models in American schools and colleges.

Schools were aided in the task of imprinting minds with the need to anglicize, to grow up with the look of America, by movies which projected images of Shirley Temple and the Andy Hardy character. Italian American homes, gardens, names, churches were embarrassing—too ornate, too foreign. It was the pristine, classic simplicity of the white New England church steeple on the village green to which taste was expected to conform, not the rococo excesses of Catholic sanctuaries—much less the gaudy, overwrought, paganized pageants of saints with which Italian Americans in some parishes annually annoyed their Irish clergy. Lines from a poem by Elaine Romaine (née Romagnano) state it succinctly, "You were always irish, god / in a church where I confessed / to being Italian)."

For the Catholicism the immigrants found here was a stern, puritanical, inhospitable version of what they had known in their homeland. In America everything was tinged by the Protestant ethic: worth was measured by material achievement, visible riches, and success, all of which is quite at odds with the Catholic harmony of everyone having worth in the sight of God and there being a divine plan in everything with hope eternal for salvation. The Protestant ethic stresses competitiveness, anxiety, struggle to succeed, to move up fast and visibly. The Catholic emphasis is on acceptance, humility, and having an internal sense of worth and dignity without the external show of prosperity that indicates Calvinist grace. It is the difference between a tolerant, live-and-let-live orientation and a chiding, judgmental one.

In order to become American, one had to learn to be alone. One had to *value* being alone.

There is in this mandate the belief in individualism which is the positive message of Protestantism, an insistence on the need to face the existential predicament of our essential aloneness and form one's self outside of and beyond family.

But growing up is difficult and filled with the traps of self-consciousness about being different and shame about the taste and smells of Italian foods, the look of grandparents, the decor of home and garden.

Imagine Italians in a Currier and Ives world: sleighing up at Christmas to a cold and isolated farm on a forest's edge instead of strolling through a village where houses are all snuggled one against the other and you can mingle in a piazza thick with people and human exchange. It's a different image of the world. The American penchant for being off alone in nature, for being Thoreau, was alien to Italian immigrants; it is part of the American mind. Henry Steele Commager's outdated *The American Mind: An Interpretation of American Thought and Character since the 1880s* viewed that mind as one in which, it has been pointed out, not a Jew, nor a Black, nor a Catholic had a presence nor, consequently, did their particular sensibilities and visions of what this country means.

Sister Blandina Segale foresaw in her journal that Establishment history, as written by "Mr. Bancroft" (in his ten-volume *History of the United States*), would not give the whole picture of what had been accomplished in American life by non-Anglos. Commenting on how the freedom-of-conscience edicts enacted by Catholic Lord Baltimore in Maryland were frequently overlooked, she charges, "Yet look at the stream of articles constantly given to the public about Plymouth Rock and the Pilgrim Fathers!" Just as those who decry the Mafia as an Italian import forget that the Ku Klux Klan is an Anglo-American invention.

In its presumption of rightness the Anglo-conformist society determined that every group but theirs was "ethnic." Thus the disingenuousness, for instance, of John Cheever, who referred to his mother as "an Englishwoman" but denied that his writing, though concentrated on a small world of Episcopalian suburbanites of British descent, was ethnic. British Americans simply take it for granted that the customs, language, and school curricula of this country are anglocentric—this, to them, isn't "ethnic," it's natural. It reflects the American imperative of giving a common frame of reference and unity to the many disparate peoples who make up this country. But its elitist and value-judgment overtones are something more—a slur against other ways and cultures that continues to wound the peoples who feel its sting.

"The truth is," wrote Joseph Alsop in his biography of Franklin D. Roosevelt, "that the America Roosevelt was born into . . . and even the America of 1932 was entirely White Anglo-Saxon Protestant by any practical test . . . the presence . . . on the citizenship-rolls of so many people of other origins did not in any real way alter the fact that America in 1932 was still a WASP country in all significant respects . . . non-WASP Americans, however able, were excluded from the normal opportunities of any moderately fortunate WASP."

The children of the immigrants immersed themselves in the texts the American schools provided, books that offered heroes and heroines who were unfamiliar in Italian American life. These models were not only alluring, they also gave Italian Americans a sense of displacement and estrangement. The Italian American self-image was never in perfect focus: one could never find who one was, only who the larger society thought one should be.

It is a delicate question of balance. Italian Americans internalized English literary culture and were certainly enriched by it, but in the process were denied knowing that their tradition had, in fact, riches and glories of its own.

America has passed through its period of isolationism and in the second half of the century following World War II has inevitably become part of the total world scene abroad and more accepting of cultural pluralism at home.

Different origins presume differences in temperament and attitudes; it was psychologically impossible for Italian Americans of earlier generations to fit themselves into the Procrustean bed of Anglo-conformity without, in fact, maiming a part of themselves.

Consider Medea: she, the barbarian princess, the foreigner,was the ultimate outsider to culturally correct Jason, the Greek insider. And her internalized rage was at his contempt for her being "other."

It is the rage which always informs the writing of those who are perceived as different. It is there in James Baldwin's *The Fire Next Time* as he grappled with the theme of American identity; over and over it appears in multicultural writing; it is in women's writing; it is in *The Dream Book* as I question why Italian American writers, particularly women, have been left out of the national literature.

"As I grow older, I think more and more about my cultural background which I unfortunately denied for many years," playwright Michele Linfante told me; she expresses the prevalence of those internal seeds of doubt, known to many ethnic groups, as to who she was supposed to be.

Would it have been different if Frances Winwar, sixty years ago, had opened the door to respect for Italian American writers by letting her highly successful books carry "by Francesca Vinciguerra" on their title pages? One can only speculate as well as recognize that other Italian American authors underwent the same self-censorship of name or fictional characters and material.

"I am really Sandra Mortola Gilbert," explained Sandra Gilbert, "and my mother's name was Caruso, so I always feel oddly falsified with this Waspish-sounding American name, which I adopted as a twenty-year-old bride who had never considered the implications of her actions!"

Names are powerful signals, and an Italian American surname sets up barriers of preconception or even prejudice in those circles of American literature that are hard to penetrate even under the best of circumstances. Italian names are analogous to the skin color of Black writers–they immediately signal difference. The Italian American women who have written with Anglo surnames are not seen as they actually are–and that is to be regretted for it feeds the notion of the missing Italian American woman writer. Exceptionally, Barbara Grizzuti Harrison has always kept her Italian birth name along with her married name.

And several women have reclaimed an Italian maiden name for their authorial signature, e.g., Rachel Guido deVries, Marianna De Marco Torgovnick, and Maria Mazziotti Gillan, one of whose books of poetry is called *Taking Back My Name*.

In her review of *The Dream Book*, Anna Quindlen wrote, "I am Italian American, my father's surname belies my mother's background. Our literature should in part reflect our lives, and mine has not. There is a world that has not appeared very often in modern

American literature, a world of insular families scorned by an English speaking society, torn by the lure of assimilation and the sure disintegration of tradition that this would bring." In her first novel, *Object Lessons,* Quindlen looked at that world.

Italian American women writers are left with questions: how to become writers out of the intercultural tensions of their lives? how to use their individual selves narratively to oppose and/or understand the Otherness of the dominant society? how best to restructure the self to fit the society?

What I find is that we write ourselves to know ourselves; we write of our differences in order to embrace them. Yet it is hard for society and the literature to accept our differences. It has been said that the very essence of the creative is its novelty; hence we have no tried and tested standard by which to judge it. Substitute "different" for "creative" and the conclusion is the same.

Another difference between the Italian American woman writer and other woman writers is the degree of isolation she felt. In *Black Women Writers at Work* Toni Cade Bambara says, "what determines the shape and content of my work is the community of writers . . . writers have gotten their wagons in a circle, which gives us each something to lean against, push off against."

Not so with Italian American woman writers; most of those who appeared in *The Dream Book* thought themselves unique as writers of Italian American background. Very few knew of others. But once collected and named they became aware of each other, held joint readings, formed groups, began to appear in collections, were asked to talk at colleges and at women's history month events. With Emelise Aleandri's 1987 staging of "The Dream Book Revue" at the CUNY Graduate Center in New York, many of the women whose written work had appeared in the anthology were visibly brought together for the first time as a collective presence and voice.

"What is the way out of this dilemma?" asks Sandra Gilbert in an essay on Sylvia Plath, as she considers the paradox of Plath's (or any creative woman's) life: that even as she longs for the freedom of flight, she fears the risks of freedom. Interestingly, Gilbert states that double bind in terms that describe the Italian American sensibility: "How does a woman reconcile the exigencies of the species—her desire for stasis, her sense of her ancestry, her devotion to the house in which she has lived–with the urgencies of her own self? I don't know the answer."

Already some of the myths about women embedded in the culture have crumbled. Jean Baker Miller's *Toward a New Psychology of Women* identifies growth as the most dynamic quality of being human. Growth means change, and human growth equals psychological change; it means that personal creativity is a lifelong imperative for having a fulfilled life. Miller's cogent insights acutely question the "desire for stasis" which Gilbert posited as a female exigency and make it more a social construct.

Woman's traditional role as static bearer of the past must be rethought in terms of what reality shows, i.e., women are involved through child care in witnessing and fostering constant change and growth. Women, raising children, have absorbed lessons for change, not fixity. By twisting reality and going against the grain of their nature and the very texture of their experience, society has conditioned women to desire stasis and to appear as compliant upholders of traditions in which men have a major vested interest. That interest is premised on the maintenance of status quo. The price to women has been the thwarting of creative growth and change in themselves.

Can it be (what societies have long denied) that women are *more* change-oriented than men, more flexible and tolerant, have always longed for the psychological excitement of growth and change rather than their statuary calm?

Iris Sangiuliano in 1978 published *In Her Time,* a work which defines the common life journeys of women and the crises that trigger growth. It is a false dilemma, Sangiuliano said, for women to think they have to choose between family and career for they can have both. Life, she finds, unfolds not predictably, but in "great surges of billowing change; and it is the unpredictable which is the seminal female ingredient for change: conflicts + contradictions = change."

Italian American women in particular have projected their feelings of worth outward, making affiliation central to their lives. Waiting to be confirmed by others, they often have a woefully undeveloped central core of self. Women's nature has been defined for them by the other sex, and woman's graceful compliance to male authority (whether in home situations or in public institutions) has been made to seem the measure of their femininity.

While Tillie Olsen in her story "Tell Me a Riddle" gave us a glimpse of the myth deflated, Italian American women were still internalizing the myths of the "sacrificial mother" and "everyone else first before me."

Philosopher Martha Nussbaum, in an essay review of *Reclaiming a Conversation: The Ideal of the Educated Woman,* found that past theorists of woman's role, from Plato who imposed on women a male notion of the Good Life, have always described a female life that lacked something. Solutions, Nussbaum says, are not to be found in the past philosophical tradition; rather, a new chapter remains to be written by both men and women trying to live fuller lives in a joint human experience. What she foresees is that we will face a plurality of different lives, sometimes conflicting and sometimes enriching each other. In daily choices, we will construct new and fuller meanings for the ideal of "the complete human life."

If this is a dilemma for all Italian Americans, it is more so for the writer, and utmost for the writer who is a woman. As Cynthia Ozick has reckoned, "You can't be the good citizen doing petitions and making chicken soup for your sick neighbor, and still be an artist." Ozick has the self-confidence to be the artist; Italian American women writers, according to which generation they belong to, have not had the confidence, or have acquired it with misgivings, or have never had the problem.

For it is the woman who, at the core of the family, is the transmitter of its traditions and upholder of its values. Can *she* defect from the one institution Italians believe in, the family? Can she at least redefine the ancient laws for her advantage?

This is the paradox: being at the heart of things, it is Italian American women who, breaking the silence imposed on them by family loyalty, thereupon become best suited to make literary use of the material implicit in family struggles. What was in the past an obstacle to the writing now provides the thematic material.

Emerging from the redoubt called Family Loyalty, many Italian American women writers have used writing as an act of public assertiveness. From Di Donato on, Italian American writers have openly aired the family secrets. Family has been their theme more than such "American" ones as angst, personal ambition, spiritual struggle, or the hard working out of the sexual relationship. Italian American women writers, like all writers, crack the hard nut of secrecy by publishing personal material. That sufficiently gives the lie to Gay Talese's perverse "revelation" that there are no Italian American novelists because the would-be authors are in dread of offending family and are thus bound by a code of silence. But it does not explain why the *New York Times* gave front-page prominence to Talese's exercise unless it was a willful editorial decision to perpetuate the negative stereotypes of Italian Americans. "They are the last ethnic group America can comfortably mock," playwright John Patrick Shanley noted about some of his own material in a *Time* magazine interview. This assessment was reaffirmed in the *New York Post* by investigative reporter Jack Newfield, who wrote that in America, "Prejudice against Italian Americans is the most tolerated intolerance."

That Italian American women became writers at all is a triumph of assertion and faith over formidable obstacles. Italian American women were taught to keep out of public view: don't step out of line and be noticed, don't be the envy of others, don't attract the jealous fates who will punish success. Italian American women were not brought up with the confidence that makes Jewish women such splendid social activists, such demanding wives and able promoters of themselves; nor have they had the long experience of self-reliance and expressivity in the English language (oral as well as written) that Black women have had. They are not incited and brought together by ancient wrongs as are the Native Americans and Chicanos.

They were, instead, susceptible to the idea that excelling, drawing attention to oneself, was not womanly, not good. This notion was prevalent in a society in which belief in *malocchio*–the evil eye– was present on all levels. One mustn't disconnect from one's immediate group, as a writer must in order to get perspective and unique vision; and one mustn't try to see too much either into oneself or into others; all will bring upon one the curse of separation. The taboo is against being seen as excelling in anything, or in that close seeing which is self-knowledge. Those who see too far–Tiresias, Milton, Galileo–go blind, or, like Cassandra, go unheeded.

Many Italian American women have had a hard time overcoming inner blocks to creative expression because they were not empowered, as female children, to be independent. Typical are women who have had to disengage themselves from internalized messages of unworthiness. Poet Kathy Freeperson, née Telesco, changed her name to indicate her changed perception of herself after leaving her father's tyrannical household. "Shut up—you're not a boy," was what she and her sisters heard growing up. Many Italian American women have heard the same message: "What right have you got to think?" or, "Girls can't have opinions."

Other Italian American writers have undergone a de-ethnicizing influence in higher education and have rejected their own experience (too often portrayed in film and TV as backward and ignorant) in pursuit of so-called universal values which are, transparently, Anglo-American ones. It is, in fact, absurd to think that one can universalize only from Anglo-American models. Jewish writing in America has disproved this.

There is another reason, beyond the question of leisure time and education, that Italian American women have taken long to become writers: they have not been used to intense self-inspection, to writing their thoughts in daily journals; they expressed themselves only in the condoned relief of the confessional where a male figure exonerated and blessed them.

But now the phenomenon of rising expectations has reached everyone. Italian American women have a generation or more of higher education, economic independence has been reached, and many have moved in adulthood from the working class of their birth to the professional middle class.

It is the era of self-birthing, an experience well known to women of ethnic minorities who, lacking models, have, in fact, made their own by creating themselves. Therefore, Tillie Olsen in her splendid book *Silences* says to all the silent women: create yourselves. There is much that is unwritten that needs to be written. Bring into literature what is not there now.

The words of Native American poet Joy Harjo are pertinent: "As I write I create myself again and again . . . We have learned to only touch so much. That is why I write. I want to touch more . . . it frees me to believe in myself . . . to have voice, because I have to; it is my survival."

Italian American women have long been denied the possibility of finding themselves in literature. How could they affirm an identity without becoming familiar with the models by which to perceive themselves? We are what we read, but, in the case of Italian American women writers, we could seldom read who we are.

It is unfortunate that Grazia Deledda, a strong, relevant, and highly pertinent model of an internationally significant writer embodying female values, someone for Italian Americans to emulate, is so little known here.

Unfortunately it was Simone de Beauvoir who became a model for some feminists; the myth of the tough dame, as Mary Gordon has pointed out, took hold as women looked to emulate those who seemed to have made it on their own terms. Contrarian Camille Paglia has championed Madonna as a feminist. But most women have been cruelly deceived in their images of seemingly independent models like Simone de Beauvoir, Katharine Hepburn, and Lillian Hellman, who have all actually revealed in biographies that their man and his interests came first. As Mary Gordon pointed out, de Beauvoir, "the mother of us all . . . died telling us she would have been nothing without the man she loved," i.e., Jean-Paul Sartre, who demeaned her, betrayed her publicly, used her as a procurer for his sexual adventures, expected her to drop her work to help him, and then at the end cruelly humiliated her by depriving her of all access to their joint papers and possessions by naming a young woman, his mistress, as his executor. De Beauvoir is no model: she betrayed the very words she wrote. She wanted other women to do as she said, not as she did. Are women to be left with disturbing questions about choices and no answers?

Ironically, de Beauvoir's biographer, Deirdre Bair (who also wrote a biography of Anaïs Nin, another dubious model), is, despite a nonidentifying first name and married name, of Italian American background, a fact undisclosed in personal accounts of herself. One can only speculate on the positive images she could have brought to many women by using her great skills on other biographical subjects.

Much more relevant as model woman and writer, especially to Italian American women, is Grazia Deledda. It is she who most captures the ideal of accomplishing her life's mission both in her art and in her personal life. She was a self-motivated achieving woman whose sense of her personal mission, movingly depicted in her autobiographical novel *Cosima,* was not set aside for marriage and maternity but successfully combined with those womanly roles.

Born in the most backward and isolated part of Sardinia in 1871, Deledda received only three years of schooling, but continued to teach herself and set herself the task of making her country live in literature. She not only produced a steady stream of literary work (thirty-three novels, eighteen collections of stories, and other writings) in the face of great odds, but saw her life's work honored with a Nobel Prize for Literature in 1926.

Not to be underestimated is the equal achievement of Deledda's having combined family and art in her life. Grazia Deledda was not in the Anglo-American style of the childless great women writers like Jane Austen, George Eliot, Emily Dickinson, Willa Cather, Edith Wharton, Virginia Woolf; she had the support of her Northern Italian husband for her writing career. He and their sons, and family life as a whole, were the necessary sustenance to her art. She needed both.

Deledda fashioned her own destiny to become what she was told (by her family of origin and by society at large) was impossible: a great writer and a happily married mother. And she did it on her terms without denying herself her art or the family she created. She is an amazing figure of achievement—more generous and honest toward life and work than the deceptive, coldly intellectual de Beauvoir.

The name and story of Grazia Deledda were not in schoolbooks as I was growing up, but that is hardly surprising; what surprises is that even with the new surge of interest in women writers and the resurrection of old and forgotten authors, Deledda remains a forgotten woman.

Ellen Moers' *Literary Women,* for instance, is a thick compendium of the great women writers, concentrating mainly on some sixty English, American, and French women of literature, with textual and bibliographic references to worldwide women authors. Grazia Deledda is omitted; the only Italian authors mentioned are in the back-of-the-book appendix: a line for Renaissance poet Vittoria Colonna, two for contemporary novelist Natalia Ginzburg.

That Deledda should be so little known, so overlooked by publishers intent on rescuing so-called lost women writers from oblivion, so missing from the consciousness of Italian American women writers who need precisely and desperately the kind of validation she gives, is just another of the instances of silence in which we have seemed to struggle alone without models, without inspiration.

Unlike Christina Rossetti, who wrote from an internal agony of renunciation and whose art was the bitter fruit of a masochistic abnegation, Deledda did not deny herself. She said she believed in only two things, the family and art for its own sake; these were the only beautiful and true things in life. It has a very Italian ring, and a very sound psychological basis in the feminist theory of Jean Baker Miller, as well as in the earlier writings of eminent psychologist Karen Horney, who identified the dubious split in a woman of public versus domestic life (a dichotomy de Beauvoir insisted on) as "The Flight from Womanhood."

Another undiscovered Italian author is Sibilla Aleramo (1876–1960), whose novel *Una Donna* created a sensation in Europe at the beginning of this century, anticipating feminism and women's liberation by many decades. It was, in fact, in this autobiographical novel that the word "feminism" was used for the first time, and the author's personal suffering was related to the condition of all women. Aleramo's novel has been translated into English as *A Woman* and is a gripping account of the psychological anguish of a creative woman's marriage to a small-minded and stultifying oppressor, and her flight from him at great personal expense. It is a story of courage in a time and place that made her action and subsequent book utterly remarkable. But Aleramo, too, has been missing from the Italian American woman's reservoir of models.

Poets Jean Feraca and Rita Signorelli-Pappas are among a growing number of Italian American writers who have journeyed to Italy and have brought to bear on the ancestral land the unique vision of the American Italian. Feraca's collection *South from Rome: Il Mezzogiorno* is a strong evocation of a deeply felt archetypal Italy as veritable motherland, not merely a tourist pleasure land. And so, too, are Signorelli-Pappas' delicately incised "snapshot" poem-memories of Florence, Venice, Sicily.

Even the relatively few literate and educated Italian women who emigrated to this country would have brought few models of women writers from their culture and few incentives to imitate them. This lack of a literary ancestry from the original culture has presented a significant problem to Italian American women. Whereas English and French women writers have always been strong within their national literatures, the tradition of women writers in Italy, noted by critic Sergio Pacifici in *A Guide to Contemporary Italian Literature*, is relatively recent (notwithstanding those Renaissance exemplars who are often cited to prove that Italian women have long had voice and stature as authors but prove only that women writers in Italy were an isolated class phenomenon, not a national trend). The emergence of nationally known women authors coincided in the late nineteenth century with the unification of Italy as a nation, and the limited social emancipation of women. The liberated postwar Italy of the late 1940s, and the later feminist movement, saw an increase of notable women writers, and, says Pacifici, "Their increasing popularity with the public and the critics represents a significant cultural phenomenon, that may well herald a new era." Previously, relatively few women attained literary distinction, and this, Pacifici asserts, was not surprising in a country where the social order was shaped so exclusively by men. The lack of critical attention he ascribes "Less to an objective question of artistic merit than to critical negligence or a pronounced prejudice against female talent."

This is true no longer in Italy, where some very notable women have attained critical acclaim, but it was until recently notoriously true of Italian American literary men and scholars. The shadows into which Italian American women writers seem to have been cast come not only from male critics, but quite surprisingly also from feminist critics.

In Annis Pratt's introduction to her *Archetypal Patterns in Women's Fiction,* she acknowledges having done, for that study, "close readings of more than three hundred women's novels." Not one of those novels is by an Italian American woman. Writing on the novel of development, Pratt notes that in women's fiction it is more often the story of women "growing down" rather than "growing up." Yet Italian American women are writing of rising expectations and the quest for self-realization. One of these is Dorothy Bryant, whose novel *Ella Price's Journal* is a classic example of the novel of growth–in this case, not of a young male, but of a middle-aged wife and mother.

Bryant's married name, under which she writes, cloaks her Italian American background; and her character–Ella Price–is an Anglo-Saxon Everywoman; but just as the outsider experience is heightened when told from the point of view of the double outsider (the Black, or the Jew), so, too, the woman's experience of being stifled in a male world might have been made even more compelling if Bryant had used her own Italian American background from which to create the story of a woman's growth toward autonomy. The weight of her tradition makes the Italian American woman's experience in moving out of marriage toward autonomy even more dramatic than that of the more assertive Anglo-Saxon or Jewish woman. Did Bryant feel that her book would be given more consideration if she made her characters more "American"? That is a kind of self-censorship to which Italian American writers could be particularly susceptible.

Diana Cavallo's sensitive and introspective novel *A Bridge of Leaves* is written in the first-person voice of a young man whose thoughts and memories record his inner journey from an early self-contained world to full immersion in the world of others that brings him to the crisis and resolution of his maturity. It is a true bildungsroman, and yet the opportunity to narrate it in the female voice to reflect the experience of the Italian American woman was not taken.

Many non-Wasp writers have come to the fore brilliantly—Jewish women writers, African American, Asian American, Native American, Chicano, all have been collected, given critical attention, and, thereby, given presence. The Italian American woman writer seems to belong nowhere. Not minority, not mainstream as Jewish and Black writers now are, she remains without champions or advocates or interpreters. The Italian American woman writer seems to have been stranded in a no-woman's-land where there is small choice: either follow the omnipresent models that do not speak to her own particular experience, or write of her experience and know that it will be treated as of no importance, too "different" for critical attention.

All is not family; it is a dominant theme but not an exclusive one in Italian American literature. Present also is the same theme of alienation in an uncomprehending society that has been so well used by Black and Jewish writers. Cultural dichotomy; divided loyalties; the problems between generations; intermarriage and the problems between the sexes as men and women search for new roles; the tragic consequences of self-doubt and self-hate, of placing honor before truth and possessive "love" before understanding; the stress on "catching up" with America; the loss of heritage—the Italian American experience has it all, and it has all to be told.

Italian American women who write are in the process of redefining themselves and family patterns; they are writing to create models that were never there for themselves; they are writing to know themselves. They write with positive affirmations. The personages they write about are afflated with hope, with the sense of change, with inspiration. They do not affect the "deflation" style of many Anglo-American women writers whose work documents a long period of emptiness and futility in the wispy, stylish voice of mini-malism. Italian American women write from the passion of the out-sider experience, as women whose time has come. They are emerg-ing, not receding, writers.

In a very true sense, the Italian American woman writer had to be a self-made person; lacking a literary tradition, she worked in isolation without models and interpretive critics, struggling with an internal dialectic that was a barometer not only of inner doubts but also of subtle discrimination and rejection; she struggled to become an author, sustained only by the need and impetus of what she is doing.

Why this is so has to do not only with the inner blocks of her tra-dition, but very much, also, with the external obstacles of the sur-rounding society and its prevailing literary hegemonies.

Literary Hegemonies and Oversights: The External Blocks

It becomes usual to hear that there are no Italian American writers of any value; established critics make it so by not noticing them, professors of American literature say it in defense of why Italian American writing is not presented in course work, and an Italian American author of some prominence like Gay Talese says it in the confidence of being the exception. Readers believe it for the simple reason that except for *The Godfather,* they've heard of no other work; no author has been made familiar enough to them to come to mind. It is easy to dismiss what one doesn't know.

The spurious and circular reasoning is this: if there had been any Italian American first-rate authors one would have heard of them. But once that was said of women as a group, too; women writers and women's experience were by definition minor—the male expe-rience was presented as the universal human one. Now we know better.

It is not that Italian Americans have not written work of value; it is that the dominant culture, working under its own rules and mod-els, with a tight network of insiders who are editors, agents, sales-men, reviewers, and critics, is not eager to recognize and include in its lists that which does not reflect its own style, taste, and sense of what is worthwhile, or, more basically, the stereotypes that sell. Af-ter *The Godfather* phenomenon, Mafia themes proved profitable; therefore the rash of books like Nicholas Pileggi's *Wiseguy: Life in a*

Mafia Family and his cousin Gay Talese's *Honor Thy Father* on crime boss Joseph Bonanno, which in turn spawned the editorial decision to have wife Rosalie Bonanno "write" a mass-market book, *Mafia Marriage: My Story*. *Mafia Princess: Growing Up in Sam Giancana's Family,* by Antoinette Giancana and Thomas C. Renner, *Mafia Wife* by Robin Moore with Barbara Fuca, Richard Condon's Prizzi books, and others belong to this subgenre; they were then spun off into feature films and television miniseries. Thus a skewed and stereotypical vision linked to market potential drives out those books which do not deal with the Italian American experience in market-determined ways. Having first created a Mafia market for the general public, publishers then defend their rejection of worthy Italian American material by saying there is no Italian American market for it!

Italian American novelists are not generically second-rate; they handle different material and handle it with the newness, and perhaps rawness—but also drive—of the just-born and self-made writer. Referring to the vividness of her heritage, a Jewish character in Rita Ciresi's title story from the collection *Mother Rocket* says to her Wasp boyfriend, "you're so normal . . . so *American*. I mean, what do you people who aren't ethnic think about all day?"

Literature is not only in the great and practiced writer. It is also in the new voices which add to the store of human experience; in the voices which, by enriching and extending the national literary achievement, become of permanent value.

Italian Americans who accept, uncritically, the estimate of their denigrators that they are unworthy of attention have let themselves be defined in a way that writers of other ethnic groups will no longer tolerate. Rather than examine an excluding system and question its premises, critics have accepted that Italian Americans don't read, therefore they don't buy books, therefore publishers are justified in not publishing Italian American writers. This is not valid reasoning; it is prejudice expressed as market research.

We are long past the stage when Italian Americans were represented by hordes of illiterate just-arrived immigrants. At the end of the twentieth century it is egregiously discriminatory still to single out that ethnic group and say its members don't read or buy books. Yet publishers continue to use this worn-out red herring to justify not publishing more Italian American authors, even though Italian Americans do not write to be read only by Italian Americans any more than the West Indian American author Derek Walcott writes only for West Indian Americans. When Amy Tan's *Joy Luck Club* was published and became an enormous best seller it was not because it was aimed at a restricted Asian American market—*everyone* bought and read the book. It is inconceivable that the publishers of Richard Rodriguez or Sandra Cisneros think only in terms of a Hispanic market for their work or that Louise Erdrich's books are only for a Native American market. The fact is that all those writers are Americans, writing for the whole American public and not just parts of it. The same is true of Italian Americans.

A subcategory of "ethnic writing" was contrived as the catchall for what didn't fit mainstream. This is itself a peculiar notion: a mainstream is not a body unto itself but exists by being fed from tributaries, and in literature those tributaries are the feeders which contribute to the whole body of the national literature. That the writings of some American writers are marginal and not part of the cultural mainstream of the American literary world but exist, at best, in a backwater of folklore and curiosities, is an outdated concept that is finally being addressed in the outpouring of multicultural writing. In 1992 this was officially recognized when Derek Walcott was awarded the Nobel Prize in Literature for his "multicultural vision and commitment." The opening may have come at last for many writers who have been overlooked as ethnic or marginal because of the homogenizing tendency to portray a society of uniform values rather than the lively cultural pluralism which is the reality of American life.

It can be fairly claimed that Italian American writing in a limited amount *did* and *does* get published; that there is no concerted effort to keep Italian American authors from being published. Thus, John Fante's inspired production (*Wait until Spring, Bandini!, Ask the Dust,* and *Dago Red*) and other novels did get published. But they were not really noticed or taken up in any way. They languished and died for want of advocates.

It can be said, also, that there is no concerted conspiracy of silence on the part of reviewers or literary critics to exclude mention of Italian American writing. How could there be! To organize a conspiracy would imply recognition of a body of literature that is, instead, more conveniently marginalized by simply being ignored.

A novel using Italian American material, when written by an Italian American author, is all but invisible, while the use of that material by authors of other backgrounds seems to receive attention as, for instance, *The Immigrants* by Howard Fast; *The Little Conquerors* by Ann Abelson; *Principato* by Thomas McHale; *Household Saints* by Francine Prose; *Fly Away Home* by Marge Piercy; and the very successful theater and screenplays *Moonstruck* and *Italian American Reconciliation* by John Patrick Shanley.

In a country this size, comprising such rich and varied strains, there is room for all facets of literary expression, and there should be the opportunity to become familiar with them. But that is not the case. There are hierarchies and hegemonies which, consciously or not, promote and decide what is literature and what is not. The facts of literary life are elementary: it is not simply publication, but attention before and after that counts.

Mary Gordon once told an Authors Guild symposium, "reviews have a tremendous impact on book sales . . . books which are not reviewed are buried." And that is what happens to the overwhelming majority of books that are published without being signaled for attention by powerful names: they die. And unfortunately Italian American authors have no national advocates either within their group or without.

Nothing exists comparable to the so-called Jewish family of editors and critics who promote their own; or the group of Black writers who, feeling that Toni Morrison was not receiving adequate recognition, published in the *New York Times Book Review* a "testament of thanks" to Morrison for advancing "the moral and artistic standards by which we must measure the daring and the love of our national imagination and our collective intelligence as people." *That* is support.

Books that are not reviewed in the *New York Times,* the closest thing we have to a national paper, are seldom picked up elsewhere along the tightly linked chain of literary life. Literary achievement is gauged by appearance in required reading lists, literature course outlines, textbooks, anthologies, critical appraisals, book reviews, bibliographies, and even jacket blurbs. All things that Italian American writers have been largely excluded from because they lack the interest and support of well-placed people to boost them.

Strategies exist to exclude writing that is considered marginal. Jules Chametzky, a scholar of cultural pluralism as reflected in American literature, has shown how the publication of regional literature became, toward the end of the nineteenth century, "a strategy for ignoring or minimizing social issues of great significance." Regional novels substituted for those dealing with race, class, the new money power, America's new ethnic composition, and the challenges to engrained social assumptions and mores. Ignoring the themes that called for serious literary treatment but could upset notions of a unified national culture, local color and regional literature, which reinforced notions of a basically homogenous rather than a conflicted nation and culture, was focused on by editors and accepted by the public.

Katherine Newman, a literary scholar and critic, sees as one characteristic of American literature (particularly relevant from the ethnic perspective) eccentricity in its exact meaning of off-center, asymmetrical, irregular, uneven. That explains the uniqueness and marvelous strangeness of Pietro Di Donato's powerful 1939 novel, *Christ in Concrete*. That explains, also, other facets of Italian American fiction, with its "extraneous" material, eccentricity of style and language, distortions of character like the raging father in John Fante's *Brotherhood of the Grape,* and the often ambiguous attitude of the implied authors. That is not to be wondered at; Newman quotes other studies to show that implied authors of ethnic novels tend to be schizoid, that is, in conflict between the values of their ethnic groups and those of the majority group.

This very off-centeredness—and it is relevant to note that Barbara Grizzuti Harrison's collection of intelligent essays is aptly entitled *Off Center*—of Italian American literature should be valuable in itself; ethnic literary scholarship stands for understanding material that, before, under a policy of literary apartheid, was often excluded because measured by nonapplicable standards.

Like the feminists, ethnic literary scholars opt for a humanist criticism that transcends narrow views of what people are or should be; it should breach the Establishment walls that Mario Puzo, in his own way, set out to scale by writing *The Godfather.* For it was when he made the deliberate effort to embrace the condoned formulae and stereotypical characters of mainstream writing that Puzo was admitted to the club of visible writers. Applauding him for playing the game was Rose Basile Green in *The Italian American Novel* when she noted, "An Italian American novelist, Mario Puzo, has pried open the box that has secreted the sacred blackballs of the American literary club."

But it is not that kind of pandering to violent themes or the deliberate commercialization of the story that should relate Italian American fiction to the American mainstream. Rather, it is another characteristic of American literature that Newman identified as deriving from the pressure of pluralism: "The chief preoccupation of our writers is *choice-making....*"

The necessity of choice—the old ways or the new? one's loyalty to family or self?—has always been implicit in the main thrust of Italian American writing. Italian Americans are laden with conflicted choices in loyalties and roles, with contradictions within the tradition, with ambivalence in life. It is not always a cause for optimism—seeking resolution of conflict is painful—but it *is* affirmation, it is using one's native strength and wit, it is autonomy. And that seems to be the direction in which Italian American writing is propelled.

The women authors of Italian American background who have dealt with their ethnic material have been the ephemerids of literature, fated to have a creative lifespan as brief as that of the mayfly. They were born, in a literary sense, already out of step by virtue of their themes. They were given no notice by reviewers, which meant they went out of print swiftly and receded into the silence from which they came without having made a ripple in the mainstream of American writing. It is a demoralizing and chastising experience. A writer must be given the opportunity to publish at least two or three books in order to have a substantial voice, a presence. Many Italian American women never get beyond the first book because the lack of response and attention makes a publisher unwilling to risk further. Frequently a complete literary oeuvre remains unknown, unavailable. Italian American male authors have undoubtedly faced these same barriers as well.

We falsify literary history if we don't record all voices and give access to these voices by publishing, keeping in print, and making part of study courses those writers who are not merely the commercially prominent ones of the dominant tradition. As Newman says, the critical function is to examine works on their own aesthetic terms, to relate them to the entire corpus of American literature, and to overcome the internalized stereotypes and cultural myths that have caused critical myopia.

Publishers have been slow to receive Italian Americans outside of the safe stereotypes of a warm people with comical behavior (*Mount Allegro, Brotherhood of the Grape*) or Mafia criminals and connections. They are cool to the complexities of human nature portrayed in minority or ethnic groups–they prefer racial tensions for Blacks, gangsterism and family solidarity for Italians, and complicated emotions or angst only in Wasps or Jews.

Genevieve Belfiglio, publisher of *Real Fiction,* explains that she founded that publication of short stories out of frustration, because her experience was that "Major publishing firms attempt to mainstream fiction, at the expense not only of writers, but readers as well since only a narrow range of experience and style is acceptable." This is confirmed by publishers who accept material which conforms to their notion of what the market wants; such an attitude fosters sales, not literature.

Publishers say they cannot afford to be crusaders. But Black writer Zora Neale Hurston replied that she refused to be humbled by second place in a contest she never designed, and she identified what comes out of safe, marketable publishing as candidates for the American Museum of Unnatural History, i.e., a weird collection of stereotypes and nondimensional figures that can be taken in at a glance: the expressionless American Indian, the shuffling Negro, the nonarticulate Italian, and so on.

Before it was published in 1986, my novel *Love in the Middle Ages* was rejected by one publisher because it didn't "seem right" that the Italian American woman character was the achiever and her Jewish lover was not; it was said to appear anti-Semitic, and the publisher suggested that the roles be reversed. Of course! Then the formula would have been observed–the same one that John Sayles used in his film *Baby, It's You,* which is the story of two high school lovers: he's an Italian greaser who takes woodwork and she's a Jewish princess who's the president of the drama club and headed for Sarah Lawrence. She, it's understood, will get over her transitory sexual attraction to Sheik (his nickname derives from a condom) because she is going to be someone and he isn't. Hardly anyone of Italian American background hasn't encountered that slur in real life. With Dorothy Bryant (who was then Dorothy Calvetti, and at the top of her class), it occurred when a teacher said to her, "You can't be Italian, where were your people from?" Near Turin, said Dorothy. Then, said the teacher, relieved, they could be of Germanic origin.

The exclusionary practices in the publishing world where Italian Americans are not perceived as literary writers but, at best, writers of romance, suspense, or young adult books, seem to parallel the school's tracking ones: Italian Americans were routinely tracked into vocational courses rather than college-oriented ones. In her lead essay in *Crossing Ocean Parkway: Readings by an Italian American Daughter,* Marianna De Marco Torgovnick described her high school experience: "Although my scores are superb, the guidance counselor has recommended the secretarial track; when I protested, the conference with my parents was arranged. . . . My father also prefers the secretarial track, but he wavers, half proud of my aberrantly high scores, half worried. I press the attack, saying that if I were Jewish I would have been placed, without question, in the academic track. . . . I am allowed to insist on the change into the academic track."

Publishers do not like Italian American characters to be individuals, to be complex, to be alive and contradictory, subject to the pulls of tensions and defeats of doubt, subject to losses and gains and changes. Instead the cultural myth perceives them in very rigid, demeaning, stick-figure dimensions. And so Italian American authors often get around this by giving their characters non-Italian names, disguising their material.

That Italian American women writers have been underpublished is undeniable; just as exclusionary, however, is that the few who are published are not kept on record and made accessible, even bibliographically, in libraries and in study courses. Not only do Italian American women writing their own stories publish with great difficulty, but once in print they must confront an established cadre of criticism that seems totally devoid of the kind of insight that could relate to their work.

Italian American names were notably missing in essays such as the *New York Times*'s "Women Playwrights: New Voice for the Theater," where no mention was made of Donna DeMatteo, Karen Malpedet or even Nina Faso, producer of *Godspell*. In the *Times* piece "Brooklyn, Borough of Writers," a lot of names were dropped but not those of authors Barbara Grizzuti Harrison or Daniela Gioseffi, who were both published Brooklynites at that time.

It is not only in reviews and essays, but also in feature articles and in letters it chooses not to print that the *Times* can marginalize authors and practice a kind of censorship.

Herbert Mitgang began a *Times* review of Italian stories with this statement: "Sicily is better known as the spawning ground of the Mafia than as the home place of an unusually large number of pioneering novelists, poets and playwrights." Certainly a backhanded way of acknowledging (without naming them) literary giants like Verga, Pirandello, Vittorini, Sciascia, and Lampedusa. And even as Mitgang managed to slip in the *Times*'s favorite M-word.

Times film reviewer Caryn James wrote of the film *Once Around,* "It is too obvious to say that Francis Ford Coppola and Martin Scorsese capture the texture of Italian-American families more sharply than Lasse Hallstrom [director of *Once Around*]. What matters is that *The Godfather* and *Goodfellas* create *believable* ethnic characters instead of shallow ethnic types."

This weighted verdict on "believable" Italian American characters is all the more offensive since Ms. James has previously been on record as sensitive to poor depictions of other ethnic groups: reviewing the Spike Lee film *Mo' Better Blues,* she called the seamy characterizations of Mo and Josh Flatbush "disturbing Jewish stereotypes." It is not unusual that the prevailing climate at the *Times* allows a double standard for what is "good" stereotyping as against what is "disturbing."

By not reviewing authors, by the almost zero presence of Italian American surnames on bylines, and even by neglecting our letters to the editor, the *Times* contributes to a perceived lack of Italian American status, and a negative cultural image. This, in turn, reinforces the low self-esteem that has been documented among Italian American students as contributing to a high dropout rate in the city school system.

On the other hand, coverage of Italian American affairs becomes full when a reputed Mafia godfather or an incident of racism is being covered. It was apparent in reading the reportage of the Bensonhurst or Howard Beach incidents that there was a peculiar slant in the way Italian Americans were depicted and their speech was reported, while no probing effort was made to understand the complexity of their community fears and frustrations. Disconcerting was the *New York Times*'s emphasis on Italian Americans' poor use of language on the one hand, while on the other it seems to exclude from its pages many of us who are practiced writers.

Then there were the weighted descriptions of people in the neighborhood: "Young women with baroque hair and their names spelled out in gold necklaces wear tight slacks and spike heels." Were there ever equivalent stories on Blacks or Hispanics or Jews or Koreans so peppered with odd words and phrases, or such personal descriptions, to single them out in a deprecating way? Such personalizing has even appeared gratuitously in a theater review, where critic David Richards took note of "Laura San Giacomo's vulgarity" and "native sullenness" and then decided that this fine actress (just think of her in *Sex, Lies, and Videotape*) has little acting skill to accompany those offensive personal attributes.

Multiplied inexorably, year after year, author after author, and never redressed, or even acknowledged, this kind of press adds to a general misperception and mockery of a whole group, coupled with a reluctance to review their books.

After the reviewer, it is the critic who takes the long view and decides what becomes part of the canon. The African American critic Henry Louis Gates, Jr., has done extraordinary service to the career of Toni Morrison. He has written of her and brought her to national attention. There has been no equivalent Italian American critic either with a national audience, or with an agenda to further the career of an Italian American writer.

Next in the ring of exclusion are editors of collections and bibliographic tools, like the powerful H. W. Wilson Company, who deny admittance into their bibliographic retrieval tools to those who have not been reviewed in the publications which the Wilson Company chooses to scan. The *Book Review Digest* lists fiction reviewed in at least four journals on Wilson's approved list of some one hundred sources (compared with the Gale Company's *Book Review Index* which reports on any book reviewed, no matter how often and no matter where, from four hundred twenty-two sources). The Wilson Company effectively discriminates against ethnic, counterculture, or minority writers who are reviewed in journals outside conventional sources. In effect, the reviewing medium, not the book itself, is being judged. Omitted from the *Book Review Digest,* for instance, have been books by Mary Caponegro, Cris Mazza, Jeanne Schinto, and Mary-Ann Tirone Smith. Such a distorted selection of what writing by and about a particular ethnic group will be part of the national literature is another aspect of literary apartheid.

When teachers, editors, and compilers consult the Wilson volumes for, say, the names of authors who are writing about Italian Americans so that they can be included in syllabi, presented at conferences, studied and commented on, they are naturally led to the conclusion that there are pitifully few Italian American authors, and of those few, *no women at all*. Without entry in Wilson's *Short Story*

Index, Fiction Catalog, Book Review Digest, Standard Catalog for Public Libraries, etc., the nonlisted author becomes a "lost" one—difficult for a teacher, compiler, or researcher to pick up except by hearsay.

I would never suggest that only Italian Americans can write of themselves. But to emphasize, as the *Fiction Catalog* does, that the "the best fiction" on Italian Americans is done by non–Italian American authors is to create a record that is skewed, biased, and eminently flawed.

By ignoring the cultural and literary pluralism reality of the second half of this century in the United States, the Wilson library tools have made themselves irrelevant to what is happening in American literature and cannot be consulted as a reliable guide to what fiction is being produced, published, and read in representation of various American ethnic groups.

William Vance, who produced the notable two-volume work *America's Rome* (1989), included only three Italian American writers (William Murray, John Ciardi, and Dana Gioia) in his examination of American fiction writers and poets in Rome, noting that a lack of visibility led him to conclude that possibly there weren't many Italian American writers.

The lack of visibility Professor Vance referred to is directly related to exclusions from the *Fiction Catalog*. From the inception of subject listings in 1941 through the thirteenth edition of 1996, the listings under the subject heads "Italian Americans" or "Italians in the United States" have been quite ludicrous.

The Wilson Company persists in demeaning the category "Italian Americans" with its longest-running entry (listed since 1957!), Max Shulman's outdated satire of suburbia, *Rally Round the Flag, Boys*. Even when available, Shulman's slight novel was entirely inappropriate as representative of Italian Americans, using them only as stereotypes along with the two other groups being lampooned, New England Yankees and New York commuters. The only other entries in the *Fiction Catalog* under "Italian American" were for Reynolds Price and Anna Quindlen.

Almost equally equivocal is a previous listing under "Italians–New York, NY," which lists Jimmy Breslin, Bernard Malamud, Howard Fast, Mario Puzo, Francine Prose, Richard Condon, and Robert J. Waller as having written on the subject. One has to wonder why only one Italian American–Mario Puzo, represented not by his

most respected book, *The Fortunate Pilgrim* but by *The Godfather*–
was thought to have written meaningfully on the subject. Or why,
in one edition, Mary Lee Settle's book about Italian coal miners in
West Virginia was featured, but not Denise Giardina's well-received
works on the same subject, *Storming Heaven* and *The Unquiet Earth*.
Or why there was a heading "Jews in Vermont" but none for "Italians in Vermont," thus overlooking Mari Tomasi's novel *Like Lesser
Gods* on the Italian granite workers.

When law professor Thomas Shaffer sent me a reprint of his
article from the *Notre Dame Law Review* where novels on Italian
Americans were mentioned, he wrote, "I turned up *Umbertina* as
soon as I began to do research on Italian Americans. I cannot remember who recommended it. . . . If I were asked today where to
begin such an inquiry I would recommend *Umbertina* above all
else." And yet, if he had tried to locate source material through reference guides such as the Wilson *Fiction Catalog,* he would never
have found my work listed, nor that of any Italian American woman
writer.

Novels by Italian American women writers on Italian American
subjects have never been listed by the Wilson Catalog, except one
by the unidentifiably Italian American Anna Quindlen.

It is, again, for Italian American women writers like never having
been published at all except for that minute inner circle of friends
who may have heard personally of the event–certainly such work is
not "published" in the true sense of being made public and accessible. It's as if the writing of Italian American women were some fas-
tidiously secret pursuit, a distilling of a rare liqueur not to be shared.

There are other areas of bibliographic oversight:

- No Italian American novels were listed in the category of family chronicles in the bibliography of *American Historical Fiction* until the fifth edition.
- Through the fourth revision of *The Literary History of the United
  States,* which is still the current edition in library holdings, no
  mention is made of authors of Italian American background
  except for the eighteenth-century political writer Filippo Maz-
  zei and for Mozart's librettist, Lorenzo Da Ponte.
- *Contemporary Literary Critics* (1977) lists 115 American and
  British critics. Missing, along with the eminent critic Bernard
  De Voto, is any other Italian name.

- In *The Ethnic American Woman* (1978), a collection of writings
  of ninety-five women authors from twenty-four ethnic groups,
  the Italian American group is represented by one entry, the
  writer of a scholarly paper, as compared with other groups
  amply represented by literary writers of novels and poetry.
- *The Columbia Literary History of the United States* (1988) is woefully inadequate in citing two nineteenth-century authors of
  "ghetto" novels and then skipping entire generations of Italian American writers such as Di Donato, Tomasi, Fante, et al.
  only to arrive at the "new journalism" as practiced by Gay
  Talese.
- *American Women Writers* (1983) includes one Italian American woman writer (again, unidentifiable by name), Frances
  Winwar. Lina Mainiero, editor of that four-volume set and of
  Italian background herself, told me she was predisposed to
  include Italian American women but said there were none
  that she could find; unless writers had been carried in anthologies or mentioned in literary criticism, or had won awards,
  there was no way to locate them.

  That justification was not really credible: Mari Tomasi had
  been named one of ten outstanding novelists of the year in
  1940; *Buying Time: An Anthology Celebrating Twenty Years of the
  Literature Program of the National Endowment for the Arts,* published prior to the time of Mainiero's compilation, lists Italian American award recipients Helen Barolini, Diane diPrima,
  Joan Castagnoni Eades, and Leslie Scalapino. The UNICO
  national literary awards for Italian American authors have
  been in operation since before the Mainiero compilation and
  Jeanne Schinto was a recipient in 1982. Perhaps an expecta-
  tion that there would be no Italian American women writers
  canceled out the motivation for a search.
- *American Women Poets* (1986), of which Harold Bloom is the
  editor, and *Modern American Women Writers* (1991), edited by
  Elaine Showalter, both omit Diane diPrima, the most important counterculture woman poet of the fifties and still actively
  writing.

These examples reinforce the self-perpetuating myth on the part of
readers, editors, professors (and the demoralizing perception among
Italian Americans themselves) that Italian American literature *is*
second rate because if it weren't, it would be included in reference

tools and collections; would be issued in paperback or series; would be anthologized, collected, selected, recommended, discussed, analyzed, and put in course offerings.

Exclusion leads Italian American writers to the Kafkaesque conviction that their writing is not worthy of being included. To emerge from this dismal swamp requires enlightenment on the part of denigrators; an end to stereotyping of Italian Americans in the media and in publishing; a wide diffusion of the literary contributions made by Italian American writers; an increase on the part of reviewers and critics in sensitivity and ability to explicate the particular experience and relate it to the dominant culture–and of teachers who will promulgate the work because they need it and want it but have to know *it is there!*

Among ethnic groups, Jews have become excellent critics, literary scholars, tastemakers. The officially recognized minority groups–Hispanic Americans, Asian Americans, African Americans, and Native Americans–have benefited from grants and the critical attention of liberals eager to right the wrongs of racism, and are doing some of the most interesting work published today. There is an abundance of multicultural anthologies and collections featuring minority authors. They have been championed by the Before Columbus Foundation, which has been giving out American Book Awards since 1978 that, for the first time, respect and honor excellence in American literature without regard to best-seller lists or publishers' promotion.

In the wake of the feminist movement, the lost women writers of the past have been exhumed, explained, reprinted, and made known. They have been published by the Feminist Press and university presses, and have become entries in the volumes of *Notable American Women* and other sets. Naturally, Anglo-American women predominate, but entries from other groups can be found–all, that is, except for the Italian American group; one is left to ask why Sister Blandina Segale or Renata Brunorini, a playwright and actress at the beginning of this century, or novelist Mari Tomasi is not entered when many more marginal women of Anglo-American background are. The Feminist Press since its inception in 1976 has had a mission of recuperating women authors who were lost or neglected but it wasn't until 1997 that Tina DeRosa's *Paper Fish* became the first Italian American novel on their list.

Editors and publishers have engaged in a great deal of "vertical" expansion with still more diaries and autobiographies of unknown "American housewives and writers," predominantly of Anglo-Saxon origin, and always documenting the same experiences; little attempt has been made to go horizontally into truly new areas to find other voices and to reach into experience that is not the conformist Anglo-American one. Recently Louise DeSalvo's memoir *Vertigo* and Barbara Grizzuti Harrison's *An Accidental Autobiography* have broken new ground, and there's been a reissue of Diane diPrima's *Memoirs of a Beatnik*.

In the last decade and a half of the century, Italian American women writers have received awards for work of distinction: Mary Bush and Cris Mazza received PEN/Nelson Algren awards for fiction; Jeanne Schinto's story "Caddies' Day" was among the twenty selected for *Best American Stories 1984*, where Mary Caponegro was listed in the Honorable Mentions. Helen Barolini's "How I Learned to Speak Italian" was selected for *The Best American Essays 1998*. Caponegro has had the American Academy's Prix de Rome; Agnes Rossi's first collection of short stories was awarded New York University's first fiction prize and publication by that press; Rita Ciresi's collection *Mother Rocket* won a Flannery O'Connor Award for Short Fiction; and Donna Masini's poetry collection *That Kind of Danger* was the winner of the 1993 Barnard New Women Poets Prize. The May Sarton Award to Maria Mazziotti Gillan was in recognition not only of her poetry, but also of her efforts to diffuse poetry to unreached audiences through her founding and directing of the Paterson Poetry Center.

The difference between neglect and respect can be the network of support which one has in the academic world, in the publishing industry, in the media. Recommendations for writers' colonies, panel appearances, grants, readings all count. It is an America still to be discovered by Italian American women writers.

Affirmations

Though the exclusions for Italian American women as writers have been great and the barriers formidable, still, there is an answer. If others have not taken the subject of Italian American writing seriously, the writers can do so by becoming themselves the teachers and critics of their experience. That is what Black women writers have said and done. And that is what our own tradition counsels: in the Sicilian version of the Noah's Ark story, after God chose two of all His creatures to go aboard the ark, the fleas found they had been forgotten. So they slipped on by getting into Noah's beard. As the Sicilians say, "If God forgets us, we must use our own wits."

An answer also lies in time, time for Italian American women writers to become economically able to support their writing, time to add depth to the habit of writing, to explore and experiment stylistically with the language, to retell old stories with new insights, to articulate in an authentic way the Italian American experience.

The evidence shows that an Italian American literary record exists and that women are part of it. Yet that body of work remains largely unreissued by publishers and unexamined by critics; it has still to be made known to a wide public, and put into libraries and on reading lists. For Italian American women it is a continuing "ordeal of the woman writer"—the words identifying a tape-recorded conversation among Erica Jong, Marge Piercy, and Toni Morrison to discuss the difficulties *they* faced in getting recognition. Each published and reviewed at the time, if those three prominent writers could speak of "ordeal," it makes all the more compelling by comparison the hurdles faced by disadvantaged Italian American women writers. Earlier, Virginia Woolf, though privileged by birth with connections to the English literary milieu and intellectual elite, had lamented the obstacles and self-doubt inherent in being a woman writer. How hollow those laments sound to the aspiring writer with the wrong name, with no contacts or associations within the publishing network, and with few or no literary antecedents! For Italian American women who have been struggling under burdens of poor education, dependency, traditional roles, and prejudicial stereotyping in the publishing world, the obstacles to their acceptance as writers are still formidable.

A whole new form of literary criticism based on psychoanalyst Karen Horney's theories, and the new insights from ethnotherapy, could most appropriately be applied to developing Italian American writing. Horney had a comprehensive approach to experience, and, proceeding from her studies of alienation, her work focused on the unblocking of neuroses which hindered growth of personality and the full maturation of a person. Her concrete focus is extremely relevant to an analysis of realistic literature and very applicable to the feelings of unworthiness, low expectations, and self-doubt experienced and revealed by Italian American women. Dr. Bernard

Paris, applying Horney's theories to the study of literature, has identified a Third Force psychology which goes beyond Freudianism and behaviorism to recognize a third principle—the evolutionary and constructive force in human beings which represents the drive toward self-actualization. This formulation seems extremely applicable to the growth-oriented direction of Italian American writing, which often proceeds from a sense of alienation to reach toward newly articulated self-awareness. Further, cultures themselves can be evaluated in terms of a universal norm of psychological health, for misguided values can also manifest themselves in societies as a whole. As Dr. Paris has stated, "Those things are good in a culture which satisfy the basic needs of its members and foster their full human growth, those things are bad which frustrate the basic needs and induce self-alienation."

Depth psychologist Angelyn Spignesi set out on a bold new track in her first book, *Starving Women*. Exploring the female psyche, she finds the anorexic woman enacts a war against traditions binding her to earth, food, body, reproduction. In wording seemingly colored by her own background, she identifies the anorexic as "the carrier of the starving woman in every person, the female starving to be nourished by the underworld from which she has been cut off for centuries," confined as she was to the world of matter (*mater*) and the literal kitchen, and identified exclusively with aspects of emotion and nurturance, while men were free to scale the heights of intellectual soaring or descend to the imaginative night realm of the other "under" world. An unwitting affirmation of Spignesi's starving woman theory was given me by the novelist Kenny Marotta when he observed of the female characters in *Umbertina*, "all those psychically malnourished, starving women, all women with a doomed wish for a nurturing mother, all with the painful vacuum they must mourn."

More recently Donna Masini's poem "Hunger" in her award-winning collection *That Kind of Danger* reiterates the theme:

> Deprived of a kind of salt I grew
> to an insatiable craving.
> I tried to eat rocks. I snapped
> shut on a terrible hunger.

Spignesi's search for the female self is quite opposite to Camille Paglia's defense of a patriarchal vision of culture; in Spignesi's view, an artificial opposition between Mother and Father resulted in the male-female dichotomy that is at the bottom of Western civilization. The culture has been set up to perpetuate opposition—the separation between Father and Mother and all that it implies in right/wrong, good/bad.

Spignesi does not propose destroying Father to enthrone Mother, but reviewing the narrow domination of one psyche (the male) and its one "way-of-seeing" while more deeply exploring the female psyche. She suggests (quite in contrast to Paglia's old-fashioned and contentious system of opposition between Apollonian male and Dionysian female) that we no longer imagine the female as opposite; by refusing to think in opposites, we can instead take "Mother and Father as continually in motion, without hierarchy, within one another yet with precise distinction and differentiation."

Spignesi, more original and independent than Paglia, ventures into the new realm of women's unconscious rather than seconding what has been predetermined by *previous male* texts. Spignesi's work is an incisive insight into the position of women vis-à-vis their mothers, and especially pertinent to Italian American women, for whose mothers sons come first, and then husbands—a finding reinforced by Dr. Aileen Riotto Sirey's work in ethnotherapy.

Spignesi's is a clear call to creative women: "an invitation to all of us 'hysterics' to begin to write on our own from the psyche which is our own and inherently that of woman. . . . It is time for women to enter the unfamiliar chasm of our own psychological terrain and to carry this up in aesthetic endeavour." Her emphasis on that goal is very much in the tradition of those who articulated the bridge from the dream realm to literary imagination.

Among the theoretical questions that scholar Katherine Newman poses for a critical framework by which to evaluate ethnic literature is this: what are the causes that bring about the production of literature by writers of an ethnic group? To which Italian American women could answer: the need to know ourselves, to create our models, to write the stories that need telling, and to bring into being the works that are missing and that need to be read.

In the broadest sense, that is the function of literature. Literature gives us ourselves.

As a group, Italian American women have angles of vision and particular perceptions which are a needed part of the revitalizing multicultural factor in this country's national literature. Using the strengths of their foremothers, but now for artistic rather than economic growth, Italian American women can authorize themselves to give their story to waiting readers.

Perhaps the first step is the keeping of journals, the writing of autobiography or memoirs. The volume *Women's Autobiography* contains a whole chapter entitled "In Search of the Black Self," affords much material by Anglo-American and Jewish women, but has not a single entry for an Italian American woman—no excerpt from Sister Blandina's journal, Bella Visono Dodd's *School of Darkness,* Barbara Grizzuti Harrison's *Visions of Glory,* or Diane diPrima's *Memoirs of a Beatnik.*

A body of autobiographical work has still to be developed to illuminate points of contact with a common past as well as to reveal the inner lives of Italian American women. Black women have realized the importance of the personal voice as part of the long, united march toward recognition. Black autobiographies, they say, help rend the veil of white definitions that misrepresent a person to him- or herself and to the world. Creating a new identity can create a new literature.

In the past the Italian American woman expressed herself orally. The oral-history narrators were natural poets, as in the case of "Hands: A Love Poem" transcribed from his mother's spoken words by Ross Talarico and appearing in Janet Zandy's collection, *Calling Home: Working Class Women Writing.*

The great range of poetry by Italian American women extends from the oral tradition to today's stylistic sophistication and eroticism. Italian American women have "made their bones" in poetry, from the intimate revelations of poets Daniela Gioseffi and Maria Mazziotti Gillan, to Sandra Gilbert's accomplished and warmly personal family recollections in her collection *Blood Pressure* (1988) and to the recent poetry collection so aptly titled *Campanile* with its Italian echo of one's home place by Southwestern poet Linda Monacelli-Johnson. Or the poet might be her own publisher. "Show respect! Subscribe!" badgers Rose Romano of malafemmina press. Like a stand-up comedian, in a collection called *Vendetta,* she stresses a blue-collar past and present, writes fast and smart, and presents herself defiantly vaunting all her differences ("I'm a Sicilian-Italian-American Lesbian / the scum of the scum of the scum"). At a total stylistic remove is the linguistic and surrealist transcendence of Ree Dragonette and Leslie Scalapino.

Unique in her half-century of writing is Diane diPrima who, having started on an academic route, dropped out to use her drive in a highly original way. She has become the most enduring of the fifties counterculture poets, a Zen teacher, an activist in social causes, and the founder of a school in San Francisco. Even when not specifically evoking an Italian American milieu, Diane diPrima's prodigious material has a rich thread of her Italian American background running through it—her preoccupation with the children, the meals, the honoring of her anarchist grandfather.

The Italian American woman is more confident now of her place in the world, and this is reflected in the emergence of an educated and emancipated generation which is more given to looking out at a world greater than that mirrored in family. These are the young women who continue their education, have careers, marry outside their group, and ecumenically fashion a mode of living from both traditions.

They signify a new school of young women writers of Italian American background who easily "pass" into the American mainstream of writing without overt ethnic tones in their material to keep them marginalized; some, despite Italian surnames, are only partially of Italian heritage, as, for instance, Tina DeRosa, Carole Maso, Leslie Scalapino, Mary Caponegro, Anna Quindlen, and Agnes Rossi. Intermarriage has bequeathed a new generation of writers who bring a differing viewpoint to their material.

Carole Maso's acclaimed first novel, *Ghost Dance,* introduced two Italian American grandparents portrayed with remarkable insight and understanding, who nonetheless remained free of the emotional overlay of either reverence or bitterness with which an older generation of Italian American writers might have imbued them. Maso writes with great literary mastery, deliberately eschewing the linear narrative mode (associated with male dominance of the novel form) for a more circular weaving and interlacing—female skills—of tempi and themes.

Mary Bush (originally Bucci) writes obliquely of the Italian American experience, but it can be intuited in her short fiction collection *A Place of Light* which was called "compelling stories of everyday existence . . . a treasury of the working-class American voice." Also in that voice are certain nuances and overtones which are strongly Italian American. In her collection, the story "Bread" centers on a young girl's impressions as she recovers from an operation, not yet convinced she's survived, and it's set against an easily recognizable

Italian American background. Ole Papa in her story "Difficult Passage" has all the resonance of the old Italian patriarch. Both stories are not Italian American per se, but the authenticity of tone identifies them.

Jeanne Schinto (the spelling of whose surname, Scinto, was remedied to help Americans pronounce it in the Italian way) is a fiction writer of great promise, who moves easily between stories of an Italian American milieu such as "The Boathouse," "The Disappearance," and "Before Sewing, One Must Cut" from her collection *Shadow Bands* to those of the larger experience as exemplified in her novel *Children of Men* with its focus on a black-white relationship.

Anna Quindlen's fiction focuses on family relationships in a very contemporary way. Ellen, a character in *One True Thing,* reflects, "How much of family life is a vast web of misunderstandings—a tinted and touched-up family portrait, an accurate representation of fact that leaves out only the essential truth." *Object Lessons* deals with a young girl's coming of age, and in *Black and Blue* a battered wife strives to reinvent the idea of family for herself and her son from the sorry remnants of what went before.

Quindlen seems a transition figure in the passage from the older storyteller to the newer generation of fiction writer. The case of Anna Quindlen is unusual in another respect. As with Mary Gordon, though her name masks it, she is part Italian on her mother's side; she was formerly in a position of high visibility on the *New York Times* and had unparalleled exposure and national name recognition through her syndicated column. From *Living out Loud,* a collection of her *New York Times* columns, Quindlen gave her history: "I believe in my own past. . . . I could no more say I am not Catholic than say I am not Irish, not Italian."

All these younger women are stylistically adept, and some more detached from narrative than others. The old robust vitality and passion for storytelling, for telling and retelling the story of the Italian exodus to the new world and what happened to displaced peasants in the great urban ghettoes and what became of their dually conflicted children seem to be gone now. The focus is more on interior life; little moments are prolonged and evoked in a minimalist manner more attuned to mainstream writing.

Mary Caponegro's "Sebastian," from her collection *The Star Café,* is a story of an Englishman and his disconcertions. The writing is certainly crafted, brilliant, and well reviewed; but it is also mannered and studied, and the sense of struggle that moved the earlier women to write is now absorbed into the writing itself. The themes of earlier novels—how to make one's place in a seeming alien society; how to become educated and evolved enough to move into that society; how to combine work and family; how, in fact, to separate from family in order to hang onto one's self without losing everything—have almost been put aside in favor of internal moments told in polished prose.

It was creativity itself that captured the imagination of Carole Maso in *Ghost Dance*, as it does in Mary Caponegro's story "Materia Prima." In this finely written, well-conceived parable of the will to creative expression which brooks no constraints, a young girl's obsession for ornithology is the metaphor for any creative passion. Paralleling Spignesi's "starving woman," Caponegro's character, when sent away to boarding school by her parents in an attempt to curb her obsession, stops eating and finds with satisfaction that she has also stopped her menstrual cycle: she becomes anorexic and thus attains the control over herself that her parents had thwarted.

The allusions to birds intersperse the narrative with great acuity and design and early establish the importance of "learning to fly on one's own. . . . Then, when it is on its own, there are no confusions. The break is clean; independence is clarity."

Again, as with Maso, the art form is strong in Caponegro. They both express the need for freedom that is realized in the service of self to art. Both are supreme stylists for whom the *materia prima* of background has indeed been transformed into a universal art with surrealistic and mysterious overlay. Curiously, the title of Maso's novel *Ava* also suggests bird flight and freedom.

Some Italian American women writers have a specific Italian American frame of reference; for others it is so attenuated as to seem nonexistent except as a muted echo. For Agnes Rossi, the Italian American background is attenuated into accents of detail and character. Marie Russo, the character through whom the title novella is narrated from her collection *The Quick,* is grounded in an Italian American family where the father still rages against children who don't fulfill his expectations, but the larger story is one of loss and has resonances for all families.

The new younger writers have a commonality—a boldness of voice and sureness of style that signal a true liberation from whatever roles and stereotypes of Italian American women prevailed in the past. They write of a gritty reality where women have faced the violence of today's life and survived, as in Jeanne Schinto's novel *Children of Men;* or they write with a new humor that is not the self-parody of the old stories, which made comic characters out of Italian Americans who acted and talked funny, but is now a controlled and knowing irony, as in the accomplished auto-erotic fantasy of Mary Capognegro's title story from *The Star Café.* The Italian American is no longer the object of humor but the distanced distiller of it, as what is nightmarish is filtered through an ironic eye.

In the imaginative storytelling of one of Cris Mazza's fictions, a story entitled "From Hunger," a striving artist is so hungry for her art (and human attention) she literally eats the paint from her canvas, another of Spignesi's starving woman. Mary-Ann Tirone Smith's characters are strikingly freewheeling young women who challenge the notions of prescribed conduct. One of them, from *The Book of Phoebe,* is named for Holden Caulfield's younger sister in the cult book of the 1950s, J. D. Salinger's *The Catcher in the Rye.* Taking as her subject matter the strains and hardships of a rural Vermont family who have no connection whatsoever with her Italian American background, Dalia Pagani has made an impressive debut with her first novel, *Mercy Road,* which received a great deal of advance praise for its lyrical style.

These newer Italian American writers have mostly taken a stance away from direct ethnic identification, one that engages in free imaginative roaming. Mary-Ann Tirone Smith put it this way in her letter to the *New York Times* in response to Talese's "Where are the Italian American Novelists?": "As an Italian American novelist, I haven't any interest in creating fiction centered on Sicilian goatherds and crowded ships poignantly pulling away from Neapolitan docks; or Ellis Island, or men carrying a statue of the Virgin through the streets of Little Italy, or the canonization of Joe DiMaggio. . . ." Rather, Smith states, what is explored is "the inevitable tragic consequences we must suffer when loyalty and honor are placed above truth. *That* is the Italian American experience."

Like other American writers, the contemporary Italian American woman writer transcends ethnic and gender group, writing in the fullness of her exposure to, and experience of, a national literature which mirrors a pluralistic society. American literature is an ocean, says Black novelist Ishmael Reed, and it's large enough for all the currents that run through it.

Referring to her first book, *Gone Primitive: Savage Intellects, Modern Lives*, Marianna De Marco Torgovnick wrote, "Eventually I write the book I like best about primitive others as they figure within Western obsessions, my identification with 'the Other,' my sense of being 'Other,' surfaces at last." Her sense of otherness, of course, comes from being Italian American, and is pertinent to the Outsider stance of Italian American literature.

As Torgovnick disclosed in her book, the civilized West's attraction to the primitive reflects a shiver of transcendental homelessness—a form of absolute alienation from the self, from society. It is easy to have those feelings growing up Italian American and, from the personal, to project them more generally. Noting throughout *Going Primitive* how primitivism has been colored by the masculine point of view, Torgovnick also seeks to redress that imbalance (much as Spignesi does in identifying the feminine psyche through female material) by looking for the female mode and by making her work accessible.

Again, as in the manner of Spignesi (and contrary to Paglia), Torgovnick stresses the importance of alternate stories to the Western one; unlike Paglia who is beholden to male mentors and has internalized their dominant, masculine values and attitudes, Torgovnick has an independent female outlook. Her refuting the colonialist denial of the complexity of primitive societies can also be translated into a refutation of the dominant American culture's denial of the importance of minority culture.

Though Smith and others have transcended their background to range imaginatively where they will, that does not invalidate the contribution of the previous generations of Italian American women writers. Each generation has its story to tell; each will find its own version of the Italian American experience or, contrarily, will not find it relevant any longer because so embedded in the total American experience.

Italian American women have always been hard workers; in the past they worked at home, taking in lodgers, making artificial flowers, doing piecework and embroidery, cooking for others. Now they are teachers and lawyers and have added to their work at home the practice of writing. To admit intellectual and artistic endeavor as "work" is a revolutionary change in attitude and class advancement.

"Nonproductive" work such as writing was once the activity of a leisured class who could afford the indulgence. But as Beverly Donofrio relates in *Riding in Cars with Boys,* once she had willed herself an education, her life changed; she was empowered to consider writing, an intellectual endeavor, as a legitimate occupation, something that moved her from working class to middle and triumphed over the *miseria* mentality that told her she would never make it out of welfare or a factory job.

To achieve balance between one's inherited culture and the culture into which one is born is a feat of what sociologists call "creative ethnicity," that is, using one's ethnic heritage as the starting point upon which to build one's own identity in a selective and critical way. There is choice rather than unquestioning acceptance of tradition. And there is anxiety in choice. The hardships now are not the primitive ones of survival, but the more complex ones of uncertainty of direction, how to choose, weighing self-expression and autonomy against bonds to others.

Pellegrino D'Acierno, who edited *The Italian American Heritage* volume in Garland's encyclopedic series *New Ethnic American Literature and the Arts,* has a positive evaluation of the two cultural forces implicated in being Italian American: "The maintenance of two identities, two cultures, two languages," he says, "should make us dissentious within ourselves, should make us into artists." He feels that in their zeal to take on a monolithic American identity, Italian Americans once let the prevailing culture deform their own life experiences and so failed to make the most of their identity crisis and to use the experience as the crucible for artistic production.

Cultural duality is not only ambivalence, it is also advantage–to draw upon two identities, cultures, and languages is to draw riches as well as dissentiousness, once the dual identity is recognized in a positive way and so used. Aileen Riotto Sirey's findings in ethnotherapy confirm that those who identify as Italian American conceive of themselves as part of something dually glorious–the magnificent long heritage of Italy plus the unique promise of American freedom to achieve one's best.

Women in particular are able to use the dichotomy of two cultures as the crucible for artistic production. The Black women writers have been particularly fine at this, for as Nikki Giovanni put it: "Our alienation is our greatest strength." Italian American women writers, too, use strong themes, turning the paradox of their lives, which has militated *against* expressivity, *into* expressivity. As Barbara

Grizzuti Harrison said regarding her past submersion as a Jeho-vah's Witness, "Women are good at turning their desolation to their advantage." From waiting, from patience, come intensity of focus, words straining to be heard, passion, conviction, an inner voice.

The opening words of the *Decameron* of Boccaccio are *Umana cosa,* "Something human." And that encapsulates the Italian Amer-ican woman writer's particular sensibility–very human, the stuff of life. She tilts toward life, bringing to her material realism, vigor, specificity, humane understanding of the emotions, and respect for the human verities.

Italian American women writers were late in coming to the fore for historical, social, and personally inhibiting reasons having to do with the culture they came from. It is not surprising that they have taken long to give voice to that experience, or that their numbers were not greater; but it does remain surprising that recognition of them is still so elusive.

As Cynthia Ozick in an essay on feminism says, "Cultivation pre-cedes fruition. It will take many practitioners of an art to produce one great artist." And the emergence of the Italian American woman as writer, scholar, intellectual is new, incredibly new, and built on a base of all the "lost" or unthought-of writers who wrote without no-tice or encouragement.

A start is made, and then, like reverberations, one work will set off another, each new literary work responding to a previous one, provoked into being by something left unsettled in the other work and, in turn, provoking new responses as each writer stands on the shoulders of another.

It has already happened that Italian American women see them-selves as writers, not simply as upholders and transmitters of a patri-archal culture through their roles as wives and mothers. To evolve from that old and potent image has taken the whole of this century that began with the great migration from Italy.

What unites the women is that, at some point, they all derive from a common cultural context and tradition, one in which woman had a strongly defined role; it is important to see them whole and to hear in the cadence of their voices the echo of the larger group. That is not to isolate them to a separatist ethnic drawer in the bu-reau of American literature, but to identify them as an important source of American writing that has been overlooked.

Once the missing pieces have been fitted into the national literature, the unheard voices listened to, the contributions of a large group
of American life attended to, the emphasis on ethnicity, per se, will
have been transcended. Each Italian American woman writer is
what she has always been: an American writer in her own right.

Bibliography
Index

Bibliography

Abelson, Ann. *The Little Conquerors*. Random House, 1960.

Aleramo, Sibilla. *A Woman*. Trans. Rosalind Delmar. University of California Press, 1979.

Alsop, Joseph. *FDR: A Centenary Remembrance*. Thorndike Press, 1982.

Aquilino, Alma. *Seeds of Doubt*. Falmouth Publishing Co., 1940.

Baldwin, James. *The Fire Next Time*. Random House, 1963.

Bancroft, George. *History of the United States*. Appleton, 1891–92.

Barolini, Antonio. *Elegie di Croton/Croton Elegies*. Guernica, 1990.

Barolini, Helen. *Umbertina*. Seaview, 1979; Feminist Press, 1999.

Barolini, Helen. *The Dream Book: An Anthology of Writings by Italian American Women*. Schocken, 1985.

Barolini, Helen. *Love in the Middle Ages*. Morrow, 1986.

Benasutti, Marion. *No Steadyjob for Papa*. Vanguard Press, 1966.

Benvenisti, Meron. *Conflicts and Contradictions*. Villard, 1986.

Bona, Mary Jo. *The Voices We Carry: Recent Italian American Women's Fiction*. Guernica, 1994.

Bonanno, Rosalie, with Beverly Donofrio. *Mafia Marriage: My Story*. Avon, 1991.

Bruccoli, Matthew. *Some Sort of Epic Grandeur*. Harcourt, Brace, 1981.

Bryant, Dorothy. *Ella Price's Journal*. Ata Books, 1972; Feminist Press 1997.

Bryant, Dorothy. *Miss Giardino*. Ata Books, 1978; Feminist Press 1997.

Burckhardt, Jacob. *The Civilization of the Renaissance in Italy*. Random House, 1980.

Bush, Mary. *A Place of Light*. Morrow, 1990.

Caponegro, Mary. *The Star Café and Other Stories*. Scribners, 1990.

Cather, Willa. *Death Comes for the Archbishop*. Knopf, 1927.

Cavallo, Diana. *A Bridge of Leaves*. Atheneum, 1961; Guernica, 1997.

Chay, Marie. *Pilgrim's Pride*. Dodd, Mead, 1961.

Cheever, John. *The Wapshot Chronicle*. Harper, 1957.

Cheever, John. *The Wapshot Scandal*. Harper & Row, 1979.

Ciresi, Rita. *Mother Rocket*. Georgia University Press, 1993.

Ciresi, Rita. *Blue Italian*. Ecco Press, 1996

Commager, Henry Steele. *The American Mind: An Interpretation of American Thought and Character since the 1880s*. Yale University Press, 1950.

Condon, Richard. *Prizzi's Honor*. Coward, McCann & Geoghegan, 1982.

D'Acierno, Pellegrino, ed. *The Italian American Heritage*. Garland, 1998.

D'Agostino, Guido. *Olives on the Apple Tree*. Arno Press, 1940.

DeCapite, Michael. *Maria*. Day, 1943.

DeCapite, Michael. *No Bright Banner*. Day, 1944.

Deledda, Grazia. *The Mother*. Trans. Mary G. Steegman. Cherokee, 1929.

Deledda, Grazia. *Cosima*. Trans. Martha King. Italica Press, 1988.

DeRosa, Tina. *Paper Fish*. Wine Press, 1980; Feminist Press, 1996.

DeSalvo, Louise. *Vertigo: A Memoir*. Dutton, 1996.

deVries, Rachel Guido. *Tender Warriors*. Firebrand Books, 1986.

Di Donato, Pietro. *The Gospels* (unpublished).

Di Donato, Pietro. *Christ in Concrete*. Bobbs-Merrill, 1939, 1975.

Di Donato, Pietro. *Three Circles of Light*. Messner, 1960.

diPrima, Diane. *Dinners and Nightmares*. Corinth, 1961, 1974.

diPrima, Diane. *Memoirs of a Beatnik*. 1969, 1988; Viking, 1998.

Dodd, Bella Visono. *School of Darkness*. P. J. Kenedy, 1954; Devin-Adair, 1963.

Donofrio, Beverly. "My Grandma Irene." *Village Voice*, August 18, 1987.

Donofrio, Beverly. *Riding in Cars with Boys: Confessions of a Bad Girl Who Makes Good*. Morrow, 1990.

Ellison, Ralph. *Invisible Man*. Random House, 1952.

Ets, Marie Hall. *Rosa: The Life of an Italian Immigrant*. University of Minnesota Press, 1970.

Fante, John. *Wait until Spring, Bandini!* Stackpole, 1938.

Fante, John. *Ask the Dust*. Stackpole, 1939; Black Sparrow, 1986.

Fante, John. *Dago Red*. Viking, 1940.

Fast, Howard. *The Immigrants*. Houghton Mifflin, 1977.

Feraca, Jean. *South from Rome: Il Mezzogiorno*. Larkspur Press, 1976.

Fitzgerald, F. Scott. *The Short Stories of F. Scott Fitzgerald*. Scribner, 1989.

Gambino, Richard. *Blood of My Blood*. Doubleday, 1975; Guernica, 1995.

Giancana, Antoinette, and Thomas C. Renner. *Mafia Princess*. Morrow, 1984.

Giardina, Denise. *Storming Heaven*. Ivy Books, 1988

Giardina, Denise. *The Unquiet Earth*. Norton, 1992.

Gilbert, Sandra, with Susan Gubar. *The Madwoman in the Attic*. Yale University Press, 1979.

Gilbert, Sandra. *Blood Pressure*. Norton, 1988.

Gillan, Maria Mazziotti. *Taking Back My Name*. malafemmina press, 1990.

Gioseffi, Daniela. *Eggs in the Lake*. BOA Editions, 1979.

Gordon, Mary. "Zi' Marietta." In *A New Day*. UNICO National, 1976.

Gordon, Mary. "The Myth of the Tough Dame." *Mirabella,* November 1992.

Green, Rose Basile. *The Italian American Novel*. Fairleigh Dickinson University Press, 1974.

Harrison, Barbara Grizzuti. *Visions of Glory*. Simon & Schuster, 1978.

Harrison, Barbara Grizzuti. "Godfather II." In *Off Center*. Dial Press, 1980.

Hendin, Josephine Gattuso. *The Right Thing to Do*. Godine, 1988.

Hurston, Zora Neale. "What White Publishers Won't Print." In *I Love Myself.* Feminist Press, 1979.

Jelinek, Estelle, ed. *Women's Autobiography*. Indiana University Press, 1980.

Lamacchia, Grace. *Collision*. Washington Irving Publishing Co., 1974.

Levi, Primo. *The Drowned and the Saved*. Trans. Raymond Rosenthal. Vintage, 1989.

McHale, Thomas. *Principato*. Viking, 1970.

Manzoni, Alessandro. *I promessi sposi*. Sansoni, 1961.

Masini, Donna. *That Kind of Danger*. Beacon Press, 1994.

Masini, Donna. *About Yvonne*. Norton, 1997.

Maso, Carole. *Ghost Dance*. North Point Press, 1986.

Mays, Lucinda LaBella. *The Other Shore*. Atheneum, 1979.

Mazza, Cris. *Animal Acts*. Fiction Collective, 1989.

Miller, Jean Baker. *Toward a New Psychology of Women*. Beacon, 1976, 1986.

Moers, Ellen. *Literary Women*. Doubleday, 1976.

Monacelli-Johnson, Linda. *Campanile*. Drummer Press, 1998.

Moore, Robin, with Barbara Fuca. *Mafia Wife*. Macmillan, 1977.

Newman, Katherine. "An Ethnic Literary Scholar Views American Literature." MELUS, Spring 1980.

Nussbaum, Martha. Review essay of *Reclaiming a Conversation: The Ideal of the Educated Woman,* by Jane Roland Martin. *New York Review of Books,* January 30, 1986, 7–12.

Olsen, Tillie. *Tell Me a Riddle*. Dell, 1961.

Olsen, Tillie. *Silences*. Delacorte Press, 1978.

Ozick, Cynthia. "Women and Creativity." In *Woman and Sexist Society,* ed. Vivian Gornick and Barbara K. Moran. New American Library, 1971.

Pacifici, Sergio. *A Guide to Contemporary Italian Literature*. Meridian Books, 1962.

Paglia, Camille. "Reflections on Being Italian in America." In *A New Day.* UNICO National, 1976.

Paglia, Camille. *Sexual Personae.* Yale University Press, 1990.

Paris, Bernard. *A Psychological Approach to Fiction.* Indiana University Press, 1974.

Peragallo, Olga. *Italian American Authors.* Vanni, 1949.

Piercy, Marge. *Fly Away Home.* Summit Books, 1984.

Pileggi, Nicholas. *Wiseguy.* Simon & Schuster, 1985.

Pola, Antonia. *Who Can Buy the Stars?* Vantage Press, 1957.

Pratt, Annis. *Archetypal Patterns in Women's Fiction.* Indiana University Press, 1982.

Prose, Francine. *Household Saints.* St. Martin's Press, 1981.

Puzo, Mario. *The Godfather.* Putnam, 1969.

Puzo, Mario. *The Fortunate Pilgrim.* Atheneum, 1970.

Puzo, Mario. *The Godfather Papers.* Putnam, 1972.

Quindlen, Anna. *Living Out Loud.* Random House, 1988.

Quindlen, Anna. *Object Lessons.* Random House, 1991.

Quindlen, Anna. *One True Thing.* Random House, 1994.

Quindlen, Anna. *Black and Blue.* Random House, 1998.

Rolle, Andrew. *The Immigrant Upraised.* University of Oklahoma Press, 1968.

Rolle, Andrew. *The Italian Americans: Troubled Roots.* Free Press, 1980.

Romano, Rose. *Vendetta.* malafemmina press, 1990.

Rosa, Alfred. Afterword to *Like Lesser Gods,* by Mari Tomasi. New England Press, 1989.

Rossi, Agnes. *The Quick.* Norton, 1992.

Sangiuliano, Iris. *In Her Time.* Morrow, 1978.

Saroyan, William. *The Daring Young Man on the Flying Trapeze and Other Stories.* Random House, 1934.

Savarese, Julia. *The Weak and the Strong.* Putnam. 1952.

Schinto, Jeanne. *Shadow Bands.* Ontario Review Press, 1983.

Schinto, Jeanne. *Children of Men.* Persea Books, 1991.

Segale, Sister Blandina. *At the End of the Santa Fe Trail.* Bruce Publishing Co., 1948.

Shanley, John Patrick. *Moonstruck.* Screenplay, 1987.

Shanley, John Patrick. *Italian American Reconciliation.* Dramatist's Play Service, 1989.

Shulman, Max. *Rally Round the Flag, Boys.* Doubleday, 1957.

Smith, Mary-Ann Tirone. *The Book of Phoebe.* Doubleday, 1985.

Spignesi, Angelyn. *Starving Women: A Psychology of Anorexia Nervosa.* Spring Publications, 1983.

Spignesi, Angelyn. *Lyrical-Analysis: The Unconscious through Jane Eyre.* Chiron Publications, 1990.

Stein, Gertrude. *The Making of Americans.* Something Else Press, 1966.

Talese, Gay. *Honor Thy Father.* World, 1971.

Talese, Gay. *Unto the Sons*. Knopf, 1992.

Tamburri, Anthony Julian, Paolo Giordano, and Fred Gardaphé, eds. *From the Margin: Writings in Italian Americana*. Purdue University Press, 1991.

Tate, Claudia, ed. *Black Women Writers at Work*. Continuum, 1983.

Tomasi, Mari. *Deep Grow the Roots*. Lippincott, 1940.

Tomasi, Mari. *Like Lesser Gods*. Bruce, 1949; New England Press, 1988.

Torgovnick, Marianna De Marco. *Gone Primitive: Savage Intellects, Modern Lives*. University of Chicago Press, 1990.

Torgovnick, Marianna De Marco. *Crossing Ocean Parkway: Readings by an Italian American Daughter*. University of Chicago Press, 1994.

Warhol, Robyn R., and Diane Price Herndl, eds. *Feminisms: An Anthology of Literary Theory and Criticism*. Rutgers University Press, 1991.

Winwar, Frances. *The Ardent Flame*. Century, 1927.

Woolf, Virginia. *Death of the Moth and Other Essays*. Harcourt Brace, 1942.

Zandy, Janet, ed. *Calling Home: Working Class Women Writing*. Rutgers University Press, 1990.

Index

Abelson, Ann, 185
Affiliation, 173
African American writers, 108, 129,
146, 191, 195. *See also* Black writers
Agnelli Foundation, 145
Aleandri, Emelise, 172
Aleramo, Sibilla, 179
Alienation, 146, 149, 151, 153, 181,
197–98, 205, 207
Alsop, Joseph, 170
Alterity, 110. *See also* Other
American Academy of Arts and
Letters, 109; Prix de Rome, 196
American Booksellers Association, 55
American Historical Fiction, 193
American Women Poets, 194
American Women Writers, 194
Anglo-American influence, 12, 61, 63,
67, 107, 116, 149, 163, 167, 169;
Anglo-conformity, 169; Anglo-
centrism, 170, 176; Anglo-American
women writers, 181, 195; literary
history, 187
Anorexia, 198, 203
Aquilino, Alma, 167
Archetypes, literary, 122–23, 143, 145,
180
Ardizzone, Tony 119
Aristotle, 122
Asian American women writers, 181,
195
Assimilation, 119, 158, 166–67
Atlas, James, 117

Atwood, Margaret, 112
Austen, Jane, 178
Autobiography, 147, 196, 200
Autonomy, vii, 119, 156–57, 165, 180,
187, 206. *See also* Individualism

Bair, Deirdre, 177
Baldwin, Faith, 55
Baldwin, James, 107, 109, 171
Baltimore, Lord, 169
Bambara, Toni Cade, 172
Bancroft, George, 169
Barbieri, Cecilia, 76, 90
Barolini, Antonio, 35, 48–53, 70, 108,
120–21
Barolini, Helen: writing career, vii, 85,
102, 106, 112, 136; Shady Lane
Farm, 48; attends Wells College,
50; Briarcliff Manor Public Library,
52; in Rome, 70–72, 84, 86–87;
planning *Festa: Recipes & Recollections of Italian Holidays,* 71, 73–74,
81, 88; poem, "At Rosati's," 93;
farmhouse in the Marche region,
93; letters to the *New York Times,*
98; childhood in Syracuse, N.Y.,
107; *Umbertina,* 111, 119, 131, 137;
at Bellagio Center, Lake Como, 128
Barolini, Nicoletta (Niki), 71, 79, 85
Barolini, Susanna (Susi), 36–37, 71,
80–82
Barolini, Teodolinda (Linda), 71, 144
Basso, Hamilton, 113